Raising Boys' Achievement in Secondary Schools

*Mike Younger and Molly Warrington,
with Ros McLellan*

Open University Press

Open University Press
McGraw-Hill Education
McGraw-Hill House
Shoppenhangers Road
Maidenhead, Berkshire
England SL6 2QL

email: enquiries@openup.co.uk
world wide web: www.openup.co.uk

and Two Penn Plaza, New York, NY 1012–2289
USA

First published 2005

Copyright © Mike Younger and Molly Warrington 2005

A catalogue record of this book is available from the British Library

ISBN 0 335 21608 0 (pb)   0 335 21609 9 (hb)
ISBN–13: 978 0335 216086 (pb)   978 0335 216093 (hb)

Library of Congress Cataloging-in-Publication Data
CIP data has been applied for

Typeset by BookEns Ltd, Royston, Herts.
Printed and bound in Poland EU by OZGraf, S.A.
www.polskabook.pl

Contents

	Acknowledgements	vi
	Glossary	ix
1	Boys and Girls Talking	1
2	National and International Dimensions: Context and Causes	16
3	The Conundrum of the Gender Gap	30
4	What About the Girls?	46
5	Raising Boys' Achievements within an Inclusive Context	60
6	The Context of the Classroom: Pedagogies and Teaching-Learning Styles	72
7	The Context of the Individual: Target-Setting and Mentoring	94
8	Organizational Contexts: Equal Opportunities in the Single-Sex Classroom	116
9	The Socio-Cultural Key	135
10	Gender and Achievement in Special Schools	157
11	Policy Directions within an Inclusive Context	171
	References	187
	Index	205

Acknowledgements

It goes without saying that this book would have been impossible to write without the support, dedication and enthusiasm of the headteachers and deputy headteachers with whom we worked during the Raising Boys' Achievement project. From them we were able to develop the links between theory and practice which we hope this book encompasses. Particular thanks are due to Dean, Eamonn, Sue, Rob, Amanda, Ian, Colin, Pam, Keith, Sandra, Joanna, Richard and Sally, whose enthusiasms, ideas and commitment went way beyond the call of duty. Their participation across at least three years of the project made the research not only satisfying and worthwhile in an academic sense, but also made it fun, enjoyable and personally rewarding. There were other school participants – too many to mention individually – who were part of different stages of the project, and whose valuable contributions we also gratefully acknowledge.

We were ably guided throughout much of the project by the expertise of Jean Rudduck and John Gray, our co-directors, whose experience proved invaluable, and we thank them, too, for continually challenging us to think in new directions. Our thanks are also due to Pat Bricheno, who joined the project in its last year, to work as Research Assistant alongside Ros: it was good for us to be able to take on fresh perspectives, and we were glad of her patience and meticulous approach. Ruth Kershner, author of chapter 10, willingly took on management of the Special School aspects of the project, and added an important dimension to the study as a whole. Peter Jackson brought his expertise as a former deputy headteacher to work with two groups of schools, and we are grateful for this contribution.

This book would not have been written without funding from the Department for Education and Skills, and we should like to acknowledge here both that financial support, but also the support of our steering group. The ever-changing composition of that group certainly kept us on our toes! In particular, our thanks are due to Judy Sebba whose encouragement and enthusiasm we much appreciated.

Finally, we owe a real debt to the family, friends and colleagues whose interest, support, tolerance and love have sustained and motivated us during the five years of work which this project has entailed. Many names could be mentioned here, but we especially thank Glyn, Ruth, Thomas and Catherine, Emma, Nic and Simon, and Martin.

We would also like to thank Steve Hawkes, Headteacher, and Sharon Churm, Teacher Consultant/ITT Co-ordinator at Deansfield School, Wolverhampton (one of the Originator Schools), for allowing us to use the photograph on the cover of this text, and to Syreeta Crosdale (teacher), Carly Winterbottom and Michel Chambers for agreeing to appear in the photograph.

Glossary

CAT   Cognitive ability test

CSE   The Certificate of Secondary Education: examination current in England and Wales between the early 1960s and 1987, often taken at the end of their secondary schooling by children in the 20–80% ability cohort, i.e. not by the so-called 'top 20% of the ability range'.

DfES   The Department for Education and Skills, the state department responsible for schooling in England (previously titled the DfEE, the Department for Education and Employment, and the DES, the Department of Education and Science).

GCE   The General Certificate of Education: examination current in England and Wales between the early 1950s and 1987, taken at the end of their secondary schooling by children in the top 20% of the ability range.

GCSE   General Certificate of Secondary Education: the examination taken by virtually all children in England and Wales at the end of their compulsory period of schooling, at 16; a common examination which replaced the GCE/CSE examinations in 1988.

GNVQ   General National Vocational Qualifications: examination provision which supplements GCSE examinations, in vocational subjects.

Key Stages   Since the introduction of the National Curriculum (1988), the English education system has been sub-divided into six key stages: the Foundation stage (children aged 3–5 years), key stage 1 covering years 1–2 (children aged 5–7 years), key stage 2 for years 3–6 (children aged 7–11 years), key stage 3 for years 7–9 (children aged 11–14 years), key stage 4 for years 10–11 (children aged 14–16), and the post-compulsory key stage 5, years 12–13 (students aged 16–19).

Levels	National Curriculum Tests, administered in English schools, are marked in terms of levels. It is assumed that the 'average' child will have reached level 4 by the end of their primary schooling (at the age of 11), and level 5 by the end of year 9 (at the age of 14).
MidYIS	Middle Years Information System : a value-added monitoring system developed by the Curriculum Evaluation and Management Centre at the University of Durham, which provides a wide range of performance indicators for students aged 11–13, and makes possible comparisons of students against other students participating nationally in the project, by subject, student and school.
OFSTED	The Office for Standards in Education: carries out a regular system of inspections of standards in every state school.
PSHE	Personal, Social and Health Education: a pastoral programme which forms part of the compulsory, but non-examined, curriculum in English schools.
SMT	The Senior Management Team within a school, usually consisting of the Headteacher/Principal, together with the Deputy Head Teachers (and sometimes including the Assistant Headteachers). In some schools, the SMT is called the SLT, the Senior Leadership Team.
YELLIS	YEar 11 Information System: similar to MidYIS, for students aged 14–16.

1 Boys and Girls Talking

I was really rescued by my mentor; he's from our community, and he showed me what was possible ... I got awards for my poetry, I proved everybody wrong, I shocked everybody ... but it was down to my Head of Year [in Year 9] and my mentor ... it gave me a real boost, and showed the teachers that my labels were wrong ... it made some of the teachers stop and think.

(Rajinder)

He's alright. He makes you feel comfortable and relaxed, and not all tensed up. He talks to you in the corridor as well.

(Mark)

I can't be silent, I need to talk! ... but I can work as well; teachers don't understand.

(Yasha)

There's too much judging here ... some teachers hear about us before they even teach us, and then they assume we're like they hear ... but sometimes it's being spread around by one or two staff who really don't get on with us ... teachers should give us more chance.

(Luke)

I'm always copying down stuff which doesn't seem to have any point.

(Jon)

If we were given a fresh start, I'm sure we'd all be much better, whereas we made mistakes in year 7 and 8, and we're paying for them now because the teachers don't treat us that well. I don't want to be an amazing person. I just want to be treated as a normal person. We all make mistakes, don't we, but they can't let it go.

(Carl)

Rajinder, Mark, Yasha, Luke, Jon and Carl, and many others like them, were boys in the final year of their schooling, speaking from co-educational comprehensive schools in different parts of England, in the early years of a new century. They were all boys identified by their schools as 'under-achieving', as 'not likely to do as well as they ought in their GCSE examinations', boys whose school attendance was giving cause for concern or who, if they attended, were in danger through their behaviour and responses to schooling of being excluded from school. During the course of our work with secondary schools, spread over the past decade, we have spent many fascinating hours listening to the talk of such boys, as they have shared with us their need to be engaged in lessons and to have an opportunity to talk (and learn), their concerns about negative expectations and stereotypes, their frustrations with the apparent irrelevance and associated boredom of much of their time in school. They have spoken of lessons which were dominated by teacher talk and worksheets, of discipline structures which appeared pointless to them, of their school's concerns about the length (neither too long nor too short!) and colour of their hair, and the types of trainers they wore. Equally, though, their voices articulated a desire for a fresh start, their admiration of teachers who communicated openly and with a caring concern, of those in schools who had offered them new opportunities and enabled them to develop a sense of achievement and fulfilment in music, drama and poetry.

In so doing, these boys gave us a glimpse, however partial, of their world, into their constructions of reality, to what was important to them. They offered mature perspectives on the relevance of their own education, their concern with sustaining an appropriate image, their aspirations and ideals, their disaffection with aspects of the school system, and their views on teaching and on the value of their own education. Such was the degree of consensus and commonality which emerged from these specific boys, regardless of school locality, socio-economic context or the age range of students served, that we have no hesitation in acknowledging the authenticity of their voices. They represent, as Jean Rudduck and her colleagues have pointed out in many different contexts (Rudduck *et al.* 1996; Rudduck and Flutter 2000, 2004; Finney 2003), some of the realities of twenty-first-century schooling for many boys labelled by their schools as 'potentially under-achieving'.

Yet their interviews with us, conducted on an ongoing basis over four years, in friendship-based focus groups or in one-to-one sessions as we got to know them better and we all grew in confidence, revealed not only astute awareness and sharp insights about the pressures and context in which schools were operating, but also revealed the roles and responsibilities which many of them performed in 'the real world outside school'. Caring for younger brothers and sisters, looking after a disabled mother, co-ordinating a shopping network for elderly people living in flats in the middle of shopping deserts, providing entertainment for a group of residents in sheltered housing, were all activities which were initiated and sustained by such boys. The boys, perceived by their schools as epitomizing particular issues, challenges and dilemmas, assumed in their 'other life' an ability to act independently and to make decisions, a sensitivity and concern, a gentleness and affection for those they perceived to be in need, which utterly belied both the perception which the school had of them and the persona which the boys themselves presented publicly at school. It was as if these boys were different people, in and outside their schools, struggling 'to reconcile the often complex relationships and responsibilities of their life out of school with their life in school' (MacBeath *et al.* 2003: 1).

This is not to deny the contrasting reality and image which these boys presented to teachers and to other students, both girls and other boys. The heart of the paradox is, of course, that they, like so many of us, *are* different people in different contexts, with a multiplicity of social, academic and peer pressures bearing upon them (Epstein *et al.* 1998; Kenway *et al.* 1998; Collins *et al.* 2000; Francis 2000a; Frosh *et al.* 2002; Jackson 2002; Martino and Pallotta-Chiarolli 2003). To some teachers, their sheer physicality, their restiveness, their short concentration span, their failure to arrive in lessons at the right time with the right equipment and books, their boisterousness, all contributed to a sense of challenge (Younger and Warrington 1996; Barker 1997; Barton 2000; Warrington *et al.* 2000; Jones and Jones 2001; Younger *et al.* 2002). They were defying the legitimacy of the teacher, denying the value of the knowledge and understanding which the teacher was deputed to share with the boys, disputing the authority conveyed upon the teacher. Yet away from the classroom context, free of constraints of uniform, timetable and the school environment, released from feelings of inadequacy, failure and vulnerability, some of these boys were quite different people. in P. 2

The enigma of boys: girls talking

The voices of girls give us perceptive insights into the enigma which is presented by some boys today. In many schools, it was clear in our interviews with girls that boys presented them with a marked dilemma. At one level, there was a strong feeling that boys' behaviour in class was a serious source of distraction which impeded girls' learning. To Amy and many other girls, 'They try to dominate, especially when they don't understand ... they're more restless, try to show off more, less involved in work.' Many boys were seen as less willing to settle down to work, more challenging and distracting for teachers, having a negative impact on overall learning because too much time was spent on disciplining a minority of boys (Warrington and Younger 2001). A general consensus emerged among girls, almost without exception across all the schools in which we worked, that even in Years 10 and 11, many boys were *still* immature: 'I suppose they do grow up sometime, do they?' (Martha). They would only work when the parameters were made very clear, when they 'respect the teacher' or 'are scared of him' or 'when they're put under pressure'. Such boys were more aggressive and more obvious in their misbehaviour, and were justly punished: 'boys make out they know everything, even when they don't ... if they asked when they didn't know, instead of making out that they knew everything about everything, we'd have more respect for them' (Lucy).

As is evident in the work of Francis (2000a) and Frosh *et al.* (2002), boys were frequently characterized as silly, immature, too willing to ridicule the contributions of girls and other boys, unable to engage in serious dialogue about sensitive issues:

> When you come onto something important or really sensitive, they can't cope, the boys act really silly like ... if the talk is about AIDS or sex, they start laughing and making comments ... they snigger away in an immature way ... it's very distracting when you want to listen and learn about something really important.
>
> (Latoyah)

To many girls, 'boys act the fool and try to be the cool ones ... usually without success!'

There is a double edge here, though, because there were occasions when girls acknowledged that the presence of boys was appreciated and enriching (Warrington and Younger 2001). In some classroom situations, boys were seen as bringing amusement and fun, a welcome sense of distraction, offering different opinions and perspectives on issues:

> Sometimes I enjoy the little things the boys go and say; they come out with stupid and funny remarks; the boys are always there to crack the jokes, to play the clown, to lighten it all up.
>
> (Kayleigh)

> Boys aren't always a bad distraction ... they can be fun and it's nice to have guys as friends.
>
> (Nicola)

On occasions, boys were valued, too, because they had a positive impact upon the general classroom ethos, and were a constructive influence on the nature of girl–girl interactions:

At times, I miss the boys ... when the bitchiness starts or you're really bored ... sometimes the boys tell you to shut up, and the bitchiness won't happen if boys are there ... the girls will be afraid of looking stupid, shy and silly if boys are there ... some of the bitchy girls, they wouldn't say anything if a boy was listening.

(Natalie)

Girls also offered very perceptive comments about the varied roles that boys played, and boys' self-awareness of image:

You see three different sides to boys I think ... you see them in the lesson, when they act stupidly and show their immaturity ... you see them at dinner time, when they're with their mates and they act hard in a bunch all together, and then you see them out of school when – if they're by themselves – they calm down a lot and act more sensibly.

(Martha)

Many girls professed to preferring boys in their 'quiet role', when boys tried hard to act without self-consciousness or egotistically, where they were more normal and tried to establish sensitive one-to-one relationships (Kenway *et al.* 1998; Frosh *et al.* 2002). The ideal boy was often described as 'showing respect, not too much of an attitude when they're with their mates, able to act their age rather than their shoe size, not showing off and acting big in front of their friends' (Balinder), and appreciated for being aware and responsive:

It's quite nice when they don't go off and play football for ever, when they actually talk to you personally... some guys notice when you're upset and are really nice about it ... they tell you how fit you look and how good your work is, and it's not sarcastic, you know, or because they're trying to get off with you ... it's just friendly.

(Joanna)

To win the approval of such girls, boys needed to be 'all round, with a good basis of friends, kind and affectionate rather than loud'. Sadly perhaps, from the perspective of many girls, a 'caring, sharing boy' was unusual, much valued, respected and – on occasions – fought over. While boys seemed to recognize the characteristics which appealed to many girls, and the qualities they needed to show,

You want them to think that you're alright, so you have to show them that you can get on with the work ... they want to see that!

(Jake)

They want you to listen *and* to be able to talk, to be strong *and* kind, to be sort of sensitive.

(Peter)

they frequently appeared, at least from girls' perspectives, to be less able to deliver!

These girls offer perceptive insights on the enigma which is presented by some boys, and on some of the issues which impinge upon boys' 'performance' at school. They present girls' understandings of boys' dilemmas, suggest how boys (ideally) need to react differently in different situations, and offer an identification with boys' concerns.

Boys talking about boys: perplexed or arrogant? bewildered or complacent?

It is in discussing boys' reactions to their GCSE courses, in particular, that we gain some real insights into the different realities and perspectives of various groups of boys. A major theme here *was* difference. Although we focused on boys who had been identified by their schools as in danger of failing to fulfil their apparent potential, who were by definition potentially marginalized and disengaged boys, we were struck nonetheless by their variety of viewpoints and outlooks, by their different attitudes and responses.

Some boys adopted a *laissez-faire* approach, displaying a sense of bravado and an apparent self-belief that they could meet the demands of their course through frenzied activity late in the year, exhibiting a pseudo-confidence which often masked insecurity and self-doubt (Salisbury and Jackson 1996; Kenway *et al.* 1998; Warrington *et al.* 2000). For some, there appeared a genuine belief that all would fall neatly into place without undue effort: 'I've recently been allocated a mentor because apparently I'm not achieving what I'm supposed to be getting ... ' [sense of wry amusement], (Nick).

There was a confidence in the reaction of some boys, an arrogance almost, and an apparent self-belief in their own ability. There was a conviction that they would do well regardless of how little work they did, without real effort, a characteristic inherent in Mac an Ghaill's 'Real Englishmen' (Mac an Ghaill 1994) and evident in the work of Bornbolt *et al.* (1994), who noted the tendency of boys to over-rate themselves.

Boys often acknowledged the importance of homework, of revision clubs, of coursework support clubs, but seemed not to appreciate the immediacy of the need. Some of our longitudinal interviews, with individual boys through time, classically revealed a genuine sense of commitment, but – frustratingly for parents and teachers – no sense of urgency or determination:

Yes, my mum got me the revision guides; they're somewhere at home, but often I can't find them ... I'm disorganized at home.

(Chris, April, Year 11)

I will start going to Art revision class soon!

(Mark, March 30, Year 11)

I made myself go to the geography coursework club after school ... No, I didn't go to the half-term revision clubs, not in my holiday.'

(Sam, March, Year 11)

From others, there was a sense of negativity towards the initiatives which schools had developed to try to offer additional support to boys and girls. In some schools, the attitudes of a small number of peer group leaders appeared to be strongly prevalent in determining the responses of significant numbers of boys and girls within the year group, and was sufficiently strong to inhibit others from attending. Extra revision classes, twilight activities, revision activities during the Easter holiday period or over half-term, were treated with scepticism or even on occasions with contempt, eliciting a reaction of disbelief that students would sacrifice holidays to voluntarily attend school and the suggestion that such classes would inevitably be poorly attended. Some of these boys were motivated by a sense of helplessness, others by resentment, yet others by hostility to the aspirations which the school was trying to establish. Others appeared to adopt this sense of negativity as a form of self-protection, to avoid the intensity of the conflict between peer expectations and their own (sometimes latent) aspirations (Clark and Trafford 1995; West 1996; Cohen 1998; Jackson 2002).

There was also a refusal to accept responsibility for actions and for outcomes. Some boys were not willing to accept their role in classroom disruptions or their failure to reach targets; they did not believe that they could explicitly be held accountable for disengagement or unruly behaviour and activity (Younger et al. 1999). While acknowledging off-task behaviour and disruption, they argued that this stemmed from a catalogue of circumstances (Younger and Warrington 1996; Warrington et al. 2000; Frosh et al. 2002): boring lessons, teachers who could not control them, other students who distracted them, lessons which were not challenging enough, lessons where the subject matter was 'rubbish ... the same thing over and over again'. Such boys argued that the situation was beyond their control, almost inciting them towards disengagement:

I get distracted by my mates. They mess about, the teacher doesn't do anything about it, then you get dragged into it, because you're bored because no-one is paying any attention to the teacher, so

you can't learn. You don't even think about it, you just get
involved in the noise and the mucking about!

(Colin)

This sense of helplessness, linked as it was in some schools to the discourse
of blame, is neither helpful nor constructive in engaging boys in their own
learning, and in generating a sense of worthwhileness and commitment to
schooling. It is nonetheless, as Head reiterates, an essential attribute of how
some boys perceive the reality of their schooling: 'Males tend to develop a
defence mechanism of attributing success to their own efforts and failure to
external factors ... boys have to take responsibility for their own poor work'
(1996: 63). This contrasts starkly with other schools, however, where the
passionate commitment of the staff, notably the regular involvement of the
headteacher and senior staff, helped to ensure that extra sessions, even
extending into residential weekends and away days, were well attended and
highly valued by such boys (Younger *et al.* 2002). Thus:

I ain't bothered about staying after school as long as I'm getting my
coursework done. It's better than going home because you do it
more here.

(Philip, Year 10)

The teachers go quite far to get us really good grades, they'll go the
extra mile for us ... they'll help with any learning problems to get
us where we want to get to ... and late buses are provided to get us
home.

(Sandeep, Year 11)

In these contexts, some boys had come to realize that they were indeed
heading for disappointment and that they were not going to be able to fulfil
the ambitions they had established for themselves. Positive identification
with mentoring schemes (Chapter 7) often followed:

I felt a bit gutted to be involved in this, but when I thought about
it, I thought it was a good idea, otherwise I'd just carry on under-
achieving, to be honest.

(Leon)

At the start, I thought I was doing OK but then I did my mock
exams, and I thought 'yer, I am an under-achiever here', but I'm
not a major under-achiever, like some of my mates!

(Charlie)

These conflicts between image and aspirations, between realism and hope, were acknowledged less openly by girls, and appeared less stark for girls and more easily managed by them. Far fewer girls adopted a *laissez-faire* approach, or were complacent and had problems openly reconciling genuine aspirations with ambition and goals. More girls appeared cautious and realistic, appreciating that achievement needed sustained and dedicated effort through time. Girls were thus much more inclined to take responsibility upon themselves (Head 1996), acknowledging that their own liking for various subjects affected the ways in which they responded in lessons, and accepting that students themselves crucially affected the teaching–learning situation, and attributing their own lack of success to intrinsic factors linked to self rather than to external factors (Dweck 1986; Boaler 1997). Many boys, on the other hand, adopted a protective mantle, feigning lack of concern about outcomes or a seemingly arrogant self-belief that achievement would fall into place without undue effort. Many girls and boys agreed that boys were less interested in school work and were prepared to revise before GCSEs only at the last minute, whereas girls themselves admitted to more worry and anxiety about examinations: 'It's a boy thing ... girls get into gear right from the beginning, but boys don't seem to realize until there are three months left ... I was surprised when I got my target grades because I thought I was doing much better' (Gavin).

It is too simple, however, to suggest that all boys minimize their work because of this conflict between peer group image and individual aspiration. There does seem to be, among some boys at least, a genuine belief that they are preparing adequately for GCSE examinations, and a real puzzlement and increasing sense of perplexity that their teachers are suggesting that this might not be the case. Such boys seem totally unaware of the demands of their GCSE course until very late in the two-year cycle, not actively demotivated or challenging in the classroom, but rather cruising gently through their last years of schooling. The sense of frustration felt by some of the teachers of these boys is palpable! Some of these boys are articulate, charming, willing, yet in many senses unengaged (rather than disengaged) and almost untouched by the realities around them. Only very late on through the two-year course did our individual interviews with some of these boys show a sense of increasing unease, and a sense of rising panic and despair, as the truth slowly dawned.

Contrasting case studies: fulfilled potential or not?

Henry was one such boy we encountered, apparently confused and disorientated by the demands of the GCSE course, almost chastened by his experiences. Aware that he should do better, and that he was 'not working hard enough', he could not analyse why, and did not have a sense of what he needed to do: 'Some teachers feel I could try harder ... I agree .... but I don't know how to. My teachers say I need to revise, but I do ... I read my notes, and my mum tests me, but it doesn't help. I don't know what to do next'.

Our interviews with Jon exemplified similar issues. In many respects, Jon was 'a classic boy', with level 5s in all three core subjects in Year 9 National Curriculum tests, and six predicted GCSEs at grade C or above. During his GCSE course, he was identified as underperforming, with a higher than average appearance on poor behaviour lists, regularly on report for failure to complete homework, seemingly minimizing his efforts on academic work:

> I have the intelligence, but not the attitude or the behaviour. I got in the wrong group of people late on in Year 9, and behaviour stayed bad til Y11 ... I would have done better if I had concentrated more, but it's probably too late for real improvement now.

The self-reflection and increasing awareness of both Henry and Jon in May during their Year 11 studies were both painfully and astutely accurate, shown in the one grade C GCSE which Henry eventually achieved and in Jon's three grade C passes at GCSE.

Both Jon and Henry showed an increasing realization of need as GCSEs approached, but equally a sense of resignation and growing helplessness, which often translated in similar boys into low self-esteem and a lack of self-worth, into a sense of disillusionment and disengagement. Some such boys never make it to the examination hall, of course, disappearing in May under the sense of failure and disenchantment.

Craig was a similar case of potential unfulfilled. Cognitive ability test scores identified Craig as a very able boy, but his performances in National Curriculum tests at 14 were disappointing (three level 5s in the core subjects), and elements of under-performance were reflected both in his subsequent targets for GCSE (four grade C passes predicted) and in the comments from his tutor both at the end of Year 10 and at the mid-point of Year 11:

> Craig has the ability to contribute well and in general has a good understanding of his work. But he has some serious personal targets if he is to succeed ... he is not single-minded enough and, although he works well when he focuses, he needs constant reminding to stay on task; he has a good deal of ability but has yet to use it; he plays too much on his status as a talented sportsman.
>
> (June, Year 10)

> He is capable of good work on the rare occasions when he applies himself, but exam results are disappointing. All subjects speak of his need to apply himself if he is to make the most of his obvious

potential; he must catch up on all work missed, and minimize the distractions.

(February, Year 11)

Throughout the two years of his GCSE studies, Craig's ongoing interviews with us (and significantly, he usually gave the impression of interviewing us, taking the initiative, discussing his own progress, contributing articulately and confidently) were marked by an utter lack of realism, and a lack of awareness and self-analysis. In Craig's view, he 'worked well' with his teachers but 'could probably put in more effort' (February, Year 10); in June of Year 10, he was 'reasonably optimistic' about his progress in most subjects and his 'tutor was very helpful in giving after-school support and offering a place for him to work', and he was 'working much harder than in Year 10 (twice as hard), and enjoying the work', but it was 'impinging on my social life and sport'. Nevertheless, in February of Year 11 he was 'still managing to revise for up to an hour each night, but I have a break at weekends'.

His Head of Year, in contrast, described Craig as

one of the most able boys you are interviewing, but very lazy; he derives his self-worth from sporting ability (footballer) and is held in high esteem by his peers. His parents are relaxed about his school performance, despite some exclusions, and he is in serious risk of missing out at GCSE.

(December, Year 11)

By May, the scenario was much clearer still: 'he has totally lost the plot ... a very pleasant lad at one-to-one, but not working; he has recently been excluded on a short-term basis; he is intent on not performing, disrupting learning for others, and has lost all motivation in the last few months'. Craig's final performance, no higher level passes at GCSE and six grade Ds (including grade Ds in all the core subjects) confirmed that the school's analysis of Craig's performance was more accurate than his own!

There was in some boys, then, a lack of engagement with the demands of academic work in the final years of their schooling. This was sometimes evidenced through confrontational behaviour, or through a refusal to identify with the aspirations of the school. Sometimes, too, there was an arrogance, a rebuttal of what teachers and parents saw as extrinsically valuable and worthwhile. Equally, there were occasions when boys identified a lack of responsibility for their own learning, displaying the expectation that it was the teacher's responsibility to engage and motivate, and there was no sense that students must work towards their own goals. In such contexts, there was no sense of autonomy of the learner or a responsibility for self: 'if the teacher can't control us, then no work is done'.

Work was sometimes seen by some boys as a necessary evil, for the benefit of the teacher rather than for themselves: as Woods (1990) suggests, motivation came from the school's own valuation of work, and above all, the relationship with the teacher. As we have seen, boys were also more likely to blame the teachers for their lack of success, attributing their failure to external factors (Head 1996), with some expressing the view that teachers preferred girls and gave them more help (Younger and Warrington 1996, 1999). Those who had earned a bad reputation lower down the school felt that even if they did work hard, they would get no credit for it from the teachers; these boys were unable to see the value of self-motivation, and expected the impetus to come from their teachers.

This lack of engagement and resistance to school was mirrored to some degree in students' views about whether schools really have individual students' well-being and achievement as their core concerns. In most schools, this was self-evident, and both girls and boys asserted strongly that teachers really did care, offered encouragement, showed real understanding, 'they talk to you and ask your views'. There was nonetheless an ambivalence in some schools, among both girls and boys, as to the reasons for this concern. In some schools, there was a grudging acknowledgement that the school did want its students to do well, but only because of its own reputation: 'to make certain that the school is better than other schools ... they don't care about pupils, only results ... they support those pupils who will do things for the school's good name, rather than for the pupils themselves'.

An uncomfortably high number of students in some schools also subscribed to the view that 'lots of teachers don't give a damn ... they get paid anyway', and that they were more interested in GCSE grades 'so that they don't get the sack!' ... or 'so that they can cross their threshold!'. Interesting, all groups identified a minority of teachers who had talked to them explicitly in these terms. In some schools, this developed into a discussion on teacher retention: 'We haven't seen a history teacher for months! ... Teachers should come to school more!!'

Some boys whom we interviewed, however, established a very subtle balance between image, engagement and achievement. Aydin was one such boy; identified by the school as 'unlikely to achieve 5 grade Cs at GCSE, partly because of attitude and partly because of prior achievement', Aydin also achieved level 5s in all three core subjects in Year 9 National Curriculum tests. Through Year 10, he worked steadily and appeared well organized, achieving an end-of-year report which commented on his mature attitude and determination to do his best. In his interviews with us, he spoke of 'working hard because I know I have to if I am to get good grades. I usually work hard with others but sometimes I can get distracted. I am good at managing homework.'

By November of Year 11, his Head of Year was describing 'a very opinionated student, a rough diamond who might come good, difficult to teach at one level ... but also working steadily and with determination'. In November, Aydin told us that he was taking a more serious attitude to work since Y10, liking the more adult treatment from teachers, and determined to meet his targets; in January, he was beginning to attend revision classes, particularly in French.

By May, he had been appointed a prefect and 'I really like the role because it gives me a sense of being important and being able to help younger children'; he was revising two hours a night, was confident that he was making reasonable progress; and was particularly encouraged by the constant praise he received in French. To his Head of Year, he remained 'very vocal in class, occasionally too outspoken and regularly comes close to overstepping the mark in terms of the tone of his classroom comments because he is not quite sure where to draw the line at times'. Crucially, however, Aydin was also described by his Head of Year as 'working very hard on the sly, regularly requesting extra help and asking for extra exam papers, but he has worked hard to disguise this and not to show others he is doing so'.

Aydin's ultimate achievement, six GCSEs at grade B (including French) and two at grade C, illustrates what can be achieved when individual aspirations are raised, when teachers are prepared to challenge and deny their own pre-conceptions, when targets are revised in the light of performance rather than seen as having a self-fulfilling prophecy. Some students perceive that teachers have misjudged them, underestimated what they were capable of, and written them off too soon. This is understandable given the prior performances of some students. Aydin told us, however, that he was determined to do better, that a chance exchange with a young member of staff early in Year 10 had challenged him, that he became convinced that he could motivate himself 'to do better, to improve from within, and that it wasn't helpful being beaten with a stick from outside'. Equally, though, his position in the peer group, his concern with how he was thought of and viewed by his friends, meant that he could not legitimize his new-found belief in explicit action. Hence the subterfuge to sustain image and respectability through a continuing macho behaviour in the classroom; hence the conspiratorial approach to additional work, in which key teachers explicitly colluded.

We take up some of these issues in more detail in Chapter 9, when we consider socio-cultural issues. From the perspective of students' voices, however, we have to acknowledge that 'being a lad' for many boys meant the need to preserve a macho image, and that this was partly related to not achieving or engaging with school work (Francis 2000a; Warrington *et al.* 2000; Martino and Pallotta-Chiarolli 2003; Skelton 2003). At the same time, however, many lads still expressed aspirations for a good job, a wife and a car, and were able to articulate the difficulties this caused for them in reconciling conflicting images: 'If you don't do well at school, you're not going to get a decent job and a nice house. You're going to be stuck on the minimum wage.' Thus, many students had credible career plans and were aware of the need for qualifications and the liberating effects these could have. In some schools, there was a growing sense of value about external qualifications; several boys said that they 'still didn't like school, but appreciated it was doing all it could for them'. The school was seen to treat Y11 students in a more positive and adult way: 'The school does want you to do well. They keep drumming it into your head that if you don't get any GCSEs you're going nowhere so it makes people want to achieve because they want to do sommat.'

These different voices reveal some of the complexity of being a 'potentially under-achieving boy' in secondary school. For some of these boys, there were feelings of disenchantment and disillusionment, of hostility and despair, the desire for a new beginning. For others, there was an over-confidence, a complacency and a misplaced optimism that all would be well in the end. As their education proceeded, some found ways of reconciling image with covert achievement, others sank into a bewildered sense of despondency. Some boys accepted the recovery interventions which schools offered and were transformed; others found the school ethos antagonistic and unfriendly and were unable to respond. In their perplexity or their arrogance, their bewilderment or their complacency, their hope or their determination, these voices stress the complexity which many teachers and parents face as they themselves frame responses to the issue of apparently 'under-achieving' boys.

Evolving an agenda for change?

Children are expert witnesses regarding ... the conditions of learning at school, how regimes and relationships shape their sense of status as individuals and as members of the community and, consequently, affect their sense of commitment to learning in school.

(Rudduck and Flutter 2000: 76)

We place considerable emphasis on the perspectives of apparently 'under-achieving' boys at the beginning of this book because we believe that students offer us rich insights into their own experiences of schooling and learning, and the factors which motivate or demotivate, engage or disengage, challenge or bore them, as learners. In addressing issues of achievement and 'under-achievement', we acknowledge the value and power of students' perspectives as an integral part of the evidence base which needs to be collected (Pollard *et al.* 2000; MacBeath *et al.* 2003; Rudduck and Flutter 2004) if intervention strategies devised to address under-achievement are to be rigorously founded and effective. The causes of 'under-achievement' are multi-faceted, as we explore in Chapter 2, but we will only gain a fuller appreciation of the motives of individual boys and girls, be able to analyse the validity (or not) of some of the many stereotypes, be aware of the frustrations, tensions, bewilderment and hostility which some students feel, if we are prepared to listen to them carefully, to engage with them, to focus – however imperfectly – on their own constructions of the reality in which they exist. We hope these voices will inform and add realism to the positions we take, and will portray the essence of the realities which these students face.

Subsequent chapters in this book explore issues associated with raising boys' achievements in secondary school, and are underpinned by research which we have conducted in schools over the past ten years, particularly by our work on the Raising Boys' Achievement Project, 2000–4, which was sponsored by the Department for Education and Skills. This study of *boys'* 'under-achievement' takes us into a highly contested field, as we discuss in Chapter 5. Not only is the very concept of 'under-achievement' much disputed, as we show in Chapter 3, but the emphasis on boys that emerged in the mid-1990s has been rigorously challenged, and rightly so, by many who feel that disadvantage and invisibility remains the destiny for too many girls in too many schools (Chapter 4). We hope we address these concerns throughout this book, not only by recognizing diverse constructions of masculinity and femininity, but by emphasizing the need to seek intervention strategies that address achievement issues for all students, and that operate in a context of inclusivity to transform achievement and opportunity for girls as well as boys. We may not always have succeeded, but our aim, in working directly with secondary schools in contrasting socio-economic environments in different parts of England, has been to identify, help to refine and subsequently evaluate intervention strategies, in both mainstream and special schools (as described in Chapters 6–10) which are equally accessible to girls as well as boys, which can be located within gender relational contexts, and which do not disadvantage or work against any student, whatever their gender, sexual disposition, ethnicity or class.

2 National and International Dimensions
Context and Causes

The dilemma facing boys like Craig and Aydin in the latter years of their secondary schooling, and the apparent failure of many boys to fulfil their 'potential', encapsulated one of the themes which relentlessly persisted in English secondary schools in the 1990s and in the early years of the twenty-first century. In the media, the issue of boys' under-achievement and the gender gap captured the headlines in a stark and insistent way. Each summer, the publication of GCSE results brought forward a catalogue of alarming assertions, with powerful educational establishment figures reflecting on the failure of working-class boys, and the media pronouncing on the need to address 'the crisis' of male under-achievement (Bright 1998), and to devise 'rescue plans for the weaker sex' (Lee-Potter 2003). In the mid-1990s, the determination of successive Conservative administrations to publish league tables, based upon GCSE results at 16+ but without meaningful contextualization, merely exacerbated these concerns, and although the initial reactions of the 1997 incoming Labour administration seemed to embody recognition, at least in rhetoric, that league tables and value-added needed a more sophisticated and complex approach than those previously acknowledged indicators (Gray and Wilcox 1995; Gray *et al.* 1996; Thomas and Mortimore 1996; Whitty *et al.* 1998), the tone and substance of the debate did not change. A cascade of consultancy advice, research projects and in-service provision focused attention on how to improve boys' performances. In popular and government debate, the emphasis was not on girls' achievements, nor on the improved levels of performance of both girls and boys, but simply and starkly on male under-achievement, on the failure of boys at whatever age within the secondary school system to achieve similar levels of attainment to those of girls.

Similar concerns were voiced at the same time by academic researchers elsewhere in the United Kingdom (Riddell 1998; Gorard *et al.* 1999; Tinklin *et al.* 2001). In Australia, too, perceptions of 'underachieving and underprivileged' boys (Gilbert and Gilbert 2001; Martino and Berrill 2003), and of boys as the 'new disadvantaged' (Kenway *et al.* 1998; Martino and Meyenn 2002) emerged in response to Australian boys' apparently inferior performances academically (Teese *et al.* 1995; Yates 1997), their skewed subject choices and their lower retention rates at school (Collins *et al.* 2000). The rhetoric on 'failing boys' was also driven by 'a backlash mentality which is informed by the presumption that boys experience educational disadvantage in ways which are comparable to that of girls' (Foster *et al.* 2001: 7), and by notions that 'boys were being sissified and expected to give in to the feminisation of the world' (Australian Member of Parliament, quoted by Rowan *et al.* 2002: 31). To some Australian academic commentators, meanwhile, there was a sense of foreboding (Kenway *et al.* 1998; Lingard and Douglas 1999; Gilbert and Gilbert 2001), a danger that the entire debate on achievement and equal opportunities was being captured and refocused, such that 'policies on gender equity are being hastily rewritten to give more prominence to the needs of boys' (Yates 1997: 337).

In the United States, there emerged a similar proliferation of texts on the theme of how to 'protect' boys, on how teachers, counsellors and therapists might identify and respond to boys' hidden despondency and depression, on ways in which boys might be 'rescued'. Some commentators argued that elementary schools were feminizing boys (Gurian 1998), refusing to acknowledge that boys needed to be encouraged to be boys, and giving the message that 'boyhood is defective' (Foster *et al.* 2001: 12). Weaver-Hightower described how 'progressive groups are already working with boys, seeking to mollify their disadvantages' (2003a: 479), particularly providing 'African-American and other ethnic minority boys with tutoring, mentoring, recreational and educational activities, and sometimes spiritual guidance, to help them overcome the severe disadvantages that they face in schools and other aspects of life' (2003a: 490). Similarly, Majors (2001) outlined 'rites of passage' programmes which focused on teaching boys how to negotiate with dignity, how to manage anger, how to deal with perceived snubs and put-downs.

The educational scene in mainland Europe echoed similar concerns, although the tone was more measured and reflective, and less alarmist. Nonetheless, it has been acknowledged that more girls than boys have been achieving the baccalaureate in France since the 1970s, and in Germany girls have been obtaining better school marks than boys, repeating classes less often and gaining school certificates more successfully (Sutherland 1999). In Belgium, research suggested that boys' culture was less study-oriented than girls' and that, not surprisingly, this impacted upon differential achievement of girls and boys in their secondary schooling (Van Houtte 2004). In Sweden, there were concerns that boys learnt less in schools about democratic values than did girls and were more attracted to anti-democratic ideals, and voices were raised in favour of putting more effort into developing boys' social competence and democratic understanding (Ohrn 2001). Teachers' perspectives on differences in teaching boys and girls, of single-sex settings as learning contexts for boys and girls and of boys' and girls' differing prospects in school and into the future, also entered the public domain in Finland (Gordon 1996), in Denmark (Kruse 1996), and in Iceland (Johannesson 2004). Further afield, in Malaysia, there are emerging signs that the research agenda on gender issues is turning to address the under-achievement of boys during their secondary education and their subsequent under-representation in all subjects in university education (Lebor, personal correspondence, 2003).

In England, this construction of the debate in terms of a preoccupation with boys' 'under-achievement' ought not to surprise us. The whole ethos and structure of the English educational system, through the establishment of public schools, through the weighting of grammar school entries to ensure the selection of at least an equal number of boys in the 11+ selection examination, through the organization of the curriculum of the comprehensive schools, have enshrined a preoccupation with boys. The discourse has been dominated by concerns with male achievement, male values, male aspirations and goals (Gipps 1996; Weiner *et al.* 1997; Arnot 2002). Although equality of opportunity initiatives of the 1980s, with the development of whole school policies which addressed issues such as differential option choices, the language of textbooks and classrooms, teaching strategies and teacher expectation (Whyte 1985; Arnot and Weiner 1987; Rudduck 1994), appeared to have been successful at one level, at least in terms of girls' levels of achievements and their expectations and ambitions, these 'successes' themselves were turned into a source of anxiety:

> It appears as if female success is viewed as a corollary to male failure. Rather than celebrating girls' achievements and aspirations, we have now a discourse of male disadvantage in which boys are viewed as falling behind in academic performance.
>
> (Weiner *et al.* 1997: 620)

It was as though the very successes of girls were seen as threatening, as undermining for boys in schools and for men generally, a threat to the group which for so long had dominated Western societies, and had retained the political, economic and social power ('Grim reading for males', *The Guardian*, 1998). This reorientation of the discourse, whether in the United Kingdom, mainland Europe, North America or Australia, is viewed in some contexts as a male reaction against the equal opportunity thrusts of the earlier decades, constituting 'a backlash against feminist successes' (Kenway 1995: 59), and responding to the perceived inadequacy of ongoing empirical and theoretical work which focused on boys and girls together (Yates 1997; Warrington and Younger 1999). As a consequence, equal opportunity initiatives which emphasized the needs of girls and young women virtually disappeared overnight (Myers 2000).

So what is it about (some) boys?

In essence, then, the debate on male under-achievement has seen a re-emerging concern with boys in their own right, rather than simply as players whose attitudes and approaches had to be changed if female disadvantage was to be eliminated (Kenway 1997; Yates 1997). There is an increasing unease, however, with some aspects of this reoriented discourse (Epstein *et al.* 1998; Lingard and Douglas 1999; Francis and Skelton 2001; Martino and Berrill 2003) and the sense of moral panic which this has induced in some commentators and governments. As we make clear in Chapters 4 and 5, we share this unease, not least because the notion of male disadvantage is one which is difficult to sustain in the labour market of Western economies and in the wider context of a patriarchal society, and because the issue is far more complex and pluralistic than often is presented, with the need for discussion of more sophisticated relational rather than oppositional interpretations (Francis 2000a; Gilbert and Gilbert 2001; Arnot 2002; Skelton and Francis 2003).

Nonetheless, this unease does not negate a concern over the achievement levels of some boys. This 're-discovery' of a gender gap between the achievements of boys and girls in many secondary schools in England is a major challenge for those concerned with raising standards in those secondary schools. Work in individual school contexts (Rudduck *et al.* 1995; Pickering 1997; Younger *et al.* 1999; Younger *et al.* 2002) emphasizes that more boys than girls *are* disengaged, that more discipline problems *are* perceived to be caused by boys, that more boys *are* excluded from secondary schooling. Similarly, more sophisticated attempts at value-added analysis (DfES 2004a) and of the progress made by girls and boys who achieved similar levels of achievement at the ages of 11 and 14 (as measured in National Curriculum tests and teacher assessments), suggest that more girls than boys make significantly more progress between the ages of 14 and 16, over the course of Key Stage 4 in English secondary schools:

> There is a real problem with boys, especially between 10 and 16, and nobody seems to know what to do with them … at the moment too many schools just passively react to boys' disruption. A policy of containment or just getting by seems to be the order of the day.
>
> (Jackson and Salisbury 1996: 104)

> I don't know why I mess around. I got sent out of a lesson yesterday for chatting and giving it back. I don't know why I give it back, I don't like to back down. I just mouth back.
>
> (Jake, Year 10)

So what is it about some boys? What motivates them to behave as they do, to challenge, to undermine the learning of other boys and many girls? Why do they resist the often careful and painstaking attempts of their teachers to interest and engage them in learning? What helps to explain the failure of some boys to achieve at the same levels as girls of similar ability?

The literature addressing these issues is extensive, wide-ranging and profound. To some commentators, causal explanations should be sought essentially in biological accounts, centred on essentialist approaches that maintain that gender difference is genetically determined and that each gender is characterized by a distinct set of physical, emotional and psychological traits (Kehily 2001). Thus, differing characteristics are rooted in the extent of brain differences between girls and boys (Sommers 2000; Gurian 2001), with links to boys' testosterone and the 'natural' development of boys (Biddulph 1998). Similarly, Archer, J. (2004) argues for a biological construction of masculinity, citing studies that show behavioural sex differences at a very early age, before children are able to form any notions of socially constructed gender (Connellan et al. 2000; Archer and Lloyd 2002; Baron-Cohen 2003). There are, according to Archer: 'consistent patterns of masculinity across nations and history that can be understood from an evolutionary perspective ... behavioural sex differences arise out of biological differences that are apparent early in development' (2004: 136).

Much of the debate in educational circles has tended to accept that discussion about the relative importance of socialization and biology is unhelpful, however, since it is extremely difficult to isolate the one from the other; indeed, some commentators go further: 'the significance of "brain difference" for gendered behaviour continues to be challenged, and there appears to be little new evidence to suggest that gender differences are the result of physiology' (Skelton and Francis 2003: 13).

The main thrust of the educational research points therefore in social constructionist directions, linking the relative under-achievement of some boys to the context and the environment in which they live, experience and move (Mills 2001; Arnot 2002; Skelton and Francis 2003). Thus, explanations are sought in the ways in which some boys conform to the 'macho' gender regime of the local community, with a disregard for authority, academic work and formal achievement (Harris et al. 1995; Rudduck et al. 1996), in differences in students' attitudes to work, and their goals and aspirations (Younger and Warrington 1996) linked to the wider social context of changing labour markets, de-industrialization, tertiarization and the changing nature of male and female employment opportunities (Wilkinson 1994; Arnot et al. 1996; Yates 1997; Kenway et al. 1998). Such writers suggest that:

> Factors affecting young people's attitudes and motivation include the nature of employment opportunities within the locality of the

school, traditional expectations in the community about patterns of 'male' and 'female' employment and perceptions of the relevance of education to future lives and life chances.

(Arnot *et al.* 1998: 90)

Other researchers have commented on differential gender interactions between pupils and teachers in the classroom, particularly as perceived by (some) boys (Younger *et al.* 1999). There has been emphasis, too, on girls' increased maturity and more effective learning strategies (Gipps 1996), with the emphasis on collaboration, talk and sharing (Askew and Ross 1988; Fennema 1996), while boys, in contrast, were seen neither as team players, nor as unwilling to collaborate to learn (Barker 1997), and less inclined to use cooperative talk and discussion to aid and support their own learning.

Of central importance in these social constructionist explanatory frameworks, however, have been discussions based on notions of masculinities and laddishness, with explorations of the ways in which boys' identification with concepts of masculinity are frequently seen to be in direct conflict with the ethos of the school; it is to these discussions which we now turn.

The role of image in attitudes to work and behaviour

The starting point for any discussion on the impact of masculinity and laddishness on the achievements of boys at school must be by acknowledging the seminal work of academics such as Mac an Ghaill (1994), Connell (1995), Sewell (1998), Arnot *et al.* (1999) and Martino and Pallotta-Chiarolli (2003), which illustrates clearly the complexity of the notion of masculinity, and rejects the argument that there is simply one type of masculinity. Equally, interpretations of masculinity may vary through time and space, they are fluid and flexible (Francis 2000a), and culturally and historically dependent (Weaver-Hightower 2003a). We stress the importance of these issues in Chapter 5. We also acknowledge, however, that in many institutional contexts, there is frequently a dominant version of masculinity (Skelton 2001), usually some construction of hegemonic masculinity which embodies the public face of male power, and that in schools many boys strive to construct and mould themselves into this version of masculinity, to become 'a real man', 'a typical lad', 'one of the boys'.

It is crucially important to many boys that they are accepted by other boys, that they are able to identify with and act in line with peer group norms, so that they are not seen as 'other' or different, but rather as belonging (Skelton 2001; Martino and Pallotta-Chiarolli 2003). Such acceptance *is* often dependent on an act, negotiating an acceptable identity, incorporating aspects of laddishness of behaviour, risk-taking and living on the edge, and a certain bravado and noisy demonstration of masculinity. Expressed in behaviour, speech, dress code and body language, such laddishness often runs counter to the expectations of the home, but such behaviour is seen as a reasonable cost by boys if it allows them to protect their macho image, and enables them to ensure their acceptance as part of the chosen social group. This has been neatly summarized by Becky Francis, in *Boys, Girls and Achievement*:

> loud, physical and sometimes aggressive and/or disruptive behaviour is an integral expression of many boys' construction of masculinity ... and is likely to impede their achievement ... While girls' construction of the female role has altered in the last two decades, having a positive effect on their achievement, boys' construction of masculinity has largely remained the same. In fact, as girls' construction of gender has become more diverse, and as girls move into areas traditionally seen as masculine, it is possible that boys have become increasingly laddish in their efforts to construct themselves.
>
> (2000a: 120)

In this context, the aspirations which many schools hold for such boys are not seen to be acceptable or legitimate to them because they can only be achieved by adopting strategies – particularly linked to academic work – which are divergent from those accepted within the peer group. Peer group pressures against the academic work ethic as a consequence often lead to male behaviour which does not acknowledge and accept boundaries. In Connell's words: 'Up against an authority structure, acts of resistance or defiance mean "getting into trouble" ' (2000: 135). Our research in many English schools over the past decade has reiterated this concern with image and the extent to which social groupings play a major role in students' lives. Boys in schools in very different socio-cultural contexts, in inner cities and in rural counties, in Southern England's commuter belt and in Northern England's former mining villages, have all stressed this common theme of the vital need to conform to peer pressure, to be part of the crowd and live up to crowd norms and expectations. Unlike girls, whose interests are quite widely spread, boys' groups mainly revolve around a football culture, and boys with little or no interest in football are often excluded or marginalized (West 1996). Some boys, particularly those in higher sets, certainly are part of a group where hard work is accepted, and others have learnt to take no notice of taunts from their peers, but for many boys, being 'one of the lads', being 'real hard', being 'really loud and having a laugh sometimes', 'not showing your emotions and having to win', 'not being walked over', embody the essence of the all-important macho image (Mac an Ghaill 1994). Thus, to Sean, Tyrone and Abdalla there is safety and security in group membership, despite the pressure that this entails:

If you achieve nowt, your mates don't laugh at you.

(Sean)

You're not allowed to get scared, it's not cool ... it's hard if you don't have mates and do as they say ... because if you don't you'll lose your mates.

(Tyrone)

Around here, it's not safe .. if you're walking on your own, plenty of stuff can happen to you, so you need a gang ... and to be in a gang, you need to be right ... you know, the hood, the trainers, the mood.

(Abdalla)

Mills describes how this risk-taking pushes at the limits of whatever social context these boys find themselves in, as they strive to impress and to demonstrate their dominance over other boys and girls:

The schoolyard fight, the sexual harassment of girls, riding motor-bikes illegally, playing contact sports, accepting dares are all forms of risk-taking which have the potential to result in harm to oneself or another ... and they all take place where others can judge the success or failure of the performance.

(2001: 57)

To gain a good reputation in the eyes of the peer group, to be sought after, particularly by girls, boys need to be assertive and noticed by teachers and peers. In this context, the challenging and aggressive behaviour of some boys not only leads to their rejection of academic work, but is part of a complex performance (Butler 1990), an 'integral part of learning to do masculinity' (Gilbert and Gilbert 2001: 7), associated with a public acknowledgement and working out of masculinity which in itself has contributed to potential under-achievement (Bohan 1997). Gaining member-ship of this group, fulfilling the entrance criteria, sustaining the group norms over time, is like 'passing an examination' (Martino and Pallotta-Chiarolli 2003). There are thus 'badges of masculinity' (Majors 2001) which can generate conflicts with authority structures, and which in turn can create communication barriers and prevent some boys from developing positive gender identities and from an engagement with learning.

These badges of masculinity differ, of course, between schools and over time. In some schools, different sub-groups of boys (and equally of girls), with different characteristics, assume leadership roles within the peer community. These students may have a high profile in terms of sport, or in the performing arts, or because they have a key role in the local youth culture based on one or more of drink, drugs or claimed sexual prowess. To boys and girls in a town in southern England, these boys were 'the townies who go round in Reeboks, hoods and sporty clothes, who get the teachers' attention and really run them ragged if they get the chance!' To students in inner Manchester, a key group of boys were 'the moshies who skate and listen to daft music and stuff, and wear dark clothes, a cap and baggy pants'. To boys and girls in an East Anglian market town, they were the PGs, the self-designated popular guys and girls who 'are loud, confident and intimidating, with the right bags, "just so" make-up and the shoes, the hairstyle and "just different" school uniform, the show which counts for everything, in the limelight the whole time'.

There is an interesting paradox in some of these responses, a mix of admiration and fear, a feeling of being intimidated yet wanting to imitate. These boys (and the fewer girls who act similarly) are highly valued in the peer group, bringing prestige and status to the girls who were associated with them, conferring high rank, kudos and social standing through association. As we discuss in Chapter 9, these boys can be key players in schools, offering positive role models in some, but equally posing very significant challenges in others, particularly when they adopt a position on the margins of school life, exhibit clear anti-school traits, and exert a strong negative influence on the levels of engagement of other students with school life.

Laddishness as a defence mechanism

This culture of laddishness is not new, of course, as the seminal work of Paul Willis makes clear (Willis 1977), but in the late 1990s the term took on new connotations, beyond the context of Willis' working-class, white, anti-school youths, so that laddish behaviour is identified across social class and ethnic group (and persists in some men, it is argued, into 'maturity' and middle age). Within the classroom context, laddish behaviour is seen to have the potential to impact negatively not only on the learning of these lads but also on others, girls as well as boys (Yates 1997; Francis 2000a). Indeed, this causal link between laddishness and the causes of boys' 'underachievement' was inevitably highlighted during the late 1990s in England following statements from school ministers and the then Chief Inspector of Schools:

> We face a genuine problem of underachievement among boys, particularly those from working class families. This underachievement is linked to a laddish culture which in many areas has grown out

of deprivation, and a lack of both self-confidence and opportunity.
(Blunkett 2000)

There are a number of issues in such a view which we would want to challenge (see Chapter 5), but there are two specific aspects of this concern with laddishness which need further discussion: one is linked to the adoption by lads of specific strategies that minimize the possibility of failure and the consequent loss of status and esteem in the group context; the second is linked to an avoidance of the feminine and the 'stigma' of homosexuality.

Avoidance of failure

Interviews with boys in many schools over the past decade have convinced us some boys use laddish strategies to protect their macho image and their social self-esteem, and make considerable efforts to avoid the culture of failure. Such boys articulate explanations – through their off-task behaviour, their self-protection through lack of effort in terms of classwork, homework and coursework, their lack of acceptance of the aims and objectives of the school – for their poor performance in school, to protect themselves against failure and competition. The possibility of failure can lead to anger, hostility and disaffection. In Hey and Creese's (2000) terminology:

> In certain contexts, competition militates against certain boys' achievements ... particularly when wannabe hegemonic boys do not 'win' ... a response is for boys to adopt a can't win, won't win and don't want to play stance ... a not trying, self-sabotaging position complicit with anti-learning.

This has implications, of course, for the use of competitive activities in classrooms to which we return later (Chapter 6), but it does resonate with studies which argue that despite the widespread evidence that competition is more effective as a motivational spur with boys than with girls (Head 1996; Boaler 1997), some boys are more inclined to withdraw from the competition, rather than be seen to fail, whereas more girls were likely to struggle to overcome their difficulties (Barker 1997; Warrington *et al.* 2000).
Carolyn Jackson (2002, 2003) has positioned these arguments persuasively within the context of self-worth theory, drawing on the work of motivation theorists such as Dweck (1999) and Covington (1998) who suggest that: 'self-worth protection or self-handicapping strategies may be provoked by situations that provide a threat to one's self-worth' (Jackson 2002: 42). For whatever reasons, some boys have quickly learnt, from an early age, that they are unable to be successful in the kinds of academic demands which schools make of them. In such a context, their own fear of failure in the academic competition is such that they prefer not to enter the compe-

tition, for to fail will impact negatively upon their own self-perception and on how their peers see them. According to Jackson, therefore, boys adopt a number of subtle and well-developed strategies to avoid this possibility of failure: procrastination, the intentional withdrawal of effort and the consequent rejection of academic work, and disruptive behaviour (Jackson 2002): 'From a self-worth perspective, adhering to laddish anti-school cultures provides an in-built excuse for boys who are not achieving academically, as the focus for academic failure is shifted from a lack of ability to a lack of effort'. The lack of effort, by definition, is self-imposed and chosen freely by the boys concerned.

There is a further aspect of this argument, linked to laddish image and esteem within the group. Epstein *et al.* (1998) argue that one of the dominant aspects of a laddish approach is not the avoidance of academic work *per se*, but the avoidance of the appearance of engaging in academic work. Among staff we have interviewed in schools over the past decade, this has been a common theme: teachers have felt that boys appeared more concerned with preserving an image of reluctant involvement or disengagement and that, for many boys, it was not acceptable to be seen to be interested or stimulated by academic work. In some contexts, there were quite sophisticated attempts by boys to conceal interest or involvement and to preserve status within the peer group:

> You'll hear them say to each other outside the classroom, 'Have you done the homework?', and the reply, 'Nah, you must be joking', but when I collect it in, it's all there. The small minority of boys who are likely to be a little bit silly in class, they are more likely to be the ones who create the immaculate work, that they've done at home ... they are stereotypical boys, witty jokes, only occasional contact, they don't give away anything in class, but they create very good work.
>
> (female English teacher, quoted in Younger and Warrington 1996: 303)

To these lads, achievement was not a problem, but to be perceived by peers as needing to work to achieve definitely was (Martino 1999). From a self-worth perspective, therefore, 'effortless achievement is the ideal; ... it also provides a convenient excuse if success is not forthcoming – failure without effort does not necessarily indicate a lack of ability, but success without effort indicates true genius' (Jackson 2002: 46).

Fear of the feminine

Extensive studies over the past decade (Mac an Ghaill 1994; Redman and Mac an Ghaill 1996; Nayak and Kehily 1996; Salisbury and Jackson 1996; Kehily and Nayak 1997; Martino and Pallotta-Chiarolli 2003) have highlighted the various ways in which – as part of the various constructions of masculinity – homosexuality has been stigmatized within youth cultures and schools. Boys who are identified as different – through their clothing, their voice, their mannerisms and gestures, their interests, their behaviour, their friendship networks, have often been exposed to homophobic abuse, most consistently from other boys (Salisbury and Jackson 1996; Epstein and Johnson 1998; Gilbert and Gilbert 1998). To many boys, this is their greatest fear: 'the potentially emasculating experience of being called "gay" haunted young men in school, and identified certain boys as different ... [such] homophobic abuse could be carefully codified and ritualised within male peer groups' (Kehily 2001: 120). In such a culture, boys must work hard to show their masculinity, to resist the risks of 'having the rip taken out of them', to avoid the derisiveness of being labelled 'boff', 'girl', 'pooftah'. Being a 'real' boy entails an oppositional position to all that is feminine (Martino 1999), and this concern with avoidance of the feminine means that in many schools boys are not 'allowed' to excel except in sport. In their discussion of policing young masculinities, Frosh *et al.* (2002) powerfully document what often happens when boys resist the prevailing masculine culture, and in particular disclaim an interest in football:

> For Oliver, football was an obsession with trivia, which made boys unable to concentrate in class or to develop friendships with girls ... the price Oliver paid for this set of attitudes and behaviours was high. He was generally seen as transgressing normal gender boundaries, and the other boys taunted him with this as a masculine insufficiency, calling him 'girl'.
>
> (p. 178)

Equally, boys who *do* perform well in 'non-masculine' areas such as music, art and drama run the risk of being rejected by the in-crowd, ridiculed, and bullied; the caring, sharing, sensitive male is not an accepted image in many crowds, despite the valuing of it by many girls, as we saw in Chapter 1. As a reaction to this, many boys cultivate what Kehily (2001) calls 'hyper-heterosexual identity', where feminized traits are derided and aggressively countered, and boys adopt explicit and sometimes extreme versions of masculinity. Significantly, though, this is not simply an issue with students, but with some of their teachers (Mac an Ghaill 1994; Davison 2000) and indeed some of their parents:

> The [equal opportunities] message isn't received by all members of staff; if you say, we need to have males who approach life in terms of being sensitive, kind, alert to the needs of others in society, they would laugh you out of court. Parents would say 'I'm not having my son beaten up on the street for being a woofter', that's why I

think it is about creating within your institution a very clear culture at all levels, and in all aspects, so that the kids are aware of it and follow it, and it has got to be done in such a way that it is not seen as a joke, and accepted by all, especially male staff and that is very difficult.

(male deputy headteacher, quoted in Warrington *et al.* 2000: 404)

To some boys, a crucial aspect of this avoidance of the feminine is the avoidance of academic work, because working hard, being cooperative, quiet and engaged in school work are perceived by many boys as part of being a girl, as a feminine activity (Walkerdine 1989; Mac an Ghaill 1994; Epstein *et al.* 1998; Skelton 2001; Jackson 2003):

If boys want to avoid the verbal and physical abuse attached to being labelled as 'feminine' or 'queer', they must avoid academic work, or at least they must *appear* to avoid academic work.

(Jackson 2002: 40)

Not only were heterosexist practices connected to specific kinds of school performance, but ... students could clearly articulate the positioning of workers and achievers as gay.

(Frank *et al.* 2003: 122)

To some boys, often those on the margins of the 'in-group' or lacking a natural affinity to sport, there is thus the need, in the face of challenge from other boys and occasionally from girls, to assert their masculinity in terms of the rejection of all things feminine (Frosh *et al.* 2002). Such a rejection can impact upon their commitment to work, on their grades and achievement, on their participation; inevitably this pressure to resist being different impacts upon behaviour, upon attitudes to homework and coursework, upon interactions with teachers and other students within classes. As these boys seek to conform and to identify with this aspect of heterosexuality, so the risk of under-achievement and failure to meet potential is exacerbated. In some contexts, there is a subject dimension to this rejection of academic work (Frank *et al.* 2003), with some boys actively disengaging from those subjects, such as English, Modern Languages, the Humanities, PSHE, which are perceived to be more 'girl-friendly' and less macho. In an Australian study, for example, one boy asserted that: 'English is more suited to girls because it's not the way guys think ... this subject is the biggest load of bull-shit I have ever done ... I hope you aren't offended by this, but most guys who like English are faggots' (Martino 1995). These feminine subjects are not for 'real' boys, because they are perceived as easy options which lack rigour and seriousness (Haywood and Mac an Ghaill 2003), because they require boys to consider their feelings and emotions as well as demanding a 'factual' and 'objective' response, they are less 'hard-edged' than the mathematical and scientific subjects (Warrington and Younger 2000).

So where does this leave us?

We began this chapter by reviewing the scope of the concerns about boys' 'under-achievement' and the different perspectives which have evolved as we have sought to try to understand this phenomenon. In this context, we acknowledge the value of studies of classroom interactions and different learning styles, of work which examines social relationships within schools and groups. We recognize, too, that the debate may be transformed as we continue to develop our understanding of neuro-scientific approaches to learning. Overall, however, in these discussions, we identify closely with social constructionist explanations, acknowledging that issues of inclusion and exclusion, of rejection and acceptance, are crucial as many boys seek to identify with images and sets of attitudes and values which help them to define their own masculinity. Such images frequently involve risk-taking and role play, conforming to anti-school behaviour, adopting anti-societal norms, challenging the purposes and aspirations of the school. Such cool, macho behaviour, with its associated notions of laddishness, is *the* legitimate male role model in many contexts, even when it is alien to the boys concerned (Frosh *et al.* 2002). It is better, apparently, for these boys to identify with such images and attitudes than to deny them, and to risk isolation, bullying and allegations of homosexuality (Martino and Pallotta-Chiarolli 2003). The debate is more nuanced and sophisticated than this, however, as we show in Chapter 5: a multiplicity of masculinities and femininities do exist, and some are more dominant and acceptable in some contexts than in others. Equally, even though issues of masculinity and laddishness are strong influences on the establishment of a dominant street culture in specific localities, this dominant culture need not be 'anti-learning' or resistant to school. To acknowledge the importance of image in impacting upon students' attitudes to work and behaviour, and to recognize the centrality of laddishness and 'ladettishness' in constructing an understanding of students' behaviours, aspirations and achievements, are not to proffer or accept a counsel of doom, but to establish a framework within which schools can construct appropriate responses and strategies, which make the transformation of aspirations and achievement acceptable to the students concerned. This is the agenda for the second part of this book!

3 The Conundrum of the Gender Gap

The nature of the gender gap

Awareness of the gender gap and the apparently synonymous 'under-achievement of boys' is not new. Cohen quotes evidence which spans the last three centuries, from the writings of John Locke and John Bennett through the findings of the Royal Commissions on Education (the Clarendon and Taunton Commissions of 1864 and 1868), into early twentieth-century texts on pedagogy and thence to recent texts and conference presentations, to question how 'the fiction of boys' potential has continued to be sustained' throughout the centuries (Cohen 1996: 133). Indeed, to Cohen, 'from the late seventeenth century to the present, boys have always under-achieved ... and though it has been of concern, under-achievement has never been treated as a problem of boys' (1998: 20). Much of the evolution of state education in England and Wales supports this notion; certainly, the history of selection to mixed grammar schools in the first 70 years of the twentieth century suggests that, although boys might perform less well than girls in the 11+ examination, this did not prevent equal or greater numbers of boys proceeding to a grammar school education (Gallagher 1997).

Since the early and mid-1990s, however, it is clear that all has changed. The discourse has been transformed as commentators have focused with a vengeance on boys' 'underachievement' and on the gender gap, and on the apparent failure of boys to 'perform' as well as girls in academic examinations at crucial transition points in their primary and secondary education. Thus, our own analysis of the relative performance of girls and boys reveals that a gender gap has been apparent in England since the first introduction of National Curriculum tests and teacher assessments at Key Stages 1, 2 and 3 in the period 1992–95 (Warrington et al. 2003). For children aged 7+, there has consistently been a significant percentage points difference between girls and boys who achieved level 2 or above in reading, writing and spelling, at the end of Key Stage 1, although data for mathematics show little difference. Similarly, national data reveal that although there has been little difference between the attainment levels of boys and girls in the National Curriculum Key Stage 2 tests in Maths and Science, taken at the age of 11, there has been a marked disparity between the attainment of boys and girls in English, with girls persistently outperforming boys, particularly in writing. The gender gap persists and widens when girls and boys are tested at the age of 14 (at the end of Key Stage 3), with a 15 percentage points difference commonly recorded in achievement levels at Level 5(+) in English and in many of the Humanities, Languages and Creative Arts subjects, although again the difference in mathematics and science is much smaller (Table 3.1).

Table 3.1 Key Stage 3 performance profiles (per cent boys and girls achieving level 5 or above in national tests)

Subject		1997	1998	1999	2000	2001	2002	2003	2004
English	boys	46	57	55	55	57	59	62	64
	girls	66	73	62	73	74	76	76	77
Mathematics	boys	60	60	62	65	64	67	70	72
	girls	60	60	62	65	68	68	72	74
Science	boys	61	57	55	60	66	67	68	65
	girls	59	64	55	59	66	67	69	67

The academic attainments of boys and girls in their GCSE examinations, taken at the end of compulsory schooling at the age of 16, reveal similar patterns of disparity at school, local education authority and national level. Data for the period 1975–95 show three distinct stages (Figure 3.1):

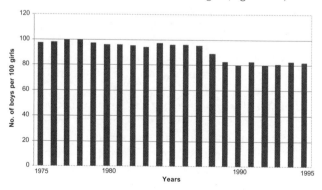

1975 -------- Period of stability / parity -------- 1987   1988–1990   1991 -------- 1995
Rapid   Period of stability /
change   Disparity.

Figure 3.1 Changing levels of performance at GCE / CSE or GCSE (1975–95) Number of boys per 100 girls achieving 5(+) A*–C grades

Source: Adapted from Arnot et al. (1998:11)

1   A period of stability and closeness to parity from 1975 through to the introduction of GCSE examinations in 1988. Here, the GCE examination restricted entry to those students who were perceived to be more able, and although the advent of CSE examinations in the mid-1960s enabled more students in secondary modern and the emerging comprehensive schools to access terminal examinations, entry patterns denied many of them access to the higher grade equivalence of the GCE examinations. Fewer students were involved in such examinations and only 31.7 per cent of girls and 28.2 per cent of boys of the national cohort achieved five or more A–C (or grade 1 CSE) grades in the last year of examination of GCE/CSE (1987).

2   The introduction of GCSE examinations and of the National Curriculum in England and Wales coincided with a period of very rapid change, with the relative difference in girls' and boys' attainments exacerbated. Thus, in 1988, the first year of the newly introduced GCSE examinations, 89 boys were achieving the five A–C benchmark grades compared to 100 girls, and by 1990 this figure had fallen to 80 boys. The gender gap had thus increased from 3.5 percentage points in 1987 to 8 percentage points in 1990, when 38 per cent of girls and 30 per cent of boys achieved the benchmark grades. This period is marked, significantly, by a higher take-up of public examinations, in terms of entry levels, and by a greater number of successful candidates, particularly of girls, for whom the introduction of the National Curriculum widened the range and often increased the number of subjects which they were enabled to take at GCSE level.

3   A period of increased stability and continuing disparity, 1991–95, with a gender gap in the region of 8–10 percentage points between the attainments of girls and boys, so that in 1995 48 per cent of girls and 38 per cent of boys entered for GCSE examinations in England and Wales achieved the five A*–C benchmark grades.

This pattern of stability and disparity has been sustained since 1995 and into the early years of the twenty-first century (Figure 3.2). A three-year rolling mean figure for England over the period 1997–99 shows that 51.6 per cent of girls and 41.5 per cent of boys achieved the benchmark grades (10.1 percentage points difference); by 2004, the gender gap was virtually unchanged, with the benchmark grades being achieved by 58.5 per cent of girls and 48.4 per cent of boys (DfES 2004e). Notably, however, this gender gap continues to exist against a background of rising levels of academic achievement of both boys and girls, although this aspect of the national performance profile has been relatively unrecognized and uncelebrated by most commentators.

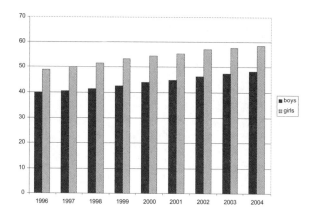

Figure 3.2 Percentage entry of boys and girls achieving 5(+) A*–C grades at GCSE/GNVQ, 1996–2004

This analysis also confirms, however, that the gender gap at the higher levels of attainment is not growing through time (Gorard *et al*. 2001), and that it has now stabilized at around 10 percentage points. It is clear also that at the lowest levels of attainment in GCSE terms, there is little evidence of a substantial gender gap; in 2004, for example, 96.6 per cent of girls and 94.9 per cent of boys achieved at least 1 A*–G GCSE grade or the GNVQ equivalent (DfES 2004e).

The other aspect of the gender gap at the end of compulsory schooling which has become more stark through time, however, has been one based upon an analysis of students' performances in different subjects. A study of English and Welsh examination data over time, undertaken for OFSTED (Arnot *et al*. 1998), concluded that: 'the size and nature of the gender gap in GCSE entries differ from subject to subject; some subjects remain male-dominated while others remain "female-dominated"' (p. 13), and that whereas 'boys secured only modest improvements … in their performance … in various subjects in comparison with girls, girls achieved sizeable improvements … in Science and Mathematics' (p. 13). This is indeed a fundamental aspect of the emergent gender gap. Those subjects perceived traditionally as boys' subjects, subjects such as Mathematics, Science, Design and Technology, Information Technology, have been colonized by girls with increasing success, whereas boys have failed to engage to a similar degree with traditional girls' subjects such as the Humanities and Modern Languages.

Thus, in 2004, as in every preceding year of the century, girls out-performed boys in virtually every mainstream subject of the National Curriculum (Table 3.2). This is apparent not only at the level of the benchmark grades, but also at the highest level of achievement at GCSE (i.e. at A* and A grade), in all subjects except for Mathematics.

Table 3.2 GCSE entries and performance levels, 2004, for subjects taken by over 20 per cent of national cohort

Subject	Gender	% A*–C grades	Gender gap	% A*–A grades	Gender gap
Art	female	77.0	19.4	27.9	14.3
	male	57.6		13.6	
Design/technology	female	64.5	16.0	21.2	10.3
	male	48.5		10.9	
English	female	67.1	14.4	18.4	7.3
	male	52.7		11.1	
English Lit	female	71.5	13.3	21.2	7.7
	male	58.2		13.5	
French	female	60.1	14.0	21.3	6.9
	male	46.1		14.4	
Geography	female	66.8	7.4	25.8	7.0
	male	59.4		18.8	
History	female	67.5	4.9	29.3	5.5
	male	62.6		23.8	
Mathematics	female	53.2	1.2	11.6	-0.5
	male	52.0		12.1	
Physical education	female	61.5	4.0	21.9	6.5
	male	57.5		15.4	
Religious studies	female	71.4	13.3	32.1	11.4
	male	58.1		20.7	
Science (double award)	female	55.8	2.2	14.0	2.6
	male	53.6		11.4	
All subjects: % of grades awarded	female	63.3	8.4	20.0	5.3
	male	54.9		14.7	

Source: DfES Autumn Package, DfES (2004e).

This accords with research we carried out in selective schools in eastern England in the late 1990s:

It is worth emphasising the existence of this gender gap, even in selective schools where there is apparent equality of performance at the five A*–C grade benchmark level; more detailed analysis, here over a six-year period, of those achieving the higher level A*–B grades, shows higher levels of achievement by girls consistently in all subjects except for mathematics and science. While a 'male tail' certainly does exist, there is no corresponding sign of a male-domination of the higher-grade results.

(Warrington and Younger 1999: 58)

Interpreting the gender gap: The case for care and vigilance

As discussed in Chapter 2, this debate on the gender gap and male 'under-achievement' has been one of the most dominant in the educational discourses of the 1990s and the early years of this century, not only in England but through the United Kingdom and in other Western economies. This debate, though, is fraught with dangers and misconceptions. As Hammersley (2001) points out, there are a number of methodological issues to which we must be alert, if we are to avoid some of the simplistic misinterpretations which bedevil the debate.

One of these is the need to distinguish between percentage point gaps and percentage changes in those gaps; thus a change in the percentage of boys achieving the benchmark grades at GCSE, from 44 per cent in 2000 to 48.4 per cent in 2004 (Figure 3.2), is a rise of 4.4 percentage points, but a 10 per cent positive change in the level of boys' performances. Gorard *et al.* draw our attention to the need to avoid what has been called the 'politician's error' (Gorard 2000) in gender analysis. 'The point difference is not the gender achievement gap, (because this) must be calculated proportional to the overall annual achievement' (Gorard *et al.* 2001: 135). Thus a point difference of around 10 points, sustained through time, becomes less significant as the overall levels of attainment rise; whereas 79 boys reached the 5(+)A*-C benchmark level in 1995 compared to every 100 girls, by 2004 that figure had increased to 83 (Table 3.3). Thus the position of boys, whilst still lagging considerably behind that of girls, has improved slowly relative to girls. The percentage gender gap has thus decreased over the last decade in England and Wales and the significance of that gap reduced, as performances have risen and the percentage of boys and girls achieving the benchmark grades has increased (Gorard 2000).

Table 3.3 Percentage point gaps and percentage changes

Year	% entry of girls who gained 5(+) A*–C grades	% entry of boys who gained 5(+) A*–C grades	Gender gap in percentage points (girls – boys)	Boy/girl ratio (boys reaching benchmark level compared to girls)
1995	48.1	3.08	10.1	0.79
1998	51.1	41.3	10.2	0.80
2001	55.4	44.8	10.6	0.81
2004	58.5	48.4	10.1	0.83

Hammersley also counsels on the need to consider examination entry figures of boys and girls, as a proportion of the cohort in the year. Certainly, in the era of performance league tables, some schools have become adept at 'massaging' their performance data through a restricted access policy which reduces the entry of some students seen more at risk of failure. Other schools have implemented policies which have involved a sophisticated targeting of students to particular examinations such as GNVQ and alternative GCSEs which, as well as being seen as offering a more appropriate curriculum for particular groups of pupils, often award dual or quadruple awards and have the effect of maximizing GCSE equivalency output profiles. There is also the danger, at a school level, of over-emphasizing yearly trends without contextualizing them in terms of school-specific issues or small sample size, particularly at subject-specific level. Equally, this talk of 'boys' ignores diversity and the centrality of issues of social class and ethnicity, as we discuss in detail in Chapter 5; certainly, there is considerable evidence (Gillborn and Mirza 2000; Phoenix 2001) to support claims that social class and ethnicity differences are more significant than gender in explanatory frameworks which consider differential achievements between and within groups of boys and girls.

We need to take care, too, in how we contextualize the debate about the gender gap. What are we seeking to achieve in contributing to such a debate? How might we identify schools which have 'successfully' addressed the issue? What underlying agendas are we seeking to address? These are important questions because too often we make assumptions, we take for granted the outcomes we are seeking and the 'success criteria' we share. Hence the conundrum in the title of this chapter: is our concern, as a society, as schools, as educators, as individuals, with a narrowing and even with an eventual elimination of the gender gap, or is it with creating contexts for raising the achievements of all individual students, girls as well as boys? Given the national context, it is understandable that the focus of the debate, particularly at the individual school level, sometimes becomes obsessively focused on the nature of the gap itself. But even in large schools, with stable catchment areas and GCSE entries in excess of 300 students each year, the pattern of GCSE results can vary markedly from year to year.

One aspect of the gender gap conundrum is well illustrated in GCSE performance data through time from an East Anglian comprehensive school (Figure 3.3). Through the period 1995–2003, the school had a stable catchment, representative of the whole ability range, serving an extensive rural area which contained both affluent commuter settlements and areas of significant social deprivation. The school became aware, in the mid-1990s, of significant differential achievement and responded with a variety of strategies designed to create an achieving culture and to reduce gender disparities. In the context of the gender gap debate, GCSE results suggested that the school had met its objectives by 1998, with virtual equality of performance between girls and boys, against a rising achievement trajectory. Continuing discussions with senior managers in the school since 1998, however, highlighted some of the dilemmas in the debate about the gender gap. In 1999, a gender gap reappeared, at a level comparable to 1996, but – in terms of the discussion above – the percentage gender achievement gap had decreased from 17 per cent to 14 per cent. In 2000, the percentage of boys and girls achieving the benchmark grades increased, but the gender gap widened in both percentage points terms *and* in terms of the percentage gender achievement gap, as girls' performances surged. But in this school, more boys and girls are achieving, in terms of the benchmark grades at GCSE, than ever before. The results' profile from the school in 2002 and 2003 add further complexity to the debate: there is virtually no gender gap in 2002, but what of the marked drop in the proportion of girls achieving the benchmark grades? Within the context of previous results, the year of 2002 is hardly a cause for celebration, despite the fact that the boys apparently 'out-performed' the girls ... or *is it*, if we knew more about the nature of the year group, the nature of the individuals and the context within which the school operated that year? Despite the fact that the gender gap widened markedly in 2003, the results here *do* appear unequivocally to be a cause for celebration, with girls' results returning to previously high levels and a higher proportion of boys achieving higher level grades than ever before? No 'under-achievement' in 2003, then? On the face of it, results in 2004 appear disappointing in the context of those of 2003, but again we need to contextualize within school-specific and cohort-specific perspectives.

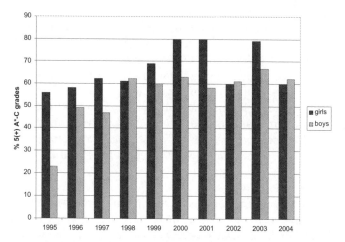

Figure 3.3 GCSE results 1994–2004: % girls and boys gaining 5(+) A*–C GCSEs – results' profile from an East Anglian comprehensive school

This somewhat cursory analysis cautions us against making simplistic generalizations and assuming too narrow a focus when discussing the gender gap. It must remain a source of disquiet that boys have consistently performed less well than girls in England's secondary schools for much of the past two decades, but an unremitting focus on the gender gap must not blind us to the fact that it is the absolute achievements of boys and girls on which we must be primarily focused, and that we must locate all our discussions about the gender gap within specific contexts at the individual school level, if we are to fully understand achievement profiles within schools.

An obsession with the 'benchmark' borderline?

Much of the discussion about the gender gap in secondary schools is framed in terms of the percentage of boys and girls who achieve the benchmark of five or more A*–C grades at GCSE. Yet there is a very real danger of focusing the debate too starkly upon one measure of 'achievement', and over-emphasizing one index which by its very nature undervalues the achievements of those boys and girls who achieve GCSE grades in the D–G range, and for whom those grades often represent a very real sense of achievement. This also creates the risk of establishing an A*–C economy (Gillborn and Youdell 2000: 12), in which resources, energy and effort are concentrated on a small number of borderline students, usually containing a high proportion of boys, who are neither secure in their chances of obtaining the benchmark grades, nor perceived as beyond hope. In such a context, the pressures to improve their competitive standing within national and particularly local league tables create a position where many schools are forced into 'a situation where almost every aspect of school life is re-evaluated for its possible contribution to (this) headline statistic' (Gillborn and Youdell 2000: 12). Gillborn and Youdell, in their forceful critique of such an approach, suggest that this understandable preoccupation of schools with the proportion of boys and girls achieving the benchmark grades, with league table position and the subsequent effect upon school reputation, student numbers and levels of resourcing, can in turn lead to schools adopting what they call 'a form of *educational triage*, a means of rationing support so that some pupils are targeted for additional time and energy':

> like medics in a crisis, teachers are increasingly seeking to identify those individuals who will benefit most from access to limited resources. In a medical emergency, *triage* is the name used to describe attempts to direct attention to those people who might

survive (with help), leaving other (less hopeful) cases to die. In school, educational triage is acting systematically to neglect certain pupils while directing additional resource to those deemed most likely to benefit (in terms of the externally judged standards).

(2000: 134)

This is strong language, but it cannot be disputed that some schools, in their anxiety to address the national agenda of raising standards, particularly of 'under-achieving' boys and improving their own local competitive position, do expend a great deal of energy on students who waiver around this five A*–C grade borderline. This need not be inevitable, however, as we show in Chapters 6–9, nor need it distract from an overall concern, in reality as well as in rhetoric, with raising achievement for all students. Indeed, the publication of performance indicators for individual schools in England by both the DfES (in the form of national benchmarking information within the 'Autumn Package' which draws upon test data provided by the Qualifications and Curriculum Agency) and OFSTED (in terms of their school-specific Performance and Assessment Reports: PANDAS) has recently placed more emphasis upon the average points score per student, using standardized conversion measures across Key Stages 1–4. This has been further refined at GCSE level, since 2002, by using the student's best eight GCSE/GNVQ results to calculate a 'capped points score'. This does add an element of further sophistication to the debate, in an attempt to shift the focus away from a simplistic interpretation based upon one arbitrary external measure such as the percentage of students who achieve the five A*–C grades. The development of performance tables which draw upon *all* qualifications which students might achieve at the end of their compulsory period of schooling, in terms, for example, of qualifications in travel and tourism, preparation for childcare, skills for working life, catering, hairdressing, using ICT, beauty therapy, ecotourism, rather than simply in terms of GCSE and GNVQ qualifications, is a further attempt to diversify provision and to acknowledge the value of qualifications gained by *all* students at *all* levels (DfES 2004a).

There is an acknowledgement, then, not least within official circles at DfES, of the dangers of adopting a form of educational triage, and an attempt

[to] create a more flexible system, with a greater emphasis and higher value placed on high quality vocational opportunities, and clear progression routes for students into skilled employment and further learning; the pilot study attempts to ensure that vocational qualifications receive the degree of credit that fairly reflects their scope and degree of difficulty.

(DfES 2004a: 1)

Both these developments – the emphasis upon a capped points score at GCSE/GNVQ equivalency and the diversification of the scope of the performance indicators to include a greater range of courses and qualifications – move the emphasis away from the percentage of students achieving the five A*–C benchmark grades, and give greater value to the achievements of all students. Inevitably, though, the construction of both these developments within the context of a more sophisticated approach to performance indicators and facilitating inter-school comparisons can reiterate the emphasis upon competition, standards and inequality of access, and there is some (long) way to go before the preoccupation of the media, government ministers, school leaders and many parents shifts from the tight focus on benchmark grades at GCSE which continues to inform and dominate the debate about the gender gap.

'Under-achievement' revisited

The debates of the past decade about the nature of the 'gender gap' and the assumption that more boys 'under-achieve' than do girls have taken place within an increasingly sophisticated context. There has been an acknowledgement that assessment tools need to be more sophisticated and wide-ranging (Gipps and Murphy 1994; Black and Wiliam 1998; James 1998), and an explicit recognition that some aspects of assessment practices by themselves can exacerbate and help to determine the gap itself. Equally, there is developing work on new modes of assessment, to facilitate the assessment of skills such as problem-solving, collaboration and decision-making (Wirth and Klieme 2003), in response to a recognition that we need to be concerned with assessing broader aspects of achievement such as students' relationships with peers and adults, their leadership skills, their sociability and sensitivity, and their involvement in community, sport and the creative arts (James 1998).

A major aspect of this increasing sophistication has been the development of value-added measures (Fitz-Gibbon 1996; DfES 2002, 2004a) to identify students' progress and attainments through time. Thus, in the secondary sector in England, it is now claimed that 'value-added' comparisons can be made between an individual student's performance in the National Curriculum tests at Key Stage 2 and their subsequent performance at the end of Key Stage 4, in their GCSE/GNVQ examinations. Significantly, the Autumn Package data from DfES also enable schools to compare the performance of their own cohort of students at GCSE/GNVQ with 'the median GCSE equivalent performance of other pupils in other schools, with the same or similar prior attainment at KS2' (DfES 2004a). Thus, it is claimed, the progress of similar students in different schools can be compared throughout their secondary schooling, specifically at the end of each key stage, and indeed, schools are encouraged to use the Autumn Package data to compare their own 'performance' against similar schools.

Secondary schools in England have increasingly used similar commercially marketed predictive measures over the past decade; the NFER cognitive ability tests (CAT), for example (Thorndike *et al.* 1986), and the battery of information systems developed by the University of Durham (MidYIS, YELLIS and ALIS[1]) are two such systems which are very widely used. Despite the fact that these measures warn against simplistic predictions (the YELLIS data, for example, are accompanied by the warning that 'predictions are not a guarantee of future performance and should be used with appropriate care as an indicator' (University of Durham Curriculum Evaluation and Management Centre 2003), their very nature implies that it is possible, within broad guidelines, to anticipate a given future level of performance for students with a given prior level of potential, as measured in psychometric type tests.

The development of the debate in these terms rests upon notions of measuring students' potential, with the idea that it is realistic to expect most students to achieve a steady and sustained rate of progress through their secondary schooling. In such a context, students who do not make such progress are often labelled 'under-achieving' against a normal level of expectation. There are many contentious issues with such a notion, however, and limitations on the credibility of aspects of value-added data (Goldstein 2001; Gray *et al.* 2003). It places heavy reliance on students' performance on a limited number of specific occasions (when they take psychometric or National Curriculum tests), it assumes reliability and validity of assessment techniques and gender-fair tests, and it can over-play the impact of students' prior educational experiences (such as limited educational experiences at primary school) on their subsequent rates of progress and their achievements. In such contexts, it is possible for the testing regime to under-estimate students' potential, and to assume fixed notions of ability which can lead schools to set targets which are too low and which can result in students being placed in educational settings (schools, bands, sets) which make insufficiently challenging demands on the students. Crucially, low expectations can then lead in turn to student disillusionment, boredom and the self-fulfilling prophecy of low levels of performance.

There are aspects of 'under-achievement' here which need to be more closely re-examined, particularly because the whole notion of 'under-achievement' causes considerable difficulty. It is, according to West and Pennell, a term which is widely used but rarely clearly defined, 'a concept about which there is no consensus, and one which has different connotations to different individuals' (2003: 4). This has particular resonance within the debate about the gender gap. We need to re-examine what we mean by 'under-achievement', what measures we might use to *reliably* identify those who under-achieve (Smith 2003) and how their under-achievement might be defined:

> One of the problems with the notion of under-achievement is, quite simply, in understanding what the under-achievement is in relation to. Is it related to some kind of innate ability on the part of the individual or is it achievement relative to that of a larger group?
>
> (Smith 2003: 576)

Clearly, 'under-achievement' is different from 'low achievement', although there is a widespread tendency to treat the two as synonymous (Smith 2002). It is possible in some schools to identify students achieving at a relatively low level, as measured against benchmark grades within the national context, but who are achieving well above their 'potential' as measured against previous attainment or against cognitive ability tests (Smith 2003). It is clearly nonsense to label such students 'under-achieving'. Equally, in previous work (Warrington and Younger 1999), we have identified groups of under-achieving boys (and a smaller number of girls) who had been identified as highly able, at least in terms of 11+ tests which had gained them access to state selective school settings. Although such boys are achieving at a relatively high level, they might be defined as 'under-achieving' against their prior attainment, although they are frequently not perceived as such; their under-performance can remain hidden, therefore, and complacency can spread through their school.

The notion of 'under-achievement' which has gained current usage in policy and practice in secondary education in England, therefore, seems to be premised on assumptions that ability is inherent, that it is fixed, that it can be measured accurately and that 'in measuring ability one is somehow getting at an underlying characteristic which explains or predicts an individual's performance in another activity such as reading [or] general educational attainment' (Kershner 2003: 45). Even when it is accepted that psychometric tests measure only what has been learnt, and where greater emphasis is placed on the role of environment, societal and cultural factors in the development of intelligence, there remains the implicit assumption that intelligence, as measured by these psychometric tests, is stable and fixed, and a good predictor of educational success and potential. Schools increasingly rely on such psychometric tests to make predictions about young people's future achievements; indeed, central to the DfES Autumn Package is the assumption that these test results give a measure of future potential for learning and achievement, and define an expected rate of progress (for example, from level 4 to levels 5/6 across Key Stage 3).

Hart *et al.* (2004), in their powerful and illuminating discussion of teaching practices and discourses which are free from such determinist beliefs about ability, identify the very real dangers intrinsic in an unthinking approach to the notion of inherent ability: of a minimalism of expectations of students' potential, of leaving many young people's talents and capabilities untapped throughout their formal education, of curtailing rather than extending opportunity and achievement, of creating a sense of powerlessness in teachers, schools and indeed parents. The presupposition is embedded that current patterns of achievement reflect stable differences in young people's potential, and that such differences cannot be challenged, moved or transformed to any real degree through their schooling. Such a view of ability, ironically, can lead to a situation where particular groups of students, notably perhaps those from some working-class backgrounds, those on free school meals, those from some minority ethnic cultures, under-achieve simply because too little is demanded of them.

Given the focus of the national agenda, and the concern with league tables, defined in Gillborn and Youdell's terms as the A–C economy, with an overriding emphasis upon competition between schools based on the currency of A*–C grades, it is understandable that in many schools, a definition of 'under-achievement' based on the notion of inherent ability 'is mobilised to allow the targeting of additional support and resources on to a limited pool of pupils where the most reward is expected. These are the suitable cases for treatment in the final rationing of education' (2000: 163).

There are some schools, however, where a definition of under-achievement in these terms does not lead to a rationing and selection approach (see Chapter 7), and where the focus rather is on maximizing the achievement of all students, regardless of their predictions and apparent potential (Chapter 9). It *is* equally true, however, that contemporary practice in many schools, informed by the national debate and by local education authority policies, is often based upon an implicit acceptance of notions of under-achievement, potential and ability which have not been made sufficiently explicit or subjected to enough critical analysis. In Gillborn and Youdell's terms, the danger then is of the establishment and persistence of a new IQism, which

> informs, and is in turn strengthened by, contemporary policy and practice. The view of 'ability' that currently dominates education, from the heart of government to individual classrooms, represents a victory for the hereditarian position, without debate and without conscience.
>
> (2000: 212)

Conclusion

This discussion on the gender gap and on 'under-achievement' highlights the complexity of the issue, and alerts us to the dangers of making simplistic generalizations and arriving at alarmist conclusions without contextualization. It is true that a gender gap continues at GCSE within English secondary schools, and that in absolute numerical terms there are a significant number of boys nationally who achieve less well than girls of apparently comparable ability. Against this, however, we must note that, over the past two decades, the percentage gender gap has decreased through time as achievement levels have risen. Equally, any discussion about the nature of the gender gap must not disguise the remarkable growth in the past two decades of the number of girls and boys achieving higher level GCSE passes, particularly noting girls' achievement levels in subjects traditionally perceived as 'boys' subjects', and the lack of comparable improvement in the achievement of boys in subjects such as English, foreign languages and the Humanities.

Notions of 'under-achievement', however, have been insufficiently clarified throughout this debate. Too often, high-achieving students who have under-achieved have not been identified or have been ignored, and those students who have achieved over their apparent potential but at relative low levels of achievement have not been given the praise and recognition that have been their due. Equally, it has become widely accepted, almost by default, that 'ability' is fixed and measurable, in terms of potential and on the basis of prior attainment, and that students' performance at 11 or 14 is an accurate indicator of achievement at 16. Such assumptions need more exploration and challenge, if we are seriously to tackle issues of under-achievement and untapped potential.

In this context, however, the use of increasingly more sophisticated value-added measures has enabled schools to make more targeted judgements about the academic performance of individuals and groups of students within their own contexts. This has created its own set of dangers, however, particularly in terms of notions of the educational triage, and the targeting and rationing of scarce resources to those perceived to be on the borderlines of benchmark grades at GCSE. Although this is understandable, given the competitive context of league tables which schools have operated within over the past decade, it has minimized the worth, value and attention accorded to some students in some schools, and diverted some schools from 'an achievement for all' ethos. In Chapters 6–10 we explore how some schools have avoided some of these dangers, and constructed their responses to the conundrum of the gender gap and issues of 'under-achievement', within a more open and inclusive context.

Note

1 MidYIS: Middle Years Information System/YELLIS (YEar 11 Information System)/ALIS (Advanced Level information System).

4 What About the Girls?

Introduction: a focus on girls too

Undertaking research focused on boys raises considerable personal issues for us as researchers who are either feminist or sympathetic towards feminist philosophies. It provokes questions as to whether we are, by promoting strategies to raise boys' achievement, somehow betraying 'the cause', or pandering to the 'moral panic' about boys' under-achievement (Epstein *et al*. 1998) engendered by the press. It necessitates defending ourselves at conferences in the face of sometimes disdainful retorts intended to remind us that the patriarchal society is alive and well, that the female sex is still disadvantaged in many areas of life, including school life. This we do not in any way dispute: we remain conscious of the fact that, while girls' achievements have exceeded those of boys in school examinations, there are still many areas of life in Britain where women are disadvantaged in relation to men. As Treneman (1998) points out, 'the statistical under-achievement of boys in schools is nothing compared with the statistical over-achievement of men in life'.

In this chapter we respond to those critics who would see our objectives as misplaced. For, while the focus of this book is indeed on boys, we want to argue that we have been conscious of girls, not as an afterthought, but as a central concern throughout our work. This was the case right at the start of our research in this area, when we selected the schools with whom we were to work. Thus, our initial selection of schools for the pilot study within the Raising Boys Achievement Project, and of the 'Originator' Schools in the main phase of the project (see Chapter 5), was made not simply from among schools where the gender gap had consistently narrowed, but where such a narrowing of the gap had not occurred *at the expense of girls*, and while it was difficult, as we point out, to find sufficient schools that met our criteria, it was never a consideration to compromise the criteria in respect of girls' achievements.

A second important principle throughout our research was the decision not to help develop and refine any strategies which we felt might impact negatively on girls, and the main concern here was not simply impacts on academic achievement, but cultural impacts such as the way in which girls were treated in the classroom. We were not supportive of approaches which would work to the detriment of girls, or marginalize them in any way, and so our work has involved talking to girls and monitoring the effects of strategies on them. We have tried, therefore, not to limit ourselves to the narrow framework set by the project's title, but to keep girls on the agenda. As a result, in one respect, the project was unsuccessful, since we have not solved the gender gap. The strategies we support have the potential, we argue, to raise boys' achievement – but they also raise girls' achievement too – sometimes more than that of boys, and so the gender gap in some schools we have been working with has actually widened, rather than narrowed, as our government sponsors had hoped!

Although girls have always been in the picture, it is true, nevertheless, that our key focus over the past decade or so has been on boys. This is not because we see most boys as somehow disadvantaged in their relationships with the opposite sex – far from it. Rather, we situate the debate over boys' achievement within the much broader context of a post-industrial economy, where those who leave school with few qualifications, whether male or female, have limited opportunities in today's labour market (Byrne 1999; Whitty 2001). While it used to be the case, in a Fordist economy, that young men leaving school with no qualifications could enter a factory or mine, where they would be able to obtain relatively well-paid and secure employment, this is no longer the case (Nayak 2003). Deindustrialization has seen the decline of primary and secondary industry in Western countries, and the shift towards a new knowledge economy has led to an increasing demand for a well-educated and skilled workforce (McDowell 2003). The concomitant unemployment and under-employment of young males impacts negatively on the social matrices of some areas, particularly areas of social exclusion (see Byrne 1999). It is in this context that our work is placed.

A triumph for 'equal opportunities'?

Women, too, of course, compete in this changed labour market, and to a much greater extent than in earlier times, when women's place was more likely to have been seen as in the home, rather than in the workplace. And, in many respects, it appears that girls, with their superior academic achievements, are well placed to participate in the new economy.

In the second half of the 1990s, parts of the British media began to highlight girls' successes at school. Articles put forward the notion that: 'today girls can have sex and brains too ... girls no longer need protection. Feminism has been a massive exercise in raising the self-esteem of a generation. Girl Power is not an invention of a pop group publicity manager: it really exists' (Phillips 1998). Taken out of context, this kind of assertion would suggest that the drive towards equal gender opportunities, initiated during the 1970s and 1980s by feminist researchers, had been successful. 'Equal opportunities' became an issue as research began to show that both the formal curriculum and the hidden curriculum were structured along gendered lines (Sharpe 1976; Deem 1980; Sharma and Meigham 1980; Griffin 1985). Girls tended to avoid subjects such as mathematics and science, which were socially constructed as masculine (Walden 1991), and opted for careers such as nursing or primary school teaching, which were traditionally associated with the so-called feminine qualities of caring. Researchers began to challenge the use of sexist language in textbooks, and to point out that girls were frequently marginalized within the classroom as boys monopolized both physical and social space and demanded more of the teachers' time (Stanworth 1981, 1987; Mahony 1985; Lafrance 1991). A full and perceptive account of many of these developments since the introduction of the Sex Discrimination Act and the establishment of the Equal Opportunities Commission in the mid-1970s can be found in Myers (2000).

This research into the experiences of girls both in Britain and further afield, did succeed in raising the profile of girls in school, and more consciously feminist ideas on curriculum development began to take form (Weiner 1994). Equal opportunities policies were put into place in many British schools, specific initiatives such as the Girls Into Science and Technology Project began (Whyte 1985), while the introduction of a National Curriculum in 1988 ensured that girls and boys followed the same basic curriculum throughout the years of compulsory schooling. No longer were girls able to drop science subjects, or to take a 'softer' scientific subject such as human biology, rather than a 'hard' science subject such as physics. Similar initiatives were introduced in other countries: in Australia, for example, the 1980s Labour governments were formally committed to programmes of gender reform related to girls (Aveling 2002), in the context of a school curriculum seen to be written largely by, for and about males (Kenway and Willis 1998). In the United States, the publication of a number of reports about girls and their educational disadvantages led to great strides in understanding the function of gender in educational contexts, and to pedagogical interventions to mediate the effects of gender (Weaver-Hightower 2003a).

Macrae and Maguire (2000) assert that the picture for women's educational achievement in the West has never been brighter or better, and it is certainly true to say that there are now many positive aspects to life for the twenty-first-century girl. As Chapter 3 points out, in statistical terms, her results both at GCSE level and increasingly at A-level, exceed those of boys in almost every subject. Participation in higher education is rising more quickly for females than for males: among entrants to higher education institutions in Britain in 2002/03, 47 per cent of 17–30-year-olds first-time entrants were female, compared with 40 per cent who were male (DfES 2004c). Women accounted for 56 per cent of graduates in 2002/03, and 58 per cent of women obtained a first or upper-second class degree, compared with 51 per cent of men. Furthermore, women are studying subjects such as engineering and computer studies, previously thought to be the domain of boys, with women comprising 48 per cent of first-degree graduates achieving a qualification in science (HESA 2004). Such achievements prompt the assertion by Cameron (1998/99) that 'whatever the problems of schools today, and of girls and women in them, from a feminist perspective, changes in education must rank among the success stories of the last twenty-five years'.

As a result of higher levels of achievement and good qualifications, young women are entering the labour market at higher levels of the occupation structure, and beginning to break through the glass ceiling at work (McDowell 1997). To some degree, at least, there is evidence of gender convergence, as some women begin to occupy traditionally masculine preserves, and gain some of the social, cultural and economic advantages that traditionally rest with men (Walby 1997).

This seems to suggest that the growing awareness of schools as gendered environments, and the equal opportunities policies of the 1970s and 1980s were successful, and that the position of girls in school, and as they leave school and participate more fully in wider society, is no longer problematic. In fact, some would say that the balance has tipped too far the other way. As the then Education Secretary, Gillian Shephard, suggested at the annual meeting of the Girls' Schools Association in 1994, although girls' academic advances were a cause for pride, there was a danger of *going too far* (Gold 1995, our emphasis). Indeed, the effects of girls' achievements, some sections of the media suggest, have been to provoke a situation that has 'reached crisis point across the country' (Bright 1998), making 'grim reading for males' (anon 1998). It is suggested that boys are being systematically disadvantaged (Sommers 2000) to the extent that we now need to refocus equal opportunities policies to redress the balance for *boys*.

We are keen to distance ourselves from these suggestions on two counts. First, as indicated in the introduction to this chapter, and as reiterated by David Bell, Her Majesty's Chief Inspector of Schools in a speech to the Fawcett Society to mark International Women's Day in March 2004 (Bell 2004), the success that girls enjoy at school is all too often not mirrored in later life. Reflecting on an Australian perspective which is, nonetheless, equally valid in the United Kingdom, Lingard and Douglas argue that while girls stay longer at school, and have higher participation rates in higher education, this

> does not convert into more equal post-education options in terms
> of career opportunities and income for women when compared to

men ... [because of] a host of reasons to do with subject choices, coherence and vocational relevance of that choice, and the gendered character of labour market and careers.

(1999: 97)

Similarly, Aveling (2002), reflecting on her longitudinal study of a group of female academic achievers in Australia, suggests that:

the discourse of equality of opportunity had failed these women in a number of respects. While they have demonstrated that they can succeed on male terms, the culture of the workplace ensured that despite equal opportunity strategies, and despite these women's hopes that their lives would be substantially different from those they had seen their mothers leading, their work patterns essentially replicated the employment patterns of women of an earlier generation ... It would be naive to assume that gender equity has been achieved.

Aveling's real argument here is that there has been no radical shift in emphasis as to who does the parenting and domestic work, and she argues that educators need to move beyond merely encouraging girls into non-traditional occupations and to be aware that the curricula, for the most part, continue to be silent about women as mothers and men as fathers. Thus, rather than focusing on ways in which boys are 'disadvantaged' through past equal opportunities strategies, policy-makers need to shift the focus to ask, for example, why boys have low levels of participation in the domestic sciences and why they have lower levels of self-discipline, socialization and relationship skills (Foster 1992).

We might also question the persistence of the discourses of caring and nurturing within schools, where girls take on the role of 'servicing' the needs of males in the classroom (Lees 1993; Macrae and Maguire 2000). Such discourses reinforce the binary division between men's and women's roles which is perpetuated beyond the classroom in wider society.

The other side of the gender gap: a glass ceiling for girls?

Our second reason for not supporting the notion that equal opportunities policies have 'gone too far' is that, as we argued in an earlier paper (Warrington and Younger 2000) there is another side to the gender gap which has so exercised politicians and the media since the beginning of the 1990s.

Evidence for this assertion comes first, from the detailed research we carried out in 20 comprehensive schools and four independent schools in Eastern England in the late 1990s, where we found a continuing alienation of some girls from traditional 'male' subjects, particularly science. Only 16 per cent of girls (from a sample of 176) named science as their favourite subject and the traditional differences between the physical and biological sciences were still clearly evident, with 63 per cent of girls liking biology, but only 22 per cent liking physics. Girls felt they had to work extremely hard to do well in science, and this perspective was echoed by some – particularly male – science teachers, who seemed to foster the view of boys having more of an innate ability to do science. While Francis (2000b) reports some blurring of traditional preferences in terms of favourite subjects among the 14–16-year-olds in her study, mathematics and science were easily the least favourite subjects for girls. Meanwhile, at A-level, where girls are able to choose their subjects, there remains, as Francis comments, a highly gendered pattern in post-compulsory subject choice. Indeed, at A-level, Delamont (1999) reiterates 'a familiar complaint': fear of mathematics among young women, and girls choosing non-science A-levels. This is partially borne out in the 2002 entries, which showed that only 23 per cent of physics, 29 per cent of computing and 37 per cent of mathematics A-level entries were female (although chemistry attracted slightly more females, 51 per cent, than males).

Such decisions can affect students' careers later in life, excluding women from well-paid scientific and technological professions. Although some evidence is available to show that girls' career aspirations are becoming less gendered (Arnot et al. 1998), our late 1990s study found that just over half the girls were considering a job such as childcare, nursing, work with animals, office work or hairdressing, where women still form the majority of employees. Only 9 per cent of girls wished to follow a career in what might be described as traditionally male jobs to become scientists, economists, pilots or fire-fighters. The career choices articulated by these girls, therefore, would lead them into poorly paid work and often low-status work. This pattern was replicated among a cohort of 122 Year 11 students at one of the secondary schools in the RBA project. Asked in a questionnaire about their aspirations at the end of compulsory schooling, 40 per cent of female students had chosen a vocational course, with almost all of them taking courses leading to low-status and poorly paid jobs such as hairdressing, beauty therapy or childcare.

There is evidence here, then, to support Walby's notion of gender polarization (1997), for while *some* women – those with higher educational attainments, in high status careers such as investment banking, the media, consultancy and medicine, usually younger women free of family 'ties' – have seen their economic opportunities transformed, others remained trapped by family commitments and family locality in part-time, less-well paid, less stable employment, and form a 'more flexible' labour force for employers.

In addition, although we argued above that girls are increasingly to be found taking science subjects at university, there are still clear gender differences, for example, in computer science, where 4,200 women obtained degrees in 2003, compared to 13,400 men, and in engineering and technology, with 3,100 women compared to 15,700 men.

Aveling (2002), however, cautions against blaming girls for making 'poor choices'. In addition, Volman *et al.* (1995), reflecting on the disappointing outcomes of research into how to increase girls' interest in traditionally masculine subjects, suggest that we try to understand the reasons behind their choices, to listen to girls themselves, and to acknowledge that: 'Showing that the gendered connotations of science and technology are historical products make it easier to argue that the attitudes of girls do not reflect misunderstanding or prejudice, but social realities.'

Girls' voices, however, are not always heard. Another finding which has emerged throughout our work, in common with other researchers (Taber 1992; Lee 1996; Francis 2000a) is the male-dominated classroom, with boys commanding a disproportionate amount of teacher time, and in some classrooms, girls feeling uncomfortable and occasionally vulnerable because of the sexist behaviour of some male teachers (Younger *et al.* 1999; Warrington and Younger 2000). A frequent complaint made by girls has been that they feel excluded by the way in which some young male staff attempt to bond with boys and thus encourage their macho behaviour, reinforcing stereotyped masculinity in boys rather than challenging its underlying assumptions (Roulsten and Mills 2000). Girls, as well as boys who do not fit the stereotype, feel left out of discussions about football or sport in general, and the jokes shared by boys and male teachers.

Furthermore, it seems to be the case, as Kenway and Willis (1998) point out, that teachers often normalize sex-based harassment by boys, absolving many boys from responsibility for their aggression, since 'boys will be boys'. Some girls we talked to felt strongly that there were different expectations:

> It's definitely different. Girls are meant to be more respectable than boys, to present yourself in a different way, to be more 'girly' ... We're supposed to be more mature, more lady-like ... boys get away with things because there are lower expectations of them, they're expected to be immature.
>
> (Year 10 girl, 2002)

The 'laddish' behaviour of boys in mixed classrooms certainly appears to have a negative effect on girls' learning (Francis 2000a). As our research in the late 1990s showed (Warrington and Younger 2000), girls in lower sets in comprehensive schools, particularly in language subjects where boys tend to be concentrated, said that their learning was affected because boys were noisy and disruptive and so much of teachers' time was taken up in trying to maintain discipline. Girls frequently found boys' behaviour distracting as well as irritating, particularly as it sometimes resulted in restrictions such as a ban, for example, on scientific experiments or on practical cookery lessons. In group work boys would frequently ignore or devalue girls' contributions, making engagement in the task in hand extremely difficult (see also Lee 1996).

Our more recent interviews with girls, in 2003, continued to emphasize this:

> The boys act really silly, sniggering in an immature way, which is very distracting when you want to listen and learn something really important.
>
> (Year 10 girl, referring to PSHE lessons)

> There is a small minority of boys in my class who are making it very difficult for me to work and learn – by ridiculing, misbehaving and taking up the teacher's time by teasing and rubbishing our views.
>
> (Year 10 girl, referring to science lessons)

We argue, then, that despite a significant volume of research over a number of years, and despite two decades of equal opportunities policies, we cannot be complacent about the educational experiences of girls in English schools: the strong educational attainments of girls do not readily convert into better life chances and career options, as they do for boys who frequently attain less impressively.

Strategies for boys ... and girls?

It is important, too, to be concerned about the impact of the current debate on the under-achievement of boys and girls. The national prioritisation of 'standards' and the revealing of a gender gap in attainment have generated a whole range of strategies to address the perceived needs of boys. Many of these are 'quick fixes' which are advocated without regard to context or ongoing evaluation, they are often put into place without adequate preparation and abandoned when another initiative seems to offer more promise. This is unlikely to benefit boys, and at the same time it may be the case that the needs of girls are marginalized or ignored.

Classes for boys

Evidence for this assertion comes from the survey we undertook on single-sex teaching in over 30 English comprehensive schools (Warrington and Younger 2003). This form of teaching was strongly advocated by the then Secretary of State for Education, David Blunkett, after publication of the 2000 GCSE results (Woodward 2000). Interestingly, single-sex teaching had been advocated as a way of addressing girls' specific needs in the 1980s, with Shaw (1984) arguing, for example, that girls-only schools could establish a basis for social solidarity around a shared gender identity, providing both models of academic excellence and the direct and collective experience of positive support. Similar arguments were made in Australia (Kenway and Willis 1998) and New Zealand (Harker 2000). However, our survey showed that girls were rarely a consideration in the 1990s, with over half the schools implementing single-sex teaching specifically to raise *boys'* achievement. It was therefore most often put into effect in English or Modern Foreign Languages, where boys' under-performance is most marked.

Fuller discussion on the subject of single-sex classes, including the positive and potentially negative impacts on girls can be found in Chapter 8. The single-sex survey is raised, here, however, because it provides a striking example of the fact that in most schools much more attention was given to boys than to girls. Not only was the strategy generally implemented to address issues of boys' achievement, but where it was abandoned (and sometimes this was after only a term), the reason given was either that boys' results had not improved, or their behaviour had worsened. Furthermore, having decided to implement single-sex classes, much more thought was apparently given over how best to teach boys' classes. Interviews with staff revealed a long list of teaching strategies, from the need for short, carefully structured tasks, a very quick pace to lessons, small-group work, the use of writing frames to give structure to learning and writing, focused question and answer sessions, competitive activities, emphasis on oral work, short-term targets, a more kinaesthetic approach, immediate feedback, the use of information and communications technology, to a focus on facts, and a greater degree of negotiation. In comparison, hardly any strategies were put forward as appropriate for girls, and those few suggested were far less specific, such as being left to get on with a task and more reading and writing.

Teaching for boys

The implication here is that all girls will succeed, regardless of the kind of teaching they experience: the National Education Breakthrough Programme for Raising Boys' Achievement in Secondary Schools (DfES

2003), describes this as 'girls' apparent ability to rise above indifferent teaching'. Boys, on the other hand, because they are said to be less likely to tolerate poor teaching, are deemed to need a much more structured and for-mulaic teaching style. Thus, 'boy-friendly' techniques are advocated by the Breakthrough Programme, including developing curricula that acknowl-edge the interest of boys, involving boys in texts and materials, investing in ICT, having a 'Boyszone' in the school library, and so on. These are the kinds of approaches evident in the practice-oriented literature on school- and classroom-based interventions which Weaver-Hightower (2003a) describe as 'boyswork'. Here we find the 'tips for teachers' advocated, for example, by Hannan (1997), Gurian (2001) and Hawkes (2001). The prob-lems with this kind of approach are that they ignore the context of indi-vidual schools, and they fail to consider the implications of strategies which barely acknowledge the presence of girls – or boys who do not conform to the expected stereotype of the dominant heterosexual male. As Martino and Berrill (2003) argue, these kinds of simplistic approaches are often based on problematic and normalizing assumptions about boys as a group.

Furthermore, such an approach suggests that girls and boys need dif-ferent kinds of teaching styles, and yet what is clearly evident from our research over the past decade is that, when asked what makes a good lesson, there is a broad consensus across the sexes. Thus, girls interviewed at one school said, for example, that they wanted well-organized and clearly struc-tured lessons, clear teacher explanations and a willingness to take a differ-ent perspective if students did not understand something, a choice of activ-ities, encouragement, variety, more discussion and a disciplined, though not authoritarian, classroom environment. These are the kinds of approaches that are said to benefit boys: in fact, they benefit all students.

Places for boys

While one strategy for improving boys' achievement takes the view that boys are better taught away from girls, another 'tip for teachers' is to mix them up with girls, both to reduce discipline problems and in the hope that girls' sup-posedly more engaged attitudes will rub off on boys. This might involve restructuring sets so that higher sets in language-based subjects are not dom-inated by girls and bottom sets not dominated by boys, as is almost always the case if students are organized according to previous attainment (Bleach 1998). While this may well have advantages for boys, it is clearly inequitable for girls demoted to lower sets to make way for the boys (Henry 2002).

Another often recommended approach is to organize classroom seating on a boy–girl–boy–girl basis. Again, this is generally seen as benefiting boys in particular, and Year 10 boys in one of the project schools where this had been tried said it could work well, because girls had a moderating or calming influence on the classroom environment. They did stress, however, that it only worked well if the girls they were seated next to were 'fit' (i.e. physically attractive), and willing to chat and to help them with their work! Most girls, on the other hand, felt strongly that they were being penalized for the bad behaviour of a few boys. Some said it was difficult to work with boys because boys 'work in different ways', 'are less involved in their work' and 'try to dominate, especially when they don't understand'.

Role models for boys

Another of the British government's strategies for raising boys' achievement has been to encourage more men to enter the teaching profession, in the light of the perceived feminized culture of schools (Hayes 2002). As Carrington and Skelton (2003) point out, initiatives to boost male recruitment have been presented in official discourse as panaceas for the recalcitrant behaviour of many working-class boys in school and their generally lower levels of achievement. As these authors also argue, however, there is no evidence to suggest that the fact that the teaching profession is predominantly female makes any significant difference to young people's educational achievement. Indeed, in the secondary sector, women do not outnumber male teachers, and in the primary sector, despite being significantly outnumbered by women, men hold almost half of primary headships (Cameron 1998/99). There is little explicit consideration in this debate, either, of the type of male role model to be recruited, although the implication seems to be that such men should be macho, straight and able to identify with boys' interests. As we have already pointed out, the danger then, of course, is that such male teachers may encourage types of bonding with boys which encourage laddish behaviour, reinforce stereotyping and marginalize girls (Skelton 2001). Equally, there is no evidence that male teachers are more effective than female teachers as teachers of boys; indeed, such evidence as exists (Thornton and Bricheno 2002) tends to suggest the converse; certainly all our student interviews confirm the view that the qualities and personality of the teacher are far more important than the teacher's gender.

We accept the principle of attracting more men into the teaching profession, but not because men will be able to identify better with boys and offer them more macho role models. Rather, with Lingard and Douglas (1999), we look forward to the recruitment of a wide diversity of men into the teaching profession, of those able to share the nurturing and caring roles with women teachers, and to work alongside female teachers, girls and boys, to construct more equal gender relations within schools and societies.

Are all girls succeeding? Girls in trouble

We argue in Chapters 2 and 5 that it is important to look beneath the stereotype of the 'normal' boy, and just as there are different kinds of boys, so there are different kinds of girls. Not all girls conform to the conscientious, hard-working and well-motivated stereotype, distracted from their endeavours by recalcitrant boys. Indeed, some girls are taking on the 'laddish' attributes of their male peers (Henry 2003; Jackson 2004). As Bell (2004) points out, boys do not have a monopoly on problems: there is a large number of girls who are disengaged, and do not reach their potential academically.

In 2004, according to figures published by the DfES (DfES 2005), while overall 58.5 per cent of girls achieved five A*–C grades or more at GCSE, this figure changes dramatically if students eligible for free school meals are considered, since only 30.2 per cent of these girls achieved at a similar level. There are also differences related to ethnicity, with, for example, only 43.8 per cent of Black Caribbean girls achieving the five A*–C level or above, compared with 57.3 per cent of girls classified as white British. At the other end of the scale, overall 3.2 per cent of girls obtained no GCSE passes, but this figure rose to 7.3 per cent of girls eligible for free school meals, and 18.7 per cent of girls in the gypsy/Roma category. Spatial variation also occurs at the local education authority scale, with the lowest average five A*–C or above score for girls in Kingston-upon-Hull (38.7 per cent), compared with 73.5 per cent in Redbridge (Outer London).

Examining gender differences in attainment in Scotland, Tinklin (2003) demonstrates that the gender gap in achievement at Standard grade (aged 16) is reversed among children with fathers in unskilled occupations, with boys performing better than girls. Generally, however, the educational failure of working-class girls, as Plummer (2000) argues, has been hidden and ignored, with statistics rarely being produced. Girls' under-achievement is scarcely mentioned, when girls misbehave, they receive inconsistent treatment, and there is a lack of specialist provision for girls with behavioural difficulties, with resources orientated towards provision for boys (Bell 2004).

These issues have been explored in a recent study focusing on girls and school exclusion (Osler *et al.* 2002), which points out that because nationally girls comprise just 17 per cent of permanent exclusions, they have been largely overlooked in school exclusion prevention strategies and research. Again, it is necessary to look at which groups of girls are excluded, since Osler and Hill (1999) suggest that black girls are eight times more likely to be excluded than their white female peers. However, permanent exclusions represent only the tip of the iceberg, the authors of the study suggest, since many of the difficulties experienced by girls in school are of a hidden nature and may lead to self-exclusion which is not recorded in official figures.

Self-exclusion may be a last-resort strategy used by some girls to manage antagonistic relations with teachers, or difficulties in managing the curriculum, but one of the most significant of the problems leading to self-exclusion was found to be bullying, sometimes coupled with racial harassment. Osler *et al.* (2002) identify gender differences in bullying, with girls more commonly engaged in verbal and psychological bullying, rather than the aggressive physical bullying which is more common among boys. However, while the girls identified bullying as one of the key reasons for self-exclusion, professionals interviewed by Osler's team found subtle psychological bullying more difficult to deal with, and accorded it lower priority. Other forms of exclusion include the informal exclusion among girls who have disengaged from learning: although physically present in school, these girls are effectively excluded. The 'invisibility' of girls' problems means that their needs tend to go unrecognized and unmet (Osler and Vincent 2003), and yet it is suggested that the majority of girls who have been excluded are extremely vulnerable, coming from disrupted family backgrounds and sometimes with a history of abuse, self-harm or early pregnancy.

There are therefore significant barriers to girls' achievement and inclusion: besides limited access to places in special schools for students with emotional and behavioural difficulties, and less access to support than boys in mainstream schools (Osler and Vincent 2003); these barriers include parentally condoned absences, low aspirations, caring responsibilities and sexual exploitation. It is therefore important, as Osler and Vincent argue, to look beyond achievement data in order to understand girls' experiences at school.

Conclusion

This chapter has demonstrated that equal opportunities policies, while improving educational opportunities for girls, did not ensure equality of experience within the classroom, and that furthermore, the 'boy turn' (Weaver-Hightower 2003a), can, in some instances, have a negative impact on girls. While for reasons already discussed, we believe that it is legitimate to examine boys' relative under-achievement, we have argued that it is imperative, in so doing, not to lose sight of the equal opportunities debate as it relates to girls. Policy-makers, practitioners and academics need to be aware of girls as a group, since 'many facets of girls' educational experience remain negatively affected by the masculinist values and expectations reflected in educational institutions' (Francis and Skelton 2001). And while we should celebrate girls' continuing academic achievements, it is nevertheless crucial to avoid an essentialist rhetoric that assumes that *all* girls are high achievers; we need, as Bell (2004) argues, to pay greater attention to the monitoring of withdrawn, quiet, 'less visible' girls, whose quietness may hide severe problems.

5 Raising Boys' Achievement within an Inclusive Context

The invitation from the Department for Education and Skills (DfES) in England to direct a research project on 'boys' under-achievement' generated some interesting dilemmas for us, some of which we have outlined in the preceding chapters. In Chapter 3, we discussed what an understanding of the concept of 'under-achievement' actually entails, and explored the extent to which such 'under-achievement' actually exists in English primary and secondary schools. In so doing, we questioned the nature of any gender gap, and considered some of the dangers in assuming a simplistic interpretation of the data. In Chapter 4, our focus on girls led us to debate the appropriateness of focusing a research and intervention project essentially on the (under-)achievements of boys, particularly in the light of the equal opportunities debate which had – throughout the 1970s and 1980s – stressed the very clear need to create equality of opportunity for girls. More controversially, we have wondered whether it *is* a matter of such grave concern if boys *do* actually under-perform in schools, given the pre-eminent position of many men in the employment market and in terms of the distribution of power within society. Crucially, we have debated among ourselves, for many long hours, how we could reconcile our central engagement in this work with our own clear empathy towards a feminist agenda.

These dilemmas have focused the mind, and have led us into a process of continual clarification and redefinition of the scope of the work we subsequently engaged in with schools. We decided to accept the invitation to direct this major research and intervention project because it was an opportunity to bring together different strands of work in which we had been engaged over the past decade (see, for example, Younger and Warrington 1996; Younger *et al.* 1999; Warrington and Younger 2000, 2003). It allowed us to participate in a crucial international debate from a perspective rooted in inclusivity rather than exclusivity, to acknowledge that the issues were complex and multi-faceted, and to recognize that the 'problem', however defined, was unlikely to yield to short-term and quick-fix 'solutions'. Directing this research also enabled us to work directly with schools in different parts of the nation and with policy-makers within DfES, in the attempt to formulate intervention strategies which were effective, supported by empirical data from school-based research, and rooted in a theoretical base as well as in pragmatism. In so doing, we attempted – in Weaver-Hightower's phrase – to 'cross the divide', to bring together the theoretical-based literature and practically orientated approaches (2003a, 2003b).

The essential philosophy of the Raising Boys' Achievement Project which emerged as a consequence is rooted in a number of deep-seated beliefs, based on our own pre-existing research and on that of others (Mac an Ghaill 1994; Rudduck *et al.* 1996; Arnot *et al.* 1999; Francis 2000a; Skelton 2001; Frosh *et al.* 2002; Martino and Pallotta-Chiarolli 2003), which have been of fundamental importance in affecting the ways in which the Project's thinking has evolved and developed. Equally we are indebted to the teachers and headteachers within the primary, secondary and special schools with whom we have worked, who have continually challenged us, and enabled us to reformulate our ideas and approaches in the light of their everyday experiences, as they have attempted to apply and refine classroom strategies and whole school approaches to gender issues.

The Raising Boys' Achievement Project: the philosophical position

The philosophy of the Raising Boys' Achievement Project has a number of central tenets which have been crucially important in influencing our ways of thinking and working.

Achievement for all: a central concern has been accessing intervention strategies and approaches, and defining the core aspects of the school ethos, which facilitate achievement for all students. The focus has been on creating learning environments and contexts which have enabled students to identify, recognize and maximize their own potential; in so doing, we have acknowledged that there are both girls and (rather more) boys currently within schools who do not achieve this (Chapter 3). In focusing upon both boys *and* girls, we attempt to distance ourselves from what Delamont (1999) has called the 'discourse of derision'; with her, we recognize that the achievements of girls in schools in England in the 1990s were not properly acknowledged or praised, and that the focus of the debate, on teachers, schools and local education authorities for failing boys in their educational needs, was inappropriate. As we showed in Chapter 4, there still remains a glass ceiling, for women in many careers, not least in higher levels in teaching, despite the fact that secondary education – as with primary education – is on the way to becoming a female-dominated activity. There remains much to be done to enable girls and young women to maximize their potential. The invisibility of girls is still an issue for us in many secondary schools (Griffiths 1998; Warrington and Younger 2000) and in an increasing number of primary schools where some girls continue to be under-valued and to under-value each other (Reay 2001; Skelton and Francis 2003).

So we have attempted to position the Project so that it has not been (nor been perceived to be) engaged in any backlash against girls, but rather has acknowledged and celebrated the achievement of girls in schools in the past decades, and has sought to explore why fewer boys have enjoyed comparable success. Inclusivity has been the watchword throughout.

Second, there are issues to do with the *homogeneity of gender*. A boy, according to many commentators, is characterized by emotional neutrality, by competitiveness, by individuality, by assertiveness. Boys define their masculinity in terms of their behaviour, their attitudes to schoolwork, their clothing, their body language (Kenway and Fitzclarence 1997; Francis 2000a; Skelton 2001). But we have been concerned, too, to offer relevance to teachers of those boys who define their sexuality differently to the 'mainstream': gentle caring boys as well as macho, football-loving boys; those boys who prefer music, dance, poetry; more sensitive, caring boys who find their comfort zone in the company of girls and women. Teachers working with us have been quick to acknowledge that some teachers impose expectations on boys in ways which value particularly (albeit sometimes covertly) the mischievous, laddish, impish boy who may be more challenging to teach and 'less boring' than some girls. In reality, boys differ and we acknowledge the need to recognize explicitly that there are different sorts of boys and multiple perspectives on masculinity, just as there are different sorts of girls and multiple perspectives on femininity (Connell 1989, 1995, 2000; Mac an Ghaill 1994; Gilbert and Gilbert 1998; Arnot *et al.* 1999; Martino 1999; Reay 2001; Frosh *et al.* 2002; Martino and Pallotta-Chiarolli 2003). Not all boys act in the same way; there are different sorts of boys, well illustrated in some schools by those boys who, on occasions, can be the most aggressive perpetuators of homophobic aggression against other boys.

While our main focus in the Raising Boys' Achievement Project has been on gender, we recognize the complex intersection of the issue with ethnicity and class, and our selection of schools with which to work has reflected the crucial role for different ethnic and social class backgrounds (Archer and Yamashita 2003). This has inevitably added to the complexity of the research, and made analysis more tentative and multi-faceted, but such is the reality in many schools, requiring 'more nuanced and less essentialist understandings of the intersection of ethnicity, gender, social class and attainment' (Phoenix 2001: 129).

Equally, we acknowledge, with Frank *et al.* (2003), that the issue of 'under-achievement' does not affect all boys, and that an uncritical view of boys as under-achieving because of a laddish masculinity ignores the fact that, in many schools, boys are achieving high levels of success in academic, community, sporting and artistic domains. Indeed, many boys have always done extremely well, and continue to do so; we need to recognize explicitly the privilege which advantages some boys over others, and over some girls, and to recognize that this usually reflects, at least in the United Kingdom, social class factors (Epstein *et al.* 1998). We need, in Gilbert and Gilbert's words, 'to substitute a more complex and inclusive set of stories about boys at school' with the emphasis on diversity and difference (2001: 1).

Throughout our work with schools, therefore, the Project team has recognized the diversity of 'boys' and 'girls', in terms of class, ethnicity and sexual orientation and the need to disaggregate the data. We have attempted to ensure that interventions identified and developed to support the learning of boys and girls in schools have not discriminated against children for whom heterosexuality is not the norm, nor assumed that strategies developed in one context are necessarily appropriate and transferable to others.

The issue is more complex than this, however. While it *is* nonsensical to accept the simplistic view that the issue is to do with the under-achievement of *most* boys (Arnot *et al.* 1999; Lingard and Douglas 1999), our own research, particularly interviews with groups of boys and with individual boys over the past decade, has shown that there *are* typical patterns of behaviour to which *many* boys conform. Gillborn and Mirza's (2000) research, too, has shown that – when educational performance of boys and girls is compared *within* social classes, or *within* ethnic groups – girls invariably do better than boys. In selective mixed schools, too, our own work (Warrington and Younger 1999) suggests that more girls achieve five A*–A (and five A*–B) grades at GCSEs than do boys. In the light of this, we think that it *is* admissible to recognize that, although boys are not an undifferentiated group, there are broad similarities within sub-groups which allow us to make valid generalizations. Within this, if we compare similar boys with similar girls, in terms of cognitive ability scores and prior attainment on National Curriculum tests at Key Stage 2 and Key Stage 3, there is often evidence of lower levels of academic attainment by boys.

Third, we do – despite the work of Gorard *et al.* (1999) – recognize *the existence of a gender gap* in many schools, and acknowledge that the gap widened in English secondary schools in the years immediately after the introduction of GCSEs (1988) and National Curriculum tests and then stabilized in many schools (Chapter 3), but we contextualize this against a background of rising achievement levels of both boys and girls, both at Key Stage 2 and Key Stage 4. We argue, therefore, that the emphasis of the current debate about 'failing boys' and 'boys' under-achievement' is misplaced, and that the issue is not so much about under-achievement, but of differential rates of *improvement*, with the excitement generated by the fact that, through time, the trajectory of the trend line of achievement for girls has been steeper than that of boys. Indeed, as we have shown in Chapter 3, the percentage gender gap has decreased over the last decade (Gorard 2000), as performances have risen in both Key Stage 2 assessments and GCSE examinations. Given this year-on-year improvement of both girls' and boys' performances, it is rather odd to talk of the under-achievement of boys compared to girls; the term appears a misnomer for what has actually occurred.

Fourth, the concern of the Project has been to define, through detailed empirical research, interventions which appear to have *the potential to impact positively upon levels of boys' and girls' academic, social and personal achievements within school*, to enable them in turn to access wider opportunities within society. We have used pre-existing research to inform and subsequently develop these interventions, to make such interventions accessible and immediate to schools. In some instances, these interventions are narrowly defined and explicitly related to one specific aspect of schooling. In other aspects, they are more wide-ranging and over-arching, and relate to socio-cultural contexts and the whole school ethos. In each case, we argue that there are no 'quick-fix' solutions and that essential pre-conditions must be in place before such interventions can hope to be effective. Our aim, though, has been to impact directly on the reality facing schools in different socio-economic contexts, and we identify issues of sustainability if these interventions are to be really transformative for the experiences of teachers and students nationwide.

Taken together, these concerns warn us that arguments must be contextualized, that simplistic 'solutions' which embrace all schools, all boys, all girls will not do, that multi-faceted and complex issues need subtle and sophisticated responses. School ethos and teacher attitude, socio-cultural context and community aspiration, are fundamental; the particular is crucial (Davies 1984; Quirke and Winter 1995; Rudduck *et al.* 1996; Younger and Warrington 1996):

> Another key Foucauldian notion is of the importance of the local, and of individuals and groups working for social justice at the local level ... any discussion of educational inequality therefore needs to address the 'parochial', the specificities of local confined settings.
>
> (Weiner *et al.* 1997: 622)

It is self-evidently dangerous, therefore, to generalize uncritically about girls and boys: issues of ethnicity (Nieto 1994; Sewell 1998; Gillborn and Mirza 2000; Phoenix 2001) and class (Lamb 1996; Lucey 2000; Plummer 2000), of individuality and sexual inclination (Jackson and Salisbury 1996; Martino 1999, 2001; Martino and Pallotta-Chiarolli 2003), differing images of femininity and masculinity (Mac an Ghaill 1994), all affect motivation, attitude and achievement. The emphasis has to be placed upon variety and plurality, rather than upon similarity and uniformity. Likewise, student interviews reveal that girls and boys often feel uneasy and express disquiet when notions of sameness are attributed to them (Kenway *et al.* 1998; Murphy 1998).

Research design

The research design which has structured our work within the Raising Boys' Achievement Project (2000–4) involved us in the identification of a number of key schools. In the secondary phase of the Project, schools were identified where differences between the average points score of boys and girls in their GCSE examinations was narrowing through time, but within the context of a rising trajectory of results for both boys and girls. Thus, schools were selected where this narrowing of the trend lines between girls' and boys' performances reflected boys' performances improving at a greater rate than girls, but in both cases trends through time indicated improvements over most of the time period studied (1996–2000). We acknowledged that, given schools' individual circumstances and relatively small sample size, the average points score of girls or boys might dip in one particular year, compared to the previous year, and we accepted a one-year tolerance within the year-on-year sustained pattern of improvement. Thus, in Figure 5.1, although the level of academic achievements of both boys and girls are lower in 1999 than in 1998 (as measured by the average points score achieved), the trajectory of achievement of both boys' and girls' achievements at GCSE) increases through time, and the gender gap narrows from 7.5 points to 5 points.

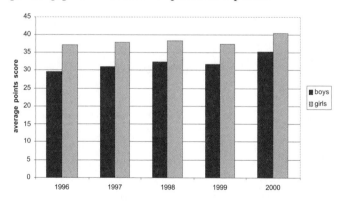

Figure 5.1 GCSE points score, by gender, through time (a hypothetical school)

Equally, schools were only selected for further involvement in the project when senior staff were able to articulate *why* this 'narrowing of the gap' was happening, and to identify the strategies which had been explicitly developed to raise boys' achievements without detracting from those of the girls within the school.

As we have discussed elsewhere (Younger *et al.* 2002), this process of identifying possible Originator Schools was an intriguing and demanding task. It was possible to identify only a very small number of schools from the existing DfES databases, and even when such schools had been identified, it was not unusual for senior staff to be unable to articulate with any precision what strategies were having such an effect on achievement patterns. Indeed, the 'whole school' nature of the basket of strategies in place frequently made it difficult to isolate the effects of specific approaches. A further complication arose even where such a results' profile *did* exist and the underlying reasons *could* be articulated realistically by the school, since the pattern of rising achievement and a narrowing of the gender gap was sometimes not sustained while the school was working with the project!

Nonetheless, in the 2000–1 academic year, we constructed eight triads of secondary schools, together with a cluster of special schools, based on our analysis of the patterns of achievement of boys and girls in each school over the four-year period 1996–2000. In each triad an Originator School appeared to have in place a strategy which had contributed towards the transformation of the achievements of boys (and girls) in the preceding four years, and two partners schools were identified, similar in socio-economic contexts, student numbers and age range, where such a transformation had not yet been effected. The aim was to identify the essence of the intervention strategy and to attempt to transfer it, with contextual specific modifications, into the partner schools. At the same time, it was envisaged that this process would support clarification of the strategy within the Originator School, and help to sharpen the focus and effectiveness of the strategy – and to further improve achievement levels – in the Originator School (Figure 5.2).

Originator School

Partner School 1

Partner School 2

Figure 5.2 Originator School and its partner schools

The development of intervention strategies

In identifying and refining intervention strategies within this Project, we have been engaged in robust debate about the effectiveness of certain approaches, and wish to challenge some aspects of the conventional wisdom which appears to have developed, particularly about the nature of boys' learning. Much of the extensive literature on intervention strategies and boys' under-achievement (see, for example, Bleach 1998; Noble and Bradford 2000; Noble *et al.* 2001) tends to emphasize pedagogic strategies which are boy-friendly, usually typified as fast-flowing lessons, which are clearly and tightly structured, and which engage boys in a variety of interactive and lively learning experiences. While this might be so, there is often little explicit recognition that such a lesson might simply describe the characteristics of good teaching, and that such pedagogies also engage and appeal to girls; as such, they are equally girl-friendly! At the same time, it has become conventional wisdom that boys respond to and benefit from competition rather than collaboration, and that pedagogies that emphasize competitive activities will engage and motivate boys more readily. It seems to us that this is equally problematic, not only because of the implicit assumption that all boys respond in this way, but also because it ignores the argument, so cogently developed by Hey *et al.* (2000) that competition can just as easily militate against certain boys' achievements as it can promote them. Competition, by its very definition, involves losers as well as winners, and the dangers of becoming a loser frequently means that boys do not risk or engage fully in learning activities, that they withdraw from the competition rather than risk failure, having recourse to a self-defence mechanism to protect their image and standing within their peer group (Jackson 2002). In such a context, then, competitive pressures have the potential to increase disengagement rather than prove an incentive for involvement in learning. Such an emphasis on competition also seems to ignore, in our view, the fact that many girls might actually perform better than many boys because they use more interactive and cooperative modes of learning (Gipps 1996), and are more willing to learn together, to be more responsive to each other, working together on an issue or a problem, rather than in isolation.

These approaches tend to be linked with recuperative masculinity politics, with a 'male-repair' agenda which seeks to confirm commonality and identity among men: 'This (recuperative masculinity) takes the form of a reestablishment of bonds of guidance and friendship between older men and boys in order to give boys a sense of ease and pride in their impending manhood' (Lingard and Douglas 1999: 133). This 'male repair agenda' has been extensively promoted in many UK schools by consultants such as Geoff Hannan (1999) and by the Boys in School Programme in Australia (Browne and Fletcher 1995). It is based on the notion that, since the 1980s, schools have developed teaching styles and approaches which have favoured girls and have generally become more feminized environments in terms of staffing, curricula and assessment. To recuperative masculinists such as Biddulph (1998) and Blankenhorn (1996), schools have opened up opportunity to girls but boys have suffered as a result, and what is now needed is a programme which incorporates approaches that emphasize men's rights, their interests and needs. Such a view sees boys as the new dis-advantaged, victims almost of girls' successes.

We have not followed this 'recuperative masculinity' approach in the Raising Boys' Achievement Project, and indeed would join with critics of this approach (Salisbury and Jackson 1996; Lingard and Douglas 1999; Skelton and Francis 2003) not just because we see it as reinforcing domi-nant versions of hegemonic masculinity, reinforcing male stereotypes, and assuming a homogeneity among boys which is difficult to recognize except at the most superficial of levels, but because we feel the effectiveness of such strategies is unproven by research or in practice. Implicit within this approach, too, is the assumption (so devastatingly exposed by Francis 2000a) that teaching girls is not problematic because – whereas 'boys are active, fun and stimulating to teach, girls are passive, boring and superficial. From this perspective, girls only engage so effectively with schoolwork because they have *nothing better to do*' (Francis 2000a: 103–4). In other words, girls will learn whatever, whereas boys need effective and dynamic teaching within a disciplined environment! Additionally, of course, there is the equally superficial assumption that all boys learn in the same way, through the same procedures, simply through being boys; all boys know about football, respond to sexual innuendo, and learn through frenzied, competitive activity, and conversely, all girls do not! Such a men's rights approach also ignores the fact that boys and men are frequently a problem, in classrooms, playgrounds, staffroom and in conferences, not only for women and girls, but for some boys and men who feel more comfortable with characteristics other than those incorporated within hegemonic mas-culinity (Kenway 1997; Warrington and Younger 2000).

At the same time, we acknowledge the wealth of new insights and understandings of gender equity issues which have been opened up by pro-feminists, and we accept the argument that many of the issues which boys face, and which impinge upon their own attainment in school, are an outcome of their own attitudes, values and behaviours within a socially constructed milieu. Thus we concur with Lingard and Douglas, when they maintain that: 'an approach which critically appraises aspects of the con-struction of masculinities is essential to positively addressing the needs of all sectors of the community' (1999: 132). The difficulty, however, is that a pro-feminist approach to the schooling of boys will not necessarily raise their achievement levels or self-esteem or enhance their valuing of women. Christine Skelton puts it concisely and with authority: pro-feminists, she writes 'offer little in terms of providing schools and teachers with practical strategies and guidance' (2003: 173) and she argues that, where such programmes exist, as in Australia, 'they tend to be couched in ways which make boys feel guilty about being boys or prevent alternative images of masculinity which boys do not find appealing' (2003: 173). There is a head-on tension here between, on the one hand, what is seen to be desirable and theoretically sound and, on the other, what is pragmatically possible in the reality of many teachers' experiences in many schools. Teaching strategies derived from pro-feminist approaches, such as *Boys-Talk: A Program for Young Men about Masculinity, Non-Violence and Relationships* (MASA 1996) and those advocated by Salisbury and Jackson (1996), profound, ambitious and far-reaching as they are, are frequently not seen to be realistic or accessible to the majority of classroom teachers. Equally, in the current performance-oriented culture, the concerns of such programmes with understanding the different constructions of masculinity and femininity, evolving just and equal social and personal relationships between men and women and exploring associated social justice issues is not high profile on government agendas, certainly not in the United Kingdom. In-service funding and course provision are rarely available to support teachers in their understanding of the ethos and rationale of such programmes, therefore, and thus the programmes themselves are frequently seen to lack credibility and applicability, and are implemented only by the brave or the idealistic!

In our experience, therefore, approaches which attempt to challenge boys' self-perceptions of masculinity, emphasize non-normalizing behaviour or require their participation in non-stereotypical curriculum activities, tend not to be the best way to engage boys in learning or to change their aspirations and self-image. Gender reform programmes that emphasize empathy and sensitivity, that invite boys to engage in workshops which explore their own sexuality, often achieve little more than make boys 'ambivalent, confused, anxious, vulnerable and hostile' (Kenway *et al.* 1998: 153). The dangers of counter-productivity are very real in such approaches. Indeed, we are not going to make boys feel more engaged with learning and with their schooling if we try to convince them that men (and boys) are *the* problem and the root cause of many of the inequalities and injustices within society.

Within the context of this project, then, we have arrived at a position which is neither based upon short-term men's rights approaches nor based on pro-feminist perspectives. Rather, a number of intervention strategies have evolved as we have tried to engage with headteachers and with teachers to address a number of fundamental issues which they have identified as crucial in affecting boys' and girls' learning. We have classified these intervention strategies into four broad groups – pedagogic, individual, organizational and socio-cultural – although inevitably no one group is exclusive of the others. Pedagogic strategies self-evidently place the emphasis on classroom-based activities, looking at classroom interactions and dynamics, and at teaching and learning styles (Chapter 6). The focus of individual strategies has usually been on some form of mentoring and target-setting, and what has intrigued us here has been the extent to which academic performance in some schools has been transformed by target-setting and mentoring, while remaining almost untouched in other schools (Chapter 7). Organizational strategies, we have defined as whole school approaches, where schools attempt to develop a school ethos and culture in which achievement in all sorts of areas is celebrated, and accepted as the norm. In this context, we are particularly interested in the potential of single-sex classes within secondary schools, on their remarkably positive impact on the achievements of attitudes of both boys and girls in some schools, and on the almost ideological resistance to the notion in other schools (Chapter 8). Finally, socio-cultural approaches are those which attempt to change images of laddish masculinity held by the peer group or perhaps the family and community, and to develop an ethos which helps to eradicate the 'it's not cool to learn' attitude among boys. Most of the approaches within these categories support learning for both girls and boys, but they sometimes have a stronger impact on boys, and one of the challenges for the project has been to try and tease out what it is in general strategies which help boys to do particularly well (Chapter 9).

Conclusion

Throughout the Raising Boys' Achievement Project, we have tried to support teachers in developing research-based knowledge about the ways in which gender – and the construction of gender by boys and by girls – affect schooling and the quality of learning opportunities for both girls and boys. We have been concerned to contribute realistically and effectively to the achievement debate, in ways that acknowledge difference between and within boys and girls, and that acknowledge that schools need support to implement effective interventions which recognize diversity and the fluidity of gender, and neither reinforce dominant versions of masculinity and femininity nor reinstate dominant versions of hegemonic masculinity in more subtle and sophisticated ways. The intervention strategies we have helped to develop, refine and monitor *do* appear – in some schools where the pre-conditions have been carefully and systematically established – to impact positively upon achievement of both boys and girls (but not necessarily, therefore, to reduce the gender gap!), but equally they appear to have the potential to engage, to motivate and to raise children's self-esteem as learners.

Our work on the Raising Boys' Achievement Project does not advocate recuperative masculinity approaches, nor pro-feminist strategies, therefore, although it will be clear in the chapters which follow, and in the interpretations and values which underpin our analysis of the debate in Chapter 2, that our sympathies are much closer to one than to the other. Rather, we have tried, as the project has evolved, to locate our work within a gender equity context, to emphasize issues of inclusivity, to develop work in schools within a gender-relational context, incorporating notions of difference and agency, and placing the emphasis on boys *and* girls. Indeed, it is our concerns for the wider academic and societal achievement of all students, with social justice and equal opportunity for all boys and girls wherever they live and go to school, with helping schools offer 'fresh starts' to the disengaged and disadvantaged boys and girls within our society, which has generated and sustained the Project. Such an approach has enabled us to attempt – to some limited degree – to 'colonise the space of practice' which Apple (2001) argues has been colonized successfully to date only by the Right and those who advocate men's rights approaches, 'not because the right has all the answers but because the left has too often evacuated that space' (2001: 228).

6 The Context of the Classroom
Pedagogies and teaching-learning styles

There is little doubt that in many secondary schools, pedagogy has been transformed in the past two decades. Inspection snapshots from OFSTED cite the improving quality of teaching and learning in many schools, and this view is broadly supported by many boys and girls whom we interviewed as part of the Raising Boys' Achievement Project. Many students readily agreed that teachers really cared and gave them encouragement and support, instilling a sense of self-belief, and they understood that the school had put in place strategies designed to enable them to become more rounded people and to achieve their potential:

> He's a real character who really leads the learning, he encourages us to contribute and to experiment, he makes Shakespeare a real lark and real fun.
>
> (Barry, Year 11)

> She does more interactive things with us, uses whiteboards, uses games and bingo so that we learn new ways of looking at and doing Maths, she uses humour and wears silly hats, she teaches in such an interesting way, it's impossible not to learn.
>
> (Sahiba, Year 10)

There has also emerged a plethora of texts (Pickering 1997; Bleach 1998; Noble and Bradford 2000; Noble *et al.* 2001), resource packs (Bradford 1996; Gardner *et al.* 1999) and sources of consultancy advice which give support and offer strategies for teaching boys more effectively. The focus is on teaching and learning styles that emphasize variety, engagement, sociable learning and the potential to transform the type of learning (Noble and Bradford 2000: 31–3). Good practice as identified by OFSTED is epitomized by lessons which have short-term targets, activity-based learning, the positive use of competition and good use of ICT, questioning which is quick-fire, lively and varied, and encompass the use of humour to good effect (2003: 19–20).

As we suggest in Chapters 4 and 5, however, such approaches are not without their dangers, especially when they are developed within a recuperative masculinity context. In some schools, there is a preoccupation with supporting boys' learning which leads to a narrow focus on boys and an implication that girls do not need to be taught in similarly interactive and investigative styles. Such an approach is self-evidently demeaning and demotivating to girls, particularly when it is assumed that particular classes, containing a majority of 'potentially under-achieving boys', have an especial need to be taught by 'better' teachers, more able to implement such an interactive, varied, humorous approach. Yet in our experience, such a view is not unusual.

Equally, there are different views about the transformation of teaching and learning:

> There's no point doing all the work we do on reducing absentee and exclusion levels unless we transform what's happening in the classroom, so that they feel that what's on offer is worth coming for!
>
> (Headteacher, 11–16 school, NW England)

> We need more of a say in what we learn, how we learn and how teachers can get better … teachers need to know about different learning styles, different ways to teach us, better and more varied teaching techniques … we know it's hard for some teachers, but they need to help us structure our learning more.
>
> (Ranjit, Year 10)

> Too many lessons are like doing time; school's fine until you get in lessons and the door closes, then it can be just so boring.
>
> (Jade, Year 11)

In expressing these sentiments, Ranjit and Jade give voice to a persistent student view, echoed by both boys and girls across many schools. It is as though rhetoric and reality fail to connect, with teaching which is sometimes unfocused, lacking challenge, without any excitement to motivate and engage.

Teaching and learning styles

One wide-ranging response to these challenges has been the development of pedagogy related to learning styles work, particularly through accelerated learning (Smith 1997, 1998) and exploring the application of Gardner's work on multiple intelligences (1983, 1999) to classroom practice. Smith's work (2001a), on 'brain-based' accelerated learning in practice (ALPS), aims to enhance pupils' motivation and achievement, and incorporates many ideas derived from research on thinking skills and cognitive styles, including Dunn and Dunn's model and instruments of learning style (Dunn 2003), Gregorc's Mind Styles Model and Style Delineator (Gregorc 1985), Kolb's Learning Style Inventory (1999) and Riding's wholist-analytic cognitive style work (2002). Smith's Accelerated Learning Framework is based on the notion that intelligence is modifiable in school, so that pupils can be taught to think and learn more effectively using a range of visual, auditory and kinaesthetic techniques (VAK), such as mindmapping, musical stimulation, physical activity and practical design activities. As such, it has clearly been very influential in some contexts, with its emphasis on learning to learn and the creation of accelerated learning schools (Wise and Lovatt 2001). Gardner's notion of multiple intelligences identifies a cluster of distinct intelligences, grounded in neurobiology, psychology and anthropology; initially a set of seven (linguistic, musical, logical-mathematical, spatial, bodily-kinaesthetic, interpersonal and intrapersonal), these have subsequently been extended to nine with the additional identification of naturalist and existential intelligences. Gardner's work has likewise been taken up by schools and local education authorities because it has seemed to acknowledge students' varying strengths and predispositions, and it has been perceived as a way of structuring school and classroom experiences to promote learning (Kershner 2003).

There has undoubtedly been some interesting and stimulating work which has originated from this work on learning styles, both in whole school contexts (Wise and Lovatt 2001) and in terms of research into teacher effectiveness (Hay McBer 2000). Intriguingly, however, there is little independent empirical research which supports the wide-ranging claims made by protagonists of accelerated learning and multiple intelligences. Indeed, Hall (2004), reporting on an extensive study commissioned by the Learning Skills and Research Council, argues that

> the theoretical and practical applications of many of the leading theories are either under-researched in educational contexts or mired in controversy. Learning style theory is complex and demanding and the desire to provide categories and groups inevitably leads to dangerous simplification in practice.

In similar vein, Klein (2003) has argued that Gardner has not shown that the distinctive claims of multiple intelligences, that each of the intelligences coheres within itself (convergent validity) and is largely independent of the other parts (divergent validity), and that students' intelligences can be assessed through completion of questionnaires (the usual mode adopted in the school context), are valid. White (1998) has also argued that Gardner has not justified the criteria he used to identify the different intelligences, and feels that, although Gardner has successfully and commend-ably opened educators' eyes to new possibilities, there are dangers in taking notions of multiple intelligences too far: 'We may escape the shackles of IQ intelligence only to find ourselves imprisoned within yet another dubious theory' (White 1998: 35).

It is significant, too, that Coffield *et al.* (2004) are highly critical of the use in educational contexts of both Dunn and Dunn's model, and Gregorc's style delineator, since both of these approaches to learning styles are based on the four modalities (visual, auditory, kinaesthetic and tactile) which underpin much of Smith's work on accelerated learning. In their review of 13 major models of learning style, Coffield *et al.*'s overall assessment of Dunn and Dunn's model is that

> Despite a large and evolving research programme, forceful claims made for impact are questionable because of limitations in many of the supporting studies and the lack of independent research on the model. Concerns raised in our review need to be addressed before use is made of the model in the UK.
>
> (2004: 24)

Similarly, they conclude that Gregorc's style delineator is 'theoretically and psychometrically flawed, and not suitable for the assessment of individuals' (2004: 26). Smith does not explicitly link his work on accelerated learning to that of Dunn and Dunn or Gregorc, although there are clear parallels. One notable aspect of Smith's work is that, while it clearly offers a wide range of practical strategies which have undoubtedly been welcomed by some teachers, it does not cite the research evidence upon which it is based, and the derivation and credence of some claims and assertions are not always clear. Indeed, Smith himself is quite explicit in this, stating that, although the leading practitioners have spent many years characterizing the typical attributes of visual, auditory and kinaesthetic learners: 'This work is not research-based. It is pragmatic and based on detailed elicitation and modelling' (Smith 2001b: 173).

Despite the limited independent evidence base, however, there has been a proliferation of in-service training and professional development on learning styles, for both secondary and primary schools. To some degree, this has been fuelled by commercial pressures and consultancy support, but there has also been active promotion of such approaches in the United Kingdom by some local education authorities and implicit endorsement by the DfES itself. Thus, for example, the DfES website on learning styles and brain-based learning uncritically references 38 programmes for teachers to resource, and talks of how brain-based learning is 'a powerful means of engaging teachers and pupils in improving the quality of learning in classrooms' (DfES 2004d). Similarly, the confidently titled support materials produced by London Challenge and the Key Stage 3 Strategy, *Ensuring the Attainment of Black Caribbean Boys*, includes materials on students' preferred learning styles and on visual, auditory and kinaesthetic learning which 'can be particularly powerful when shared with learners' (DfES/London Challenge 2004b: 17). These materials appear without context or critique, and the implicit assumption is that these are valuable tools, which can be implemented quickly and uncritically, to extend the range of teaching which these students encounter. The learning styles movement has thus gained both a self-generating momentum and a rather uncritical golden halo effect. As Coffield *et al.* note: 'In many ways, the use of different inventories of learning styles has acquired an unexamined life of its own, where the notion of learning styles itself and the various means to measure it, are accepted without question' (2004: 2).

It was against this background of competing claims – pragmatic insistence on the effectiveness of learning styles work in schools and theoretical misgivings about the validity and independence of the claims made – that we began our preliminary work on the Raising Boys Achievement Project with two Originator Schools. In both schools, there was a good deal of confidence in the potential of accelerated learning and multiple intelligences approaches to enhance boys' and girls' motivation and subsequent achievement in public examinations. Given our commitment to identify pedagogic initiatives which appeared, *from the perspective of schools*, to have such potential, this provided a natural focus for the work within these two triads. In such a context, our aim was to develop teaching and learning strategies for the classroom which would be derived from approaches which focused on accelerated learning and multiple intelligences, and to identify an evidential base, where possible, to evaluate some of the claims made about learning styles.

Case study 1: Accessing kinaesthetic learners more effectively

The Originator School and partner schools within one triad were all 13–18 upper schools in different local education authorities in East Anglia and the East Midlands. The Originator School had previously been involved in a number of regional and LEA-based projects involving the development of learning styles based upon work on accelerated learning and multiple intelligences, and there seemed some evidence, from its GCSE data through time, that this work had impacted upon students' performance data, with an upward trajectory of results and a corresponding narrowing of the gender gap.

Initial school-based research within the triad, focusing on Year 9 students, quickly revealed the complexity of analysing learning styles. At the very outset, the reliability and consistency of instruments designed to identify learning styles emerged as an important issue. Different questionnaires, purporting to identify the balance between visual, auditory and kinaesthetic (VAK) learning styles within individuals (and thus identify any dominance within their learning profiles), yielded different results when administered in the different schools, suggesting that the students in the broadly similar schools were significantly different from each other. Subsequent use of a common questionnaire[1] rejected this conclusion, however, and produced broadly comparable results across the three contexts. The analysis of individual students' dominance profiles (the balance between the visual, auditory and kinaesthetic in their preferred learning styles) suggested that – contrary to expectations derived from assertions within some of the literature – there was no significant correlation between gender and preferred learning styles. Indeed, the mean scores of 384 boys and 335 girls suggested that, if anything, there was more of a kinaesthetic tendency among the girls than the boys. Individual boys did not necessarily prefer a kinaesthetic learning style compared to visual or auditory (Table 6.1): the need for caution was becoming even more evident.

Further analysis in one partner school, however, revealed that those students (mainly boys) characterized by teachers as falling into one of a number of 'bad behaviour' categories and in danger of 'under-achieving' did record distinct patterns of dominance within their preferred learning style profile. Thus, for example, the 13 boys and 5 girls identified by teachers as 'disillusioned and negative about teachers and school' had an average learning style dominance profile which differed significantly from that of the year group as a whole, with less emphasis on visual learning and more emphasis on the kinaesthetic. Similarly, those students (8 girls, 14 boys) defined as under-achievers, those 'whose academic progress, regardless of behaviour, is below that expected', scored lower than the year group average on visual and auditory, and higher on the kinaesthetic. Similar patterns emerged in the learning styles preferences for the seven girls and eight boys classified as 'disorganized' and those 43 boys and 18 girls categorized as 'misbehavers', with poor concentration in class and offering low level disruption. In contrast, 'model' students, those 76 girls (55 per cent of girls within the year) and 85 boys (48 per cent of the boys within the year) who 'generally work well, stay on task and are positive in lessons', recorded a dominance profile which emphasized the visual and played down kinaesthetic learning.

Taken together, this initial data from one partner school tends to stress the importance of kinaesthetic modes of learning for specific students perceived by teachers as 'under-achieving' and those who are particularly challenging or misbehaving. Data about the dominance of learning styles within the teaching staff in the same partner school, however, reveal a very marked identification with the visual and a notable rejection particularly of the kinaesthetic (see Table 6.1). This exacerbates the issue, perhaps, in that it might be argued that many teachers may need particular support in developing modes of teaching which access kinaesthetic learning, because it is not a style with which they immediately identify.

Table 6.1 Balance of learning styles within dominance profiles

Group	Visual	Auditory	Kinaesthetic
Girls	32	32	36
Boys	32	33	35
Female staff	42	31	27
Male staff	42	30	28

Teaching-learning styles in lessons

Kinaesthetic learners, according to Smith, are defined in terms of their preference 'to engage with the experience physically ... (modelling) the point with hands and bodies and becoming animated as they do so. They learn through experience, movement, modelling and feel frustrated more readily with other forms of learning' (2001b: 173). Students whose learning profile is dominated more by the kinaesthetic than by the visual or auditory modes of learning are thus most critically disadvantaged by schooling which requires physical inactivity for extended periods of time. Lesson observation data, derived from student shadowing exercises in each school in the triad and subsequent interviews with key student informants, confirmed that very few lessons in 'traditional academic' subjects gave opportunities for students to learn kinaesthetically. At the outset of the research, therefore, while students' perceptions of the Arts subjects, the various Technology options, pre-vocational courses, Graphics and ICT suggested that kinaesthetic learning activities were dominant, at levels varying from 45 per cent (ICT) to 74 per cent (Dance), lessons in subjects such as English, Maths, Geography, History and Modern Languages were perceived as much less kinaesthetic (with less than 28 per cent of teaching activities defined as kinaesthetic).

In each school within the triad, however, pockets of innovative kinaesthetic practice were identified, and the process of developmental work (Figure 6.1) focused on gaining a common understanding of this good practice, and diffusing it across the three schools of the triad so that classroom teachers in each school acknowledged it as potentially effective and recognized it as credible. In the initial stages of the research, therefore, the aim was to recognize those teaching situations in all the triad's schools where kinaesthetic activities to support learning were most commonly and effectively used (Figure 6.1, stage 1) and to classify these according to different characteristics (stage 2). These school-specific teaching approaches were brought together in a teaching activities booklet (stage 3), common to all the three schools, and presented to staff development sessions in each school (stage 4). Staff were encouraged to introduce a range of these kinaesthetic activities into their teaching, to broaden their teaching repertoire to increase access to those students who had a more pronounced kinaesthetic dominance within their learning profile (stage 5).

1 Audit of subject-specific kinaesthetic activities currently used by teachers in triad schools.
2 Classification of kinaesthetic activities (e.g. students handling objects, artefacts and models to support learning; drama and role-play; investigative work using student movement and/or experimentation; *active* use of ICT to support learning; use of movement, place and space to change atmosphere and refocus students' minds; use of movement in space to capture and reinforce ideas and terminology).
3 Booklet of teaching ideas circulated to all staff.
4 Staff development sessions to introduce aims of booklet/to launch activities: to increase frequency and variety of kinaesthetic activities within lessons, with intention of promoting greater engagement in lessons / improving attainment of all, but especially of specific students with kinaesthetic dominance to their learning profile.
5 Staff self-audit of use of the defined kinaesthetic strategies/ interviews with key student informants about take-up of approaches.
6 Second edition of booklet circulated within triad schools, and in new school incorporated within 'triad'.
7 Monitoring adoption of strategies through continued staff self-audit, classroom observations and student interviews/ questionnaire responses.

Figure 6.1 The process to support the diffusion of good practice

At the same time, teachers were asked to self-monitor their use of such strategies, and to evaluate the effectiveness of these strategies in supporting the learning, motivation and engagement of their classes and of particular groups and individuals within their classes. This process was accompanied, in each school, by student interviews with key informants, identified as specific boys perceived to be in particular danger of under-achieving (stage 5). The research process in subsequent years, as the students progressed from Year 9 through to Year 11, focused on refining and extending the range of kinaesthetic teaching activities, in the light of experience in each of the triad's schools (stage 6), and monitoring the strategies in terms of their effectiveness, in the perceptions of staff and key student informants, and through classroom observations (stage 7).

The developmental process in this triad was firmly rooted in the realities of existing pedagogic practice within each school; teachers evolved their own classroom situations rather than approaches being 'top-down' or imposed from outside 'expert' practice, and thus they developed a sense of ownership of the work which the triad was developing. By the very nature of their evolution, therefore, the range of these pedagogic strategies which evolved to support kinaesthetic learning in these schools was not new, untried or experimental. In Religious Education and History, a framework provided by project work enabled students to move around classrooms, so that they could explore different types of resources – artefacts, CD-ROM, illustrations, decoding documents and symbols – at different locations within the classroom. Investigative work in Science and Maths involved mindmapping, brain gym and physical sequencing. In geography, jigsaw activities were used as part of role play, students were encouraged to use ICT publisher programs to design leaflets and poster presentations as items to support their oral assessment, and local small-scale field activities were regularly and systematically incorporated into normal pedagogic routines. In English, emphasis was placed on strategies such as hot-seating, analysing and subsequently enacting short video clips, creating themed illustrations to draw out aspects of poems and set books, handling artefacts to illustrate cross-cultural themes and to simulate creative writing. Consequently, the second edition of the resource booklet on kinaesthetic learning activities, which was circulated to all staff in all triad schools, drew on current existing practice in all four schools within the extended triad, and was extensive and wide-ranging, with over 250 subject-specific and generic proposed learning activities.

In parallel, it was recognized that this process of developing kinaesthetically orientated pedagogic activities needed to be complemented by work with students, to make more explicit for them the ideas associated with preferred learning styles. Sessions on study skills, learning styles and revision techniques were incorporated into the Personal, Social and Health Education (PSHE) programmes in each school, and keynote sessions were taught to all students. Feedback on 'VAK testing' also enabled all students to become aware of their own dominant preferred learning style, and the balance between the visual, the auditory and the kinaesthetic in their own individual profile.

Results

One of the difficulties encountered in this triad was trying to identify, with any degree of specificity, the extent to which the use of kinaesthetic teaching activities had changed over a limited time span. An analysis of students' perceptions of the extent to which teachers used kinaesthetic activities within lessons was carried out in the autumn term of Year 10, and repeated with the same students towards the end of their GCSE course of study in Year 11. Students in each school completed a subject-based audit of the diet of activities which they encountered in each lesson, using a prompt sheet to help them identify and classify teaching activities as auditory, kinaesthetic or visual. Analysis of students' responses confirmed that, at the outset of the research, much of the teaching in high status, 'traditional academic' subjects in all three schools placed more emphasis on auditory (English, French, History) and auditory and visual (Mathematics and Geography) modes of learning, with only teaching in the sciences approaching more of a balance in the learning styles encountered by the students. The end-of-course analysis of students' perceptions, six terms later, had not changed significantly in two schools, although girls in both schools acknowledged small increases in the use of kinaesthetic activities in Mathematics and French, and boys did identify similar changes in Mathematics, Geography and History. Overall, however, Science was the only subject – for either boys or girls – where learning was not dominated by auditory and visual learning in these two schools. In contrast, there were interesting variations in the other partner school, where both boys' and girls' responses suggested that there was a marked increase in the use of kinaesthetic activities in English, Mathematics, History and French; boys in Geography and girls in Science also identified an increase in kinaesthetic activities. In this partner school, students suggested that teachers had been successful, in each of these academic subjects, in introducing more variety into their lessons. Thus, in English, for example, boys' perceptions (and to a lesser extent, those of girls) indicated that they had encountered a balanced range of learning activities, across all three modalities. Similarly in French where, although auditory learning usually dominates, both boys' and girls' responses suggested a relative decline in auditory learning and a growth in kinaesthetic learning activities.

Questionnaire returns from teachers themselves tended to be inconclusive on this issue; while some of the original strategies were more prominent in some schools, other strategies were apparently used less frequently. At one level, the outcomes of the research in this triad suggests that, over a limited time period, it is difficult to change the balance of teaching activities and teaching styles used by teachers. In most of the high status academic subjects, there has been little evidence, except in partner school B, of any marked increase in teaching activities which access kinaesthetic learning, and teaching which accesses visual and auditory modes of learning continues to dominate. In part, this may be because, while teachers acknowledged the importance of introducing more kinaesthetic learning activities in order to present more of a balanced range of learning opportunities across each learning style, some teachers did not feel they had received sufficient guidance in adapting the teaching activities listed in the booklet for their own subject and context. Teachers suggested, for example, that they would have welcomed the opportunity to observe the practice of colleagues who were more experienced and confident in using kinaesthetic activities, to have had subject-specific staff development time to formulate, prepare and subsequently evaluate pilot activities, and to have had focused in-service activities to enable them to explore the detailed implications for implementing such approaches, and incorporating them into departmental medium-term planning.

At another level, however, the outcomes were more encouraging. Senior staff who had coordinated the research in each school reported that the project had impacted very positively on teachers' awareness of how students learn, and had focused staff concern on the learning process, for themselves as well as for students. They also suggested, on the basis of their extensive experiences of classroom observations across different subjects in their own schools, that there had been some significant changes, particularly in the increased use of kinaesthetic activities in middle ability and lower ability groups, and in the quality of kinaesthetic activities used by staff. This issue of quality is interesting. It was felt that teachers were now far more aware of the variety of kinaesthetic activities which were appropriate in classrooms, and how these actively supported real learning. There is a degree of subjectivity here, perhaps, mixed with optimism, but discussion with these senior staff *did* suggest that there was more reflective and thoughtful use of kinaesthetic activities, more evaluation of their effectiveness, and more integration into the structure of lessons on an ongoing basis, rather than reliance on high profile, infrequent events which might be less effective in transforming teaching and supporting learning.

In this triad, teachers' work on pedagogies has put the spotlight firmly on learning processes, and how pedagogy can most effectively support those processes through the provision of a range of high quality visual, auditory and kinaesthetic activities. This has enabled teachers to be more reflective about how they teach and how students learn, and to plan lessons which provide variety, activity and interactions, to access different modalities of learning.

Case study 2: An approach based on multiple intelligences

The nature of the intervention

The schools in the second triad served areas of extreme social and economic disadvantage, and each school exhibited features closely associated with schools in challenging circumstances. Work with the RBA project focused, in two successive years, on developing pedagogic approaches associated with accelerated learning and multiple intelligences with higher ability boys in Year 9 who were perceived as being potential under-achievers in English. Identification of the dominant learning profiles of the first cohort revealed that mathematical/logical, inter-personal and visual/spatial intelligences were more dominant than others in these boys' profiles. Among the second cohort of boys, mathematical/logical and kinaesthetic learning styles were dominant. This difference between the boys in the two cohorts is unsurprising given the small sample size, but worth noting; again it cautions us against assuming that any class of boys and girls will have a predominant preferred learning style which is gender determined.

With each cohort of students, the intervention strategy then focused on how to transform classroom practices, in the context of the teaching one of Shakespeare's plays (*Macbeth*), in the light of preferred learning styles. With the first cohort, the focus was placed specifically on the mathematical/logical and inter-personal learning styles because, although these were dominant among the learning styles of some of the boys within the cohort, in the view of the teachers concerned they were less well developed and utilized in the teaching of English. The classroom pedagogy thus required the boys to work together in small groups and teams, on jigsaw activities which focused on group interactions and presentations, on role-play activity, and on approaches that highlighted an active involvement in learning through drama. In order to develop ways of accessing and analysing the play which related to mathematical/logical learning styles, teaching approaches were devised which placed more emphasis on structure and sequence, through a series of short and sharp activities. The aim was to engage the boys in a range of activities that involved ordering ideas, sequencing events, developing a train of thought based on evidence from the play, organizing ideas and making predictions and analysis as a result of collating given information.

Work with the second cohort saw a continuing emphasis on developing pedagogy to access mathematical/logical learning styles, but also on developing teaching styles which stressed intra-personal ways of learning, since teachers felt that this was a marked weakness which restricted the boys' learning in English, and this had not been identified as a preferred learning style by many of the boys. Teachers thus attempted to devise teaching approaches which enabled the boys more effectively to visualize the activities which were being enacted within the text, to formalize their feelings and responses to incidents within the play, and to encourage the boys to reflect upon the range of emotions and experiences which the play was engendering. Particular emphasis was given to the role of talk within lessons, with boys being encouraged to work on cause and emotion through talk with each other in small groups, to ask questions of each other, to help each other in their search for understanding.

Over the two years, there was a subtle yet significant shift in emphasis, therefore, initially developing teaching strategies which focused upon boys' strengths in preferred learning styles, and then focusing upon *both* strengths and weaknesses. This reflected an evolving belief in the school that the essence of a pedagogic approach based upon preferred styles and multiple intelligences should rest (1) not just on developing a pedagogy which addresses how teachers might teach so as to access different preferred learning styles in their students, but (2) equally on alerting students to their own strengths and weaknesses as a learner, and developing their own understanding of self as learner.

Such an approach enabled teachers and students to explore with each other what learning was all about. In the words of one teacher at the Originator School:

> This more refined focus on preferred learning styles is a very powerful tool to get all students to see the link between teaching and learning ... it has facilitated a real leap in some boys' learning ... it enables them to see explicitly that what the teacher does really affects learning. 'I want students to be able to say to me: *I don't understand that; can you teach it to me in a different way please?*' I think we have empowered some boys to take on and understand their own learning.

Outcomes in the Originator School: students' views

Interviews with boys in both cohorts revealed that they had a well-developed understanding of the notion of preferred learning styles. Virtually all the boys were aware of their preferred learning styles and were able to describe them appropriately. Most boys were aware that they had a variety of preferred learning styles, that there was interplay between them, and that these might change through time. On occasions, boys showed that they were beginning to become aware of their own strengths and weaknesses as learners, and were able to discuss with each other how they learnt best.

It was also clear to many of them that some teachers were planning and teaching lessons which used a variety of different learning styles within them, and indeed explicitly identified the learning styles they intended to target in specific lessons. In both cohorts, boys' reactions to their specific study of *Macbeth* was unambiguous. The teaching had transformed their expectations and perceptions of English, particularly of Shakespeare's work, which they felt was 'interesting' and 'had some good ideas really'. The boys welcomed the school's attempt to structure the teaching to take into account the variety of preferred learning styles within the class, and felt highly valued and appreciated as a result. The variety of the teaching – the use of video, of text reading, of listening to tapes, of acting and drama led by the teacher himself – was crucial to its success, and the fact that the boys knew that the lessons were carefully planned and organized to access a variety of learning styles, and on occasions to meet their specific needs, had enabled them to develop an explicit understanding with the teacher, and a sense of being in a collaborative learning enterprise with the teacher: 'It was really good ... the way it was taught, it was just as though you are really *in* the play, you get involved and it comes alive.' Significantly, these impressions stayed with these boys through their next academic year. Interviewed again as Year 10 students in May, they spoke of the real difference which it had made to their learning, of the stimulus which had been provided by the variety of teaching styles, of the excitement and activity of the lessons:

> It was *so* good because we understood what he was trying to do ... he explained not just what we needed to learn, but how he was trying to help us learn it ... like when he play acted ... he stood on a chair and said, *I am Macbeth ... how do you feel about me?* ... so we could say ... *'Oh, Macbeth, right man ...'*, it was as though we were not talking to a teacher but to Macbeth, talking to him about how we were feeling about what he was doing. He was so very involved and engrossed in lessons ... it got us involved as well.

An interchange between a group of boys captured the essence of this in all its richness:

> The way he taught, it really helped us to remember scenes from play ... it made English lessons different, so enjoyable, like active.
>
> (b1)

> Yeah, like when he kept changing things around, so we did lots of things which involved acting, watching a video of the play, listening to music to get at the mood of the play, analysing the sequences.
>
> (b2)

> And he used rhythm from songs we knew to remember key points and quotes.
>
> (b3)

> It was fun, it involved us a lot ... you couldn't keep still ... I can still remember the lessons.
>
> (b1)

Yeah, although it was noisy, it was exciting, and it didn't matter, did it, because I can still remember lots of bits about *Macbeth* ... and it was a year ago now!

(b3)

In the end, though, he made it clear that we had to do it ourselves as well, to involve ourselves, to work out how you could help yourself when the style wasn't your own best way of learning.

(b2)

There is a sense here of real engagement and achievement, of boys who understood that the teaching had been very carefully planned and structured so as to make learning accessible and appropriate for them as a group and as individuals. Thus, boys spoke of lessons having a number of short, sharply focused activities, which were structured into a coherent whole. This structure was clearly signposted:

we knew how long we had for a task, so we'd settle quickly and get on with it, and get it done; we worked harder and achieved more.

(b1)

we enjoyed the challenge he set, really understood it because he talked about it very clearly, and then we felt good when we achieved it.

(b2)

This sense of knowing *why* they were undertaking an activity and *how* the teacher intended them to learn, established a collaborative ethic in the classroom, and contributed to a sense of combined involvement in a joint enterprise: 'We are more confident in our own ability'; 'It's been so brilliant; I didn't think I could understand a play like that.'

Outcomes in the Originator School: perspectives from the staffroom

While it would be an over-statement to claim that this approach to pedagogy had been enthusiastically adopted by all teachers in all subject departments, it was clear – from classroom observations and students' interviews – that it was high profile in a number of areas, notably in Science, Mathematics, Modern Foreign Languages, History and Music, as well as in English. Teachers in these departments felt that this approach gave them the opportunity to be more creative in their planning and teaching, and enabled them to be more analytical and reflective about their own teaching and children's learning. Several teachers spoke, for example, of being better able to understand why some members of a class might be having difficulties with a particular concept, and of attempting to teach it from a different angle, using a different approach, to access different learning styles.

Central to this approach was the sharing of ideas about preferred learning styles with students. Teachers continually engaged in dialogue with students, to make them aware of the preferred learning styles being accessed in a particular lesson, and to reassure them that their lack of understanding or difficulty with a topic was not linked to any inherent shortcomings of their own, but might be linked to the nature of the learning demanded or the way in which the topic had been taught. In the words of a senior member of staff, 'I want students to recognize the learning style I'm trying to access, and to recognize that on occasions they may need to make special efforts to access that, if it is not one of their natural learning styles.' Teachers felt that this emphasis on preferred learning styles impacted strongly upon students' motivation and subsequent learning. They spoke of boys who had 'unexpectedly come out of their shell' and were keen to take part and take on roles; of others who had responded well to textual analysis activities which required sequencing and logical deduction and scrutiny; of those who had assumed more responsibility for their own learning, been more prepared to support others collaboratively and been willing to use their own initiative to resolve learning problems they encountered. There were suggestions, too, that this approach to pedagogy had impacted very positively on student behaviour in the classroom, with students becoming more focused and engaged on the learning activities:

> There are much higher participation levels, they are keen to participate, they have been really enthusiastic and interested to perform in role [in *Macbeth*] ... I work on instilling pace, sustaining impetus, generating confidence ... the distractions and off-task behaviour has fallen massively ... there are minimal distractions in lessons, and referral rates to Head of Year for poor behaviour are much lower. I'd say, taken together, it's had a dramatic impact.
>
> (female teacher of English, reflecting on
> second year of *Macbeth* project)

The attractiveness of the approach, however, was described not simply in terms of developing students more fully as independent learners, nor in terms of the changed atmosphere within many classrooms, but in terms of increasing the enjoyment of teaching for teachers:

> When it's done well, by staff who understand the process, the difference is quite striking ... in terms of students' reactions in the classroom, their more mature interactions with others ... but also teachers here identify with the approach, because of the variety of

teaching strategies which have been made provided and made available and useable through staff development sessions.

(female Maths teacher)

Reflections on pedagogic approaches

Our work with these two triads of schools, in very different socio-economic contexts, has raised some important issues about teaching and learning within the context of an accelerated learning/multiple intelligences framework. On the one hand, there are some 'health warnings' which need to be defined, some cautionary words which need to be heeded, particularly where such frameworks are adopted uncritically. In other contexts, though, there are some promising outcomes which might be derived from such initiatives where various pre-conditions have been carefully implemented.

Cautionary words

- Work on visual, auditory and kinaesthetic learning styles does not always acknowledge the very real difficulties of defining the essential distinctiveness of each learning style. Many classroom-based activities involve all three modalities, and it is difficult simply to identify a pedagogic activity as visual or auditory or kinaesthetic, let alone in terms of Gardner's multiple intelligences. In these triads, too, it became clear that an activity planned by a teacher to access a particular learning style may well be processed by students in quite different ways. Much of the literature does not acknowledge, then, the complexity of learning through the different modalities; simplistic assumptions about learning style are often not justified in practice.
- Equally important is the need to acknowledge the difficulty of measuring and identifying students' preferred learning styles. In our first case study, different instruments (in terms of frequently used questionnaires in existence within the public domain), supposedly assessing the same phenomenon, gave different outcomes in terms of the preferred learning styles of the same students. Subsequent assumptions about students' dominance profiles were open to question and challenge, therefore, and raised questions about the clarity and validity of the different instruments.
- There is a temptation to over-simplify, to identify the preferred learning style (singular) of a student, without contextualizing this within a more balanced approach which looks at the significance of each learning style within the student's overall dominance

profile (plural). The essence of work on preferred learning styles is not to define and indulge a particular learning style, because such categorization of students is inflexible, may often be dangerously misleading and may exclude some students altogether. The focus instead must be on emphasizing a balance of different learning activities and teaching styles, and through these activities, to recognize and value diversity of need.

- Students' preferred learning styles are not fixed, but often change over the course of their secondary school education, particularly as they are exposed to a wider range of high quality teachers who might well have developed a wide repertoire of teaching strategies which access a range of learning styles. Indeed, one of the key informants in the first case study suggested that his preferred learning style differed from context to context, depending on the focus of the lesson.

These are important reservations which need to be highlighted because work on preferred learning styles is very much in vogue, is a source of a rich vein of consultancy income, and is sometimes implemented in simplistic and mechanistic ways.

Enabling factors

Nonetheless, research within these two case studies also suggests, albeit to a greater degree in some schools than in others, that work based on preferred learning styles and notions of multiple intelligences *can* help to transform the learning of some boys and some girls. For this to be the case, however, a number of enabling factors need to be established which might be defined as pre-conditions for successful implementation:

- *Placing specific emphasis on raising awareness of how learning takes place, through keynote presentations to staff and students about different modes and styles of learning.* In one triad, for example, this was consolidated and developed through an ongoing tutorial or PSHE programme which focused on appropriate study skills, and how students might acquire different study skills for different contexts. At the same time, high profile was given to the identification and open acknowledgement of students' and teachers' preferred learning styles. Executed on an ongoing basis, this ensures that students have a much better understanding of themselves as a learner: in the words of a boy in the West Midlands Originator School: 'teaching is not about teachers doing things to us, but about us understanding how we learn and how we can get better at it'.

- *As an extension of this, enabling students to recognize the implications of knowing about their preferred learning styles, and to realize what this meant for their own learning and private study* (Hart *et al.* 2004). In one school, for example, boys talked about the crucial importance of realizing that they would only learn properly when they could access learning styles which were *not* their natural preferences. Evidence in subsequent student interviews in both triads suggested that some students had adapted their learning to access a range of different learning styles, and did not feel disengaged and disempowered when teachers were teaching to a style with which they did not at first identify. This finding resonates with one of the pedagogic implications cited by Coffield *et al.* (2004). In cautioning against the uncritical use of learning styles models and instruments in schools and further education, they do nonetheless accept that

> A knowledge of learning styles can be used to increase the self-awareness of students and tutors about their strengths and weaknesses as learners. In other words, all the advantages claimed for metacognition (i.e. being aware of one's own thought and learning processes) can be gained by encouraging all learners to become knowledgeable about their own learning and that of others.
>
> (2004: 37)

- *Similarly for staff, planning lessons which explicitly addressed a variety of preferred learning styles, and enabled them to become more creative in their teaching, planning and assessing.* This is at the heart of the issue, since it focuses directly on teaching and learning, and on the need to support teachers in departments to think specifically and fundamentally about pedagogy and how it affects learning, and how learning might be made more accessible to students. On occasions, this can be a challenging and demanding task. Many teachers need explicit support, encouragement and clear exemplification of effective strategies if they are to feel really confident to use more open-ended and perhaps high risk strategies: role play, hot-seating, value-continuum lines, effective use of group work, not easily accessed by *all* teachers. There is a need for continuing in-service support to enable teachers to confidently develop and implement different teaching styles related to a range of different learning styles. Where such development work has been put in place, however, the rewards for students and teachers have been significant, as these Year 11 boys and their teacher bear witness:

> I really enjoy Maths because there is more variety ... we use rhymes and colours to understand formulae, we have classical background music to create a calmer atmosphere which is more soothing and helps concentration, we have kinaesthetic activities which involve relays and board work and lots of movement and activity.

> Every lesson there's something new ... she tries to relate the topics to our preferred learning styles and creates an environment for active learning ... we don't just sit there as though we're dead ... it's interactive and stimulating ... if she says we're to do something which seems really weird because it will help us learn, then we do it!

> It's the variety which really helps ... because you concentrate so much better when the teacher is really high profile and constantly changes the activities ... there is also loads of groupwork, which is good for me because I'm inter-personal ... and the music helps me to concentrate better, it's smoother.

> The range of teaching styles that I use now compared to two or three years ago ... it's so much more stimulating and enjoyable for me as a teacher ... and for them, I hope!

- *A recognition that these pedagogic initiatives need to be established with a wide range of staff, to provide some measure of consistency of expectation for the students, and to ensure that the gains achieved – in terms of students' attitudes, engagement and motivation – are sustained as they progress through a school.* There was some evidence, for example, that once the Macbeth project ended, some of the boys in the West Midlands Originator School found it difficult to sustain their interest, involvement and rate of progress in English, and their appreciation of Shakespeare in particular. Equally, in another partner school, the initiative failed to have as much impact as it might because, despite its enthusiastic promotion by an enthusiastic and charismatic teacher in a school leadership role, other staff were slow to identify with its potential.

Where these enabling factors are in place, the emerging evidence suggests that this approach can help transform the learning of all students, but also that it particularly helps those learners who need more help in structuring their learning, in understanding how they learn, and in offering active and varied support for learning ... and these are more often boys than girls. Our interviews suggest that it has enabled such boys to feel more valued and respected, and has engaged them as more willing and active collaborators in their own learning. In the experience of one triad, it has opened up lessons even more for students; not only are they aware of the objectives of the lesson and what the intended outcomes might be, but they also gain an insight into how the teacher is helping them to achieve the intended outcomes. In such an approach, the emphasis is centrally on the processes of learning.

Final words for the moment

We acknowledge that there are very real dangers in the learning styles debate, as it is currently constructed, especially so when it suggests that learning styles have a significant gender dimension in their distribution. We concur with the findings of Coffield *et al.* when they argue that much of the current advice proffered by a thriving commercial industry to teachers and managers on learning styles consists of 'inflated claims and sweeping conclusions which go beyond the current knowledge base and the specific recommendation of particular theories' (2004: 37) and that more independent empirical research is needed to assess the real pedagogical potential of different learning style models.

The essence of the case we have constructed here on the basis of our work with these two triads of schools, however, suggests that girls' and boys' learning styles are not stable and pre-determined in origin, but are flexible and can change through time, in response to different styles of teaching and to learning opportunities. The debate about matching similar types of teachers to similar types of learners has always been unrealistic in school contexts; the emerging research suggests that such matching would also be counter-productive and limiting for learners. The crux rather, in Hall's words, is to offer learners 'a vocabulary for understanding how they learn more effectively in different contexts at different times, [so that] learning styles may help students to become more autonomous, more motivated and more likely to continue "learning to learn" ' (2004: 35).

It is appropriate, then, that the last word rests with students in the two triads:

> Many teachers just do what suits them without much thought for us … they say 'I've always done it like this, this has always been my way and it always will, I'm not changing!', but they should, because stuff on learning styles really helps us learn, which is what we're supposed to be here for!

Some teachers open up, talk with you about how you learn and how they're trying to teach ... it makes it so much clearer, you can see what they're trying to do ... and you realize all the thought that's gone into the lesson, so that makes you think you'll work harder too, in return.

We enjoy the work, don't we, because we're not copying from books or just writing down notes that the teacher is parroting ... the lessons are active and practical, discussions, experiments ... we get the feeling the lesson has been prepared carefully and just for us, with for us to learn ... she's safe, and she only has a go at us when we need it!

I like all this stuff about preferred learning styles ... it helps me to be more confident, to try to work things out for myself, and then to ask if I don't understand.

Note

1   The questionnaire was taken from O'Brien (1991).

7 The Context of the Individual
Target-setting and mentoring

His interest helps me to attend school.

(Cathy)

I saw I could do more than I originally thought I could.

(Aaron)

My mentor opened up other possibilities for me ... he saved me from myself and my mates!

(Paul)

Mentoring in the national context

Target-setting and mentoring are well-established practices in most secondary schools in England. The establishment of the National Mentoring Network (NMN) in the mid-1990s (Colley 2003a) and a national mentoring bursary programme, launched in 1998, aimed to stimulate the take-up and use of mentoring (Golden and Sims 1999). Major government programmes, such as *Excellence in Cities* and the national careers service *Connexions*, set out to recruit both paid mentors and unpaid volunteers to help support the learning and continuing involvement in education of young people at times of crucial transitions in their lives (Benioff 1997; DfEE 2000; Colley 2003b).

The vigour with which mentoring has been promoted means that there is considerable guidance available to schools wishing to develop mentoring schemes. Mentoring needs to have a clear purpose (Sims 2002) and clearly achievable aims communicated to all participants (Reid 2002). It needs to be formalized within a clear context of where and when it is to take place (Hirom and Mitchell 1999), with clear criteria for identifying mentors and mentees (Sukhnandan *et al.* 2000). The identification and training of appropriate mentors are seen as crucial prerequisites for success (Sims *et al.* 2000), to ensure knowledge of process as well as content of what the meetings should cover (Morrison *et al.* 2000), and to facilitate appropriate listening skills and body language (Pyatt 2002). In essence, according to this literature, mentoring works when the context is empathetic, non-judgemental and understanding (Reid 2002), and when there is a balance between tutoring, guiding and counselling (Hirom and Mitchell 1999).

Much of this guidance is clear-cut and unequivocal; as researchers such as Sukhnandan *et al.* (2000) and Sims *et al.* (2000) suggest, the potential gains are clear. Mentoring has the ability to enable students to address weaknesses and improve their learning skills, to discuss targets and identify appropriate strategies to meet the targets and to offer positive role models.

There are a number of dilemmas here, however. One is related to the identification of appropriate role models for students and the need to avoid reinforcing implicit stereotyping that might arise from the involvement of external mentors such as local sporting personalities. Not all volunteers *are* appropriate mentors. Another relates back to our earlier concerns with the homogeneity of gender construction, and the tendency to generalize, to assume that it will be largely boys who need mentoring support, and that they have common needs, different from those of girls. Thus, Sukhnandam *et al.*, reviewing mentoring across eight secondary schools in England and Wales, reported that

> Staff felt that mentoring would enable them to help targeted pupils address their weaknesses and thus improve their learning skills. For boys, this often meant focusing on issues of organization, time management, revision and literacy skills whilst for girls this usually meant coping with pressure, writing succinctly and targeting specific areas of weakness in a variety of subject areas.
>
> (2000: 42)

A third dilemma relates to the need to acknowledge that mentoring is a challenging and nuanced task, involving the need to establish trust and some feeling of equality between participants, but also a recognition that the relationship has a latent power balance within it. The contextualization of mentoring is also important; successful mentoring in one school cannot necessarily be transferred to another, because the processes of human interactions which are central to it cannot be reconstructed by simply selecting from a fixed menu of options.

The research into mentoring conducted within the Raising Boys' Achievement Project was informed by these concerns and dilemmas. We acknowledged the vast growth of mentoring initiatives in schools over the past decade, but equally we were aware that formal evaluation of such schemes was limited. In those that did exist, there was a sense that the effects of mentoring were difficult to define (Golden 2000), and that mentoring may impact more upon personal development than upon academic achievement or attitudes towards school (Sukhnandam *et al.* 2000). The point is succinctly summarized by Colley:

> For the most part, this tidal wave has carried all before it in a surge of celebration. Mentoring seems to encapsulate a 'feel-good' factor ... Yet there is an irony in such a practice being sponsored so heavily by a government committed to evidence-based practice and to the pursuit of 'what works'. There is little evidence to support the use of mentoring on such a vast scale ... mentoring may be counter-productive to policy intentions for interventions with socially excluded young people, and that even where young people are enthusiastic about their experiences of being mentored, their mentors may not share this view.
>
> (2003a: 523)

Target-setting and mentoring within the Raising Boys' Achievement Project

Within the Raising Boys' Achievement Project, two triads worked on contrasting approaches to target-setting and mentoring. In one triad of schools, in urban areas in North-East England, mentoring was an explicit and direct intervention, introduced formally in the final term of Year 10, towards the end of a student's period of compulsory education. The system embraced all students, regardless of gender or ability, and mentoring was effected by senior members of staff who made a considerable time commitment to support the learning of students. Mentoring sessions were regular and frequent, normally on a monthly basis throughout the last year of 11–16 education, and were informed by a rigorous system of data collection and analysis which was fed by each subject department within the schools.

In the second triad of schools, there was more concern with developing a mentor scheme directed at the needs of students in Key Stage 3 (Years 7–9). Here a smaller number of specific students were targeted, usually boys (but with an increasing number of girls) who were identified as being 'at risk' of failing to fulfil their potential. While there were some parallels here with Gillborn and Youdell's (2000) notion of 'educational triage', the emphasis of the scheme was more appropriately defined as maximizing the schools' opportunities to recognize and work directly with students who might become seriously disaffected and disengaged before Year 10. In this second triad of schools, some mentors were Learning Mentors, funded by initiatives such as *Excellence in Cities* and not usually qualified teachers; others were teachers who did not usually teach the students they mentored, chosen for their personality and their ability to establish rapport with more challenging students. Whatever the context, mentoring here was also regular and frequent, within protected time for the students, and informed by data on behaviour, effort and quality of homework, as well as by attainment data.

The contrasting characteristics of mentoring and target-setting in these two contexts reinforce some of the real issues associated with such interventions. Given limited resources of time and energy, where should such interventions be directed if they are to be most effective? Who should be targeted by such interventions, and supported by whom, for what purpose? How do we judge 'effectiveness'? Within the achievement culture in which schools operate, how can we balance short-term gains with long-term effects?

Transforming achievement and attitudes

The schools in the first triad were 11–16 comprehensive schools on the periphery of urban areas in North-East England, serving largely white, mixed-class catchment areas of rural agricultural and commuting villages, together with large local authority housing estates within each urban area. Parts of each catchment contained areas of significant social deprivation and exclusion, with a legacy of low parental aspirations.

The Originator School had had an unexceptional achievement profile through much of the 1990s. The OFSTED report of 1998 summarized the pupils' achievements as being 'broadly in line with those expected nationally of pupils by the end of KS3 and KS4 ... and similar to those of the last inspection [in 1993]'; in 1998 34 per cent of boys and 43 per cent of girls achieved five(+) A*–C grades at GCSE. Since then, however, within the context of a broadly unchanged curriculum, an exceptional transformation in achievement had occurred, not only in terms of the percentage of students achieving the benchmark grades at GCSE (60 per cent of boys and 68 per cent of girls in 2002, 74 per cent of boys, 81 per cent of girls in 2004), but also in terms of the achievements of most students within successive cohorts in terms of average points scores (Figure 7.1).

The evidence offered by value-added data showed that the school had regularly and consistently outperformed other schools within the LEA, including those with much more favoured catchments (Table 7.1). Indeed, detailed analysis of GCSE performance against YELLIS[1] predictions for recent years revealed that a considerable number of girls and boys performed significantly better at GCSE than predicted by YELLIS data; in each year (Table 7.2), at least 50 per cent more boys and girls achieved the benchmark grades at GCSE than predicted by YELLIS.

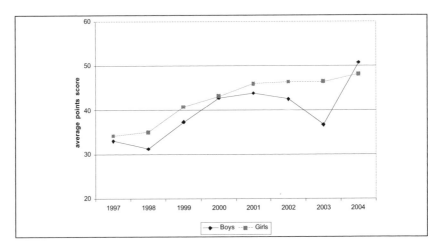

Figure 7.1 Achievement profile at GCSE (average points score)

Table 7.1 Northern LEA KS3 value-added data: Year 7–11 student transition

	MidYIS Bands achieved (data for year 7 entry) (%)						GCSE performance (year 11)
	A	*B*	*C*	*D*	*Missing*	*A + B*	*% 5 (+) A*–C*
School	16.0	23.5	25.2	30.3	5.0	39.5	65.9
LEA	25.5	26.1	22.9	24.0	1.5	51.6	47.1

Table 7.2 GCSE performance against YELLIS predictions, 2002–4

Group	YELLIS prediction % 5 A*–C grades 2002	% 5 A*–C grades 2002	YELLIS prediction % 5 A*–C grades 2003	% 5 A*–C grades 2003	YELLIS prediction % 5 A*–C grades 2004	% 5 A*–C grades 2004
boys	33%	60%	31%	61.5%	50%	74%
girls	40%	68%	43%	79.5%	52%	81%

In achievement terms, the partner schools had contrasting achievement profiles at the outset of the Project. In school A, 25 per cent of boys and 34 per cent of girls achieved A*–C grades in 2001, reflecting the challenging nature of the catchment area with extensive multiple deprivation. A new headteacher had arrived in the previous year, inheriting a recent OFSTED report which had placed the school in the 'serious weakness' category. Partner school B had higher levels of overall achievement, serving a catchment area with some more affluent areas, but a persistent gender gap similar to school B; in 2001, 49 per cent of boys and 56 per cent of girls achieved the benchmark grades.

The second triad consisted of three 11–18 inner-city comprehensive schools in culturally diverse inner-city areas of the West Midlands. Two of the schools were essentially monocultural, serving well-established Asian communities and were boy-dominated. Some 90 per cent of students spoke English as an additional language and students' basic literacy skills were poor on entry. The third served a more ethnically diverse but largely stable neighbourhood; 25 per cent of students were entitled to free school meals and 33 per cent spoke English as an additional language. The intake of all three schools was skewed towards the less able, with few very able students and the proportion of students with special educational needs was above the national average.

The Originator School established a small-scale mentoring programme in KS4 in 1997–98, targeting students who were under-achieving academically. This had an almost immediate impact on results (Figure 7.2). The mentoring programme evolved and expanded over the years and was seen by the school as being at the core of their approach to raising achievement. Cross-phase initiatives were developed, with ex-students enrolled at local HE institutions mentoring Y12, Y9 mentoring Y6 in feeder primary schools, and Y10 mentoring Y7 students, as well as a substantial programme in KS4.

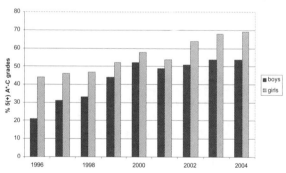

Figure 7.2 Achievement profile at GCSE for the Originator School

The partner schools had limited experience of mentoring programmes prior to involvement with the RBA Project, but they decided that action in Key Stage 3 would be more likely to have a positive impact on students' achievement, given the characteristics of the students they catered for. Consequently the partner schools implemented a mentoring programme (Activate) in Years 8 and 9. Three cohorts of 'under-achieving' boys participated in the programme over the time period of the Raising Boys'

Achievement Project, and the Key Stage 3 results' profile of these boys, comparing their actual results in English, Maths and Science against projections based on CAT scores taken on entry to secondary school, were analysed. This analysis suggested that the attainment of 74 per cent of boys in partner school A and 63 per cent of boys in school B either matched or exceeded their predicted results. Given that all students participating in Activate were felt to be under-achieving prior to their involvement in the programme, the fact that a high proportion of these students went on not only to attain at their projected level but in some cases to exceed their projections (44 per cent in school A, 32 per cent in school B) suggested the programme had real potential to raise achievement.

Target-setting and mentoring across both case studies

We acknowledged in Chapter 5 that it is frequently difficult to disentangle the differential influence of the strategies which schools have implemented to raise achievement. Thus it is with the schools in these case studies: changes at senior management level which have provided inspirational leadership and a determination to open up possibilities for students from more deprived backgrounds, a renewed emphasis on learning and teaching strategies within the classroom and an allied focus on assessment for learning, attempts to create an 'achievement for all' culture within the school, have all played important roles. Central to these initiatives, however, has been the development of a vigorous and highly interventionist form of target-setting and mentoring.

Why, though, have target-setting and mentoring in some of these case study schools been so effective in contributing to the transformation of students' achievements, attitudes and expectations, while in other schools there has been far less impact? At one level, the system of target-setting and mentoring in place appears unremarkable: introduced for a tight time period, informed by achievement data which is regularly updated, structured around ongoing dialogue between mentor and mentee. There appears little to distinguish it from schemes in many other schools. The voices of students within some of these case study schools suggests, however, that the mentoring *is* distinctive in these contexts, and it is to these that we now turn.

Students' perspectives

During the RBA Project, we observed mentoring sessions and interviewed students, both boys and girls, individually and in single-sex focus groups, as they progressed through GCSE courses and Key Stage 3. This longitudinal data offers penetrating perspectives on the strengths of mentoring in these schools, and reveals some of the key issues which schools must resolve if mentoring and target-setting are to be most effective.

To both Year 8/9 and Year 11 students in some schools within these triads, the target-setting and mentoring scheme was fundamental because it impacted so directly upon their confidence:

The regular reports and target-setting boosted my confidence and made me want to work harder. I stopped messing around, so my effort grades improved. And it gave me an idea of how I needed to work in year 10, and it's really helping now'

and opened up possibilities and raised aspirations:

My results will definitively improve ... my mentor gives me more enthusiasm to work better ... it shows you what is possible ... and helps in terms of suggesting what you can do.'

Mentoring offered an effective and supportive forum for discussions on wide-ranging issues:

It works because it's not just led by the mentor ... they give you opportunity to talk ... I feel I can start discussion myself about something that's bothering me, if it's at home or school ... we have a good conversation, it's just like talking with your mates ... well, perhaps not quite! ... but he listens well.

Mentoring established a sense of real communication and rapport between mentor and student. Students felt listened to and valued, developed a sense of self-belief, and were willing to accept praise openly, knowing that it was both genuine and realistic.

In the second triad, where the mentoring was more targeted and the scheme more selective, the group ethos generated by the scheme was particularly important in sustaining students' motivation and sense of involvement. It was particularly important also that the students could identify with others in a similar situation, and they gained strength and resolve from being part of a specially selected group: 'It's good to be part of the Activate group because you're not the Lone Ranger ... other people are trying to change as well, so there's a group feel ... and we get to do activities together.'

The structure of mentoring

It was equally clear, however, that certain structural features and distinctive characteristics contributed to the success of mentoring within these school contexts. One feature was the regularity of the mentoring system, with mentoring sessions timetabled into the yearly calendar, and administrative staff organizing monthly appointments for students. Mentors worked together to protect time for mentoring, giving it the highest priority to ensure that appointments were kept by both pupils *and* staff. A tight structure and framework were provided for students, enabling them to work with their mentor on clearly defined targets over short time periods, and to sustain the momentum of learning and motivation. Some boys, in particular, welcomed this and saw it as offering regular feedback within a supportive context. Combined with this, however, was an ethos of open access and flexibility, an informality which students saw as reinforcing the caring, supportive ethos within the school:

> All the mentors are very approachable ... even though my mentor is the headteacher, I can go and talk to him if I need to.

> If I have a real problem, I can see him between the mentoring sessions ... the mentor would sort it out, that's what he's there for.

Another feature of these mentoring systems was the way in which the agenda was set firmly within an academic context, reflecting concerns with learning and with achievement, rather than simply with broader pastoral issues. Consideration was given to topics such as strategies for learning, ways of structuring work into short, manageable units, how to focus first on aspects of work which could be met without too much difficulty before tackling more challenging aspects:

> Your mentor convinces you of what is possible ... she concentrates with you on certain subjects at a time, and discusses targets with you, and how you might do better ... she reinforces what you've done really well on, points out weaknesses and strong points ... then you become a better learner too.

There was also the concern with ensuring that students were offered strategies that helped them to minimize confrontations in the classroom and to manage their own anger. Students spoke of gaining more enjoyment from school, of being involved in less conflict with teachers and their peers, of noticing an impact on their own motivation and on how teachers in turn treated them: 'I'm hardly ever sent out of lessons now. I used to spend as much time in the corridor as in the classroom! It's better now that someone is looking out for me, to help me' or in the words of another student, 'When I get into trouble, I hear my mentor's words booming in my ears!'

Similarly, the mentor's involvement with the class teacher helped to evolve strategies which minimized distractions and loss of face:

> When my mentor asks my teacher to tell me that I had to sit in a particular place, it took the heat off in front of my friends ... it sort of gave me space to work ... I couldn't *not* have sat with them otherwise.

> I tell them I have to sit by myself to get good grades and my mates understand.

In both triads, students in some of these schools stressed that mentoring was effective because it was rooted firmly in grade predictions and target-setting. Students knew what level their teachers thought they were achieving at, and had the opportunity to discuss this with their mentors in terms of their own capabilities and strategies for improvement. Access for students to meaningful and reliable data was seen as crucial to the success of the scheme. The clear and unequivocal link with current achievement and potential was one which students found helpful and supportive, if at times daunting!

> Having access to the grades is so important ... it's given me more enthusiasm to work well because I can see what is possible ... my grades sometimes surprise me ... it's motivational ... you think you really can do it after all!

> Seeing the grades is crucial ... in my previous school mentoring wasn't linked to grades ... it wasn't very precise or helpful ... here, you get to see where you're at and to know what to do to get higher ... the targets are really important.

One might still argue, of course, that this commitment in a mentoring scheme to establishing effective rapport with students, building confidence and self-belief, organizing regular and structured meetings to an academic agenda which can be informed by reliable data, is not new. We would agree; such an approach is well documented in the literature, yet it is rare – in our experience – for all aspects of mentoring to be brought together so effectively and coherently in a whole school context, to impact so directly upon achievements and aspirations.

Collaborative mentoring

The sense of collaboration and negotiation between mentor and student was one aspect of target-setting and mentoring in these schools which was distinctive and unusual. Many students had real confidence in the system and trust in their mentors. There was a clear understanding that the mentoring scheme '[was] for us, not for the staff or the school, but for us ... it really shows that they care for us as people, about what we can achieve and are capable of'. Central to this was the notion that mentors would intercede with teachers on behalf of their mentees, and negotiate alternative opportunities and extra support where needed:

> When I'm behind with something, I can really talk about it ... my mentor will talk to the class teacher, and then to me, about how I can catch up; he'll set up extra sessions with the teacher for a group of us.
>
> (Year 11)

> I will tell the mentor stuff ... and we can work our way around a problem if I disagree with the teacher ... the mentor and the teacher are in good communication.
>
> (Year 11)

This was particularly important with Year 9 students, who might have less confidence to talk with their teachers about their learning and how they are being taught:

> Going to see a teacher on your own can be intimidating ... it helps to have your mentor, because he's talking for *you*, so it makes it easier to get the point across.

> Any of the teachers I have a problem with, or think I have a problem with, you go to your mentor and they have a quiet word, so it gets it all out of harm's way, so you don't have to deal with it. They deal with it and get back to you with what they said.

This advocacy role, with the mentor acting as an intermediary between the subject teacher and the student, was strongly applauded and welcomed by students in the schools where it had been developed. It reinforced the emphasis on academic outcomes and on strategies which would help students to achieve. Where it was most effective, students *knew* that mentors would act urgently and with immediacy to address and resolve issues which had been identified in mentor sessions:

> My mentor was an *immediate* source of help ... if, after a mentor session, we had found an issue which needed sorting out, he would do something about it the same day, straight away.

> After a mentor session, the English teacher came and gave me more help in breaking down the work and structuring it into smaller units that I could cope with.

In our experience, this is fundamental if mentoring is to have high impact. Students must have a strong belief and confidence in their mentor, convinced that the mentors are working with and for them, 'battling' for them, in the memorable words of a Year 8 girl in the West Midlands, 'when no one else, at school or at home, seems to care'. Where this negotiation is delayed or ineffective, the scheme can quickly lose credibility with those very students it needs to hold.

Equally, though, students understood that there was reciprocity within the system. Students were prepared to accept that their subject teacher might have an alternative and more legitimate view of a situation than they did, and were expected to accept the outcomes of negotiation between mentor and teacher. In the most successful mentoring contexts, it was clearly understood that the agenda was not to undermine subject teachers, but to resolve difficulties of motivation and learning, conflicts and misunderstandings, as they arose, and that students would accept their own responsibilities to implement strategies worked out in mentor meetings.

Not all the schools in these triads were able to successfully implement this aspect of mentoring and there was continuing unease in some schools, where this negotiation between mentor and student was seen as having the potential to create a feeling of complicity which might undermine subject teachers. It was equally clear, however, that mentoring was *most* effective where such open negotiation between mentor and subject teacher had been established, and where it was transparent to the student.

... and assertive mentoring

Another distinctive aspect of the target-setting and mentoring in these successful contexts was the extent to which the tone of mentoring changed as the cycle progressed. Observation of early mentoring sessions suggested that mentors usually adopted an encouraging style, offering explicit praise and gently confirming the ways in which the students were working:

> These grades are wonderful ... your mum will be over the moon ... I'll ring her and tell her how well you're doing, shall I?
>
> (girl declines offer)

> It's looking good now, from a mixed bag of Ds ... you've got the right attitude, I'm dead pleased by that.
>
> (to a 'lazy' boy)

Mentor sessions were relatively relaxed, with much of the discussion aimed at confidence building and reinforcing self-esteem...

There's always one boy who's going to get all Ds ... we've thought you're going to be that boy, haven't we? But now suddenly, you're the most successful student of the month ... coursework grades up a lot ...we're looking at 7Cs and 2 Ds now ... this is really well done ... don't take your foot off the pedal and get complacent ... are we together on this one, son?

Such mentoring was persuasive in style, gently teasing out subject issues and conflicts of personality, adopting a calm, logical manner which aimed to win-over students:

Michelle: I'm not bothered if I pass or not ... I just want to get out of his class because he's pushing me too hard.

Mr J: But who will suffer then, the teacher or you?

Michelle: Who cares ... I don't want to work for *him*!

Mr J: But you've done loads of work already; whose benefit is that for? It's your qualification which is going to be the loser if you go off in a huff, not the teacher, he won't lose.

In some mentoring sessions, however, the tone was more direct and challenging. Particular expectations were conveyed from mentor to student, and it was made clear to the student that a challenge had been set and that commitment was expected. These instances, usually in mentor sessions with specific under-performing students (mostly but not always boys), embodied a more direct interventionist style of mentoring, offering strategies and negotiation but making assertive demands in return:

I'll talk to your [subject] teacher so that you have opportunity to redo that piece of work ... You got a 5 in your SATs in Year 9 ... there's no way you're going to get a D at GCSE ... you might as well have sat in the yard instead of going to [subject] lessons these last two years ... I'll have it sorted by Monday ... see me at lunchtime .... The problem, though, is that I haven't seen you around enough in lunchtime clubs and after school clubs ... Mr D is staying behind after school, are you? ... So more effort is required, my son, ... see to it ... please ... OK?

(discussion with Y11 boy)

You've gone back on the deal we made and your grades have gone down. You need to play the game. You cannot have a minute off;

you need to be here every single day for the next five weeks. If you don't come, we'll fetch you; are you going to let yourself and me down? We've got loads to do, haven't we?

(discussion with girl who had been truanting)

This assertive mentoring attempts to establish a high level of personal involvement and to create a sense of responsibility among the students, to establish the notion that the students have a personal responsibility not only to themselves, but to honour the commitment they are making to their mentor and to their subject teachers. In establishing a personal link, using an informal style and setting up 'deals' with his mentees, the mentor is demanding that students make an equal commitment; charm and charisma are used to establish rapport, to engage the students and to get them to commit personally. Within this though, there is a direct and forceful style, with a renewed emphasis on reciprocity: 'Teachers are willing to work for you, you work for them!'

There was dialogue within these mentor sessions, however; mentors responded sensitively to what students offered; they used casual, accessible language which made immediate contact with students; the style was informal and genial, with an element of underlying humour. It was obvious, too, that mentors knew their students well, enabling them to make constant reference back to their personal and family circumstances and to issues of illness and attendance. But it was also clear where the locus of power was focused, with mentors assertive and initiating the direction of the dialogue, focusing directly on problem areas and subjects, establishing rapport and offering praise, but also challenging:

Your teacher of 20 years experience tells me you're on course for an E grade in this subject, Chris ... so whether you think you're going to get a B grade is irrelevant! Her experience, and mine, is telling you that unless you change your attitude, approach, work rate, you're in for a shock ... it's no B you're looking at, trust me on that one!

This changed tone of mentoring, with more challenge and urgency, of insistence on the students taking personal responsibility, was a marked feature of effective mentoring. Interviewed some time later, Chris appeared in retrospect to accept this as a fair deal:

My mentor could be quite scary, but that's probably just what I needed at the time. I thought I was OK and on course ... so I didn't bother much. He made me see that it would be only me who suffered. He gave me a bit of a shock at times.

The strength of the mentoring here, established through time on a regular and caring basis, with a credible and supportive mentor, was such as to sustain the relationship and the trust between mentor and student in times of stress and disengagement, and to avoid possible dangers of counter-productivity and student hostility. Thus it enabled the student to accept the challenge and engage with the choices offered by the mentor.

It is worth reiterating here, though, that there is a further aspect of this style of mentoring. We see the confrontational challenging aspect of mentoring as addressing directly issues of laddishness and macho image. The mentor in such a context provides some boys (and the occasional girl) with a way *not* to opt out. The intervention of senior staff, who are seen to be monitoring these students tightly, gives them a justification to use to their peers, to enable them to continue to work, to increase their involvement, to work to achieve targets. The school, through its strong intervention at this stage, is giving them a reason not to be laddish (or ladettish!), offering them almost a face-saving device to enable them to work without undermining their own sense of 'being a lad or a ladette'.

Pre-conditions for successful mentoring and target-setting

In at least three of the schools within these two triads, our experiences during the RBA project were very positive, and the development of mentoring and target-setting impacted very positively on students' motivation, attendance and attainment. Students made it clear that mentoring *did* help them to achieve higher level grades than might otherwise have been possible, and some were positively shocked by the high level of their achievements. Equally, though, there were difficulties and challenges, particularly in two other schools within these case studies, which meant that the impact of this intervention strategy was more limited. In one school, for example, subject staff felt that students' targets (defined by SMT in an attempt to raise staff expectations) were unrealistic; in another, students' views of their own experiences of learning and being taught were not accepted as important. The implementation of the intervention strategies has not always been smooth and successful, therefore, and it is inevitably a considerable challenge to implement significant and far-reaching change within schools. Equally, though, the relative failure of a strategy in a specific school is a further valuable source of evidence in enabling us to define some of the essential pre-conditions for successful mentoring and target-setting. It is to a discussion of these pre-conditions that we now turn.

Rationale and mutual support

A clearly defined context, justifying the purpose and intended outcomes of mentoring, and conveyed clearly to all students, is essential if the potential of any target-setting and mentoring system is to be maximized. Successful mentoring schemes develop the conviction in students that they are capable of achieving well, raise expectations where neither home nor community have high expectations of education and schooling, motivate *and* sustain motivation.

Tightly targeted mentoring schemes must overcome any feeling of stigma, and must be sensitively implemented to avoid conflicts with the laddish culture and macho images which some boys cultivate. Interviews with some boys on these schemes resonate with our earlier discussions on laddishness and raising achievement. Where hard work and extra effort are perceived to be a feminine quality and effortless achievement the aim of the macho boy, then targeted mentoring schemes are faced with a real challenge, particularly in establishing a sense of group identity with the aims and aspirations of the scheme. This is not to say, though, that such a challenge cannot be overcome:

> It was good having some of my mates on Activate ... it meant that several of us were trying to change, not just one ... so we could help each other and ignore the jibes ... I wasn't the only one, so that helped a lot.

Precise and detailed monitoring of students' progress, from Year 7 to Year 11, carried out with different cohorts through time

In some schools, target-setting is seen as a mechanistic and administrative burden, and viewed somewhat cynically as being in opposition to learning, distracting teachers from the really fundamental purposes of education. There is also the charge that the rigorous testing regime which currently permeates the English education system is counter-productive because it labels many children at too early an age, benchmarking them within a context which builds under-achievement and under-expectation into the core of the system, and resulting in an excessive focus of resources on students at the C/D borderline in GCSE examinations. We acknowledge the dangers implicit in such arguments, and accept that testing and subsequent establishment of targets can lead to a self-fulfilling prophecy on the part of teacher, parent and child.

We recognize, too, that target-setting is a complex issue. In some schools, there remains a philosophy of 'under-grading' associated with 'shocking' students into working and giving more commitment to their academic work. In other schools, teachers knowingly 'over-grade' to boost confidence and to give reassurance. Both approaches aim to increase motivation, but there are clear dangers of counter-productivity in both. Crucially, such an approach can totally invalidate mentoring and reporting since there is no secure foundation for the grades and for subsequent target-setting.

Nonetheless, we strongly believe that target-setting can be transformative and liberating. There are two important aspects here. One emphasizes the establishment of realistic grades within the context of the school's historic data, so that teachers are enabled to analyse the performance of current students in the light of the performances of past students. This contextualizes what is possible from the perspective of each school's own value-added data. In the words of one headteacher:

> It allows staff to use the historic experiences within the school to help make realistic predictions ... some staff, if unsure, will drop their prediction, for example to a D grade, and play for safety, despite their knowledge of what similar boys (particularly) have achieved in the past. If staff are not sufficiently realistic or are over-cautious, boys particularly will not cope ... they will switch off and not keep trying to improve because, as they see it, despite their best efforts, nothing is changing.

The use of past data to inform teachers and students of realistic possibilities thus not only avoids the dangers of an over-cautious approach to predictions which can demotivate and in turn contribute to the self-fulfilling prophecy of lower achievement, but it can also reassure and build confidence. The importance of this cannot be over-estimated:

> We have a target-setting system in place which is remarkably efficient, accurate and effective ... it is immensely comforting to us, and for our students, to be able to say ... 'Don't worry ... you continue working as you are, and we can predict with some assurance what you will achieve ...' it's particularly reassuring to girls, in that it reduces the stress, but it also builds up the confidence of boys ... it makes *them* more assured, visibly more confident ... it's good to confirm they're on track.

Equally, though, there has to be a recognition that historic data must be contextualized within value-added parameters and the comparable performance of similar schools. Otherwise, targets simply based on patterns of historic performances can lead to endemic under-achievement.

Time for professional dialogue!

Target-setting needs staff who understand potential data and become data-literate, and senior managers who protect time so that data analysis and target-setting are prioritized as a core activity by all staff. Such activities must be faculty-based, enabling teachers to discuss students' work and to monitor progress, to justify predicted grades and to engage in professional dialogue about teaching and learning at the level of the individual child. It reinforces and consolidates teachers' conceptual grasp of standards, and contributes to a real discussion of possible grades and targets. Such a prioritization also allows for accountability, enabling faculty heads to engage in meaningful discussion with senior managers as to why students' grade changes might have occurred, and to offer justification where grades are seen to be too low.

There are challenges here, of course, in identifying time and ensuring that staff *do* have the support which they need to become more data-literate. In one school, for example, students' targets were fixed by senior staff, using prior attainment data and informed by national data and expectations, rather than locating target-setting in subject departments where expectations were perceived as being too low. This may be an interim step necessary in some schools, but our experiences suggest that it is better to identify the time and space to stimulate professional dialogue and to challenge such perceptions of what is possible. In most schools we have worked with, it is clear that these processes of data analysis and target-setting have sharpened the thinking of some teachers about possibilities and outcomes, have led to higher expectations of students and higher predictions by staff, and subsequently generated more assurance and confidence in students. In one school, this was described to us as a 'positive, cyclical, and wholly unintended outcome which has, nonetheless, been a crucial component in the success of the scheme'. Crucially, it allows historic data, important at one level, to be challenged and to be reviewed within a context of raising expectations.

Involvement of senior staff

Where mentoring is meaningful and effective, it is a high intensity activity involving an ongoing and regular dialogue with students. But it also involves communication and feedback with subject teachers, receiving 'alert forms' and discussing grade changes so that these can be rationalized to students, as well as requiring a response to issues raised by both teachers and students.

In our experience, mentoring only impacts centrally on academic achievement when mentors are credible, accessible and committed. Although mentoring can be effective when carried out by younger members

of staff, our earlier emphasis on mentors who are well placed both to negotiate with other members of staff and to intercede on behalf of students, on
the one hand, and to challenge students, on the other, suggests that the
most effective mentors are usually members of staff with some seniority in
the school. Certainly, for students in one triad this was the defining
element of the mentoring system, the crucial aspect which contributed
strongly to the success of the scheme. In such a context, to be mentored by
a senior member of staff conferred status to the students, gave self-belief
and a feeling of value, and offered students a sense of the importance which
the school placed on mentoring. Equally, the mentor must be credible with
other staff as well as students, encouraging other teachers to value the mentoring process and accept as legitimate the concerns raised by students.
Mentors must enable teachers as well as students to 'buy into it'.

Although mentoring is demanding of senior staff, our research evidence
suggests that such a time commitment does more than support students'
learning and achievements; it offers insights into students' perspectives and
concerns about their schooling, it enables and facilitates a continuing dialogue with key student voices within the school:

> Look what I get in return, in a monthly meeting, on a one-to-one
> basis, with thirty Year 11 students, some of whom are the key
> leaders of the student peer group ... to discuss their learning, how
> they are taught, how they feel about how they are doing ... it's
> invaluable for me, both in terms of enabling and facilitating my
> continuing and regular contact with young people, and in terms of
> continually taking the temperature of the peer group leaders within
> my school.
>
> (Headteacher, North-East England comprehensive)

Accepting the student perspective

Crucial in any successful mentoring scheme is the sense of sharing, an
acknowledgement that students' perspectives on their own education are
real and that their voices are legitimate. In some schools within these triads,
this is commonly accepted practice, built into school procedures as a matter
of course, so that issues raised during mentoring are treated seriously and
students feel valued. Not all case study schools had yet established this
ethos, however, and then students sometimes felt that mentors were not
effective in negotiating with subject teachers, and mentors lacked confidence in the authenticity and value of the student voice. Some boys suggested to us that mentoring sessions were more like 'question and answer'
sessions, with little real dialogue and discussion, and little account taken of
their concerns. In the words of one Year 11 boy: 'Mentoring is so frustrating because it's just a session dominated by the mentor moaning about my

lack of progress. When I try to raise something, I can't get a word in and no-one listens anyway!' This is a far cry from mentor as mediator, 'battling for their mentee' in the words of one mentor in the West Midlands, and 'helping to keep the student together in times of stress and turmoil!'

Responsibility and intervention

One of the most vigorous debates which have taken place across schools within these triads has revolved around the philosophy underpinning mentoring approaches. How far should mentoring be directive and assertive? How realistic is the notion that mentoring should essentially aim to equip students as independent learners? What levels of responsibility and choice should be assumed differentially by students and mentors? All of these have been pressing questions, as schools have sought to develop and sustain the fine balance between the extremes of a persuasive and a more directly interventionist approach to mentoring.

Thus, in one case study school, emphasis was placed on a collaborative tone throughout, keen to develop students as independent learners well equipped for the future, anxious not to generate antagonisms with borderline and disengaged students by creating pressures and tensions. Here it was made clear to students that they must *want* to achieve, must participate fully as proactive partners in mentoring and in learning, must identify willingly and co-operatively with the aims and aspirations of the school.

This is the ideal, of course, and there is some evidence of its increasing effectiveness in this school. But there is also evidence that some students feel they need more regular support and tight target-setting, that they appreciate mentors who offer extrinsic motivation in 'forcing the pace to ensure they work', that they respond best to mentors who establish rapport with them but also make explicit and challenging demands. In some ways, too, the very students who benefit the most from mentoring are those who need more assertive guidance from mentors they respect, who need mentors to provide a context in which they are enabled to work and at the same time to sustain their own image and credibility.

We reiterate that this balance between responsibility and intervention can only be resolved in each school context, within parameters which reflect the socio-economic context and the overarching philosophy of each school. In our own experience, though, the most effective mentoring – in terms of what releases and fulfils the potential of those disengaged and marginal students within any school – is that which creates a rationale which such students can give to their peers, to justify their involvement in academic work and offer as a reason for working, which enables them to address issues of image and group credibility.

An overview

Where target-setting and mentoring have been successful in transforming the achievements and attitudes of students, there appears to have been a crucial focus on the individual, on gaining and acting upon detailed knowledge of the potential of individual students, and conveying a sense of what might be possible. The emphasis has been placed on promoting the expectations of students, particularly of those boys and girls across the ability spectrum who show evidence of disengagement and demotivation, to raise their aspirations and ambitions. In many schools this has inevitably led to an identification of more potentially 'under-achieving' boys than girls, but it has also been fundamental to establish a sense of inclusion, to create realistic and achievable targets – and effective mentoring approaches – for all students.

We suggest, then, that target-setting and mentoring have the potential to be transformative on achievements at school, on attitudes towards schooling, on attendance at school and, logically, on behaviour while at school, when they possess certain characteristics and when certain pre-conditions have been met. They can be particularly effective with potentially disengaged boys and the fewer disengaged girls when those students:

- understand and 'buy into' the reasons for target-setting, when they feel sufficient autonomy to be in control of their own learning profile, and develop the skills and attributes of independent learners;
- perceive the tone of the scheme as supportive rather than oppressive;
- understand that potential data create realistic expectations of what is possible, and gain a sense of self-esteem and confidence as learners when they realize what is indeed possible, given the historic trends within the school;
- are encouraged to make a comparison between their past self, their present self and their aspirations for their future self as learners;
- appreciate that they are offered choice by their mentor, and are (made) aware of the responsibility conferred by choice;
- are offered a context where boys (in particular) can be offered an escape from the needs to conform to a laddish, macho image, by the challenge and demands made by the mentor.

In such contexts, successful target-setting and mentoring have helped to sustain not only students' sense of membership of school and their sense of self-esteem and self-worth, but their sense of agency, of having some voice and power to impact on their own contexts and lives, to make decisions and effective choices about their own futures. Where this works well, staff talk of mentees becoming more confident and more able to articulate ideas and difficulties, developing more pride in themselves ('having that bit of magic about him'), and beginning to acknowledge that they have some responsibility for their own learning, combating the view that education and school are something that is 'done to them'.

But target-setting and mentoring, sustained through time, can also transform the expectations of teachers. Yet in some schools, too many long-serving staff – immersed in the traditions and aspirations of the local community, and teaching children of previous pupils – accept levels of achievement in which under-achievement is endemic and based on the low expectations of education within the communities which the school serve. In some schools, talk of the liberating, transformative potential of education has long been greeted with quiet cynicism, sometimes with a hostility which suggests that academic achievements are beyond many of the children 'in *this* type of school', generating in some staffrooms a somewhat resigned and weary approach to talk of targets and raising aspirations. Yet in other similar schools, sometimes in the most challenging inner city or outer rural catchments, transformations have been brought about; schools buzz with community and sporting activities, pupils are reluctant to go home as evening falls, achievements of both boys and girls rise year on year, expectations *are* transformed *and* delivered. It is appropriate, perhaps, to leave the last word to a Year 11 boy from North-East England: A good mentor

> gives you advice and support, and strategies to help you learn, but gives *you* responsibility because although they tell you what to do, you have to go and do it, to take responsibility yourself for your time-management, and your own revision.

Note

1 YELLIS (Year 11 Information System) is a value-added monitoring system developed by the Curriculum Evaluation and Management Centre at the University of Durham. The YELLIS system provides a wide range of performance indicators for students aged 14–16, and makes possible comparisons of students against other students participating nationally in the project, by subject, student and school.

8 Organizational Contexts
Equal opportunities in the single-sex classroom

Single-sex classes in mixed comprehensive schools: the issues

The comprehensive re-organization of state schooling in most areas of England in the 1960s and 1970s was based upon the assumption that comprehensive schools would be co-educational (Deem 1984; Shaw 1984). Despite the strong claims made for girls-only schools, the number of single-sex schools in the state sector fell dramatically (Robinson and Smithers 1999). Even though the debate resurfaced in the early 1980s, as evidence emerged that comprehensive schools were failing to provide equality of opportunity for girls (Arnot *et al.* 1999; Myers 2000), there was little political or educational impetus to pursue the case for single-sex comprehensive schools, or indeed for single-sex classes within co-educational comprehensive schools. Despite some advocates (Burgess 1990; Stables 1990; Faulkner 1991; Halstead 1991; Lee and Marks 1992; Fisher 1994; Leonard 1996; Ball and Gewirtz 1997; Watson 1997), there were few co-educational comprehensives which adopted single-sex classes, and the rising achievement profile of girls in the late 1980s and early 1990s appeared to have silenced the discussions.

It has been richly ironic, therefore, and a salutary indication of the extent to which the dominant discourse associated with male under-achievement has gained currency during the past decade (Gipps 1996; Weiner *et al.* 1997; Epstein *et al.* 1998; Kenway *et al.* 1998), that the resurgence of interest in single-sex teaching in co-educational schools has been almost entirely related to boys (Yates 1997). Single-sex classes are advocated, in the minds of those who support a recuperative masculinity approach, as a response to the claim that boys' performances have been limited by feminized school environments and girl-friendly teaching styles. Single-sex classes are perceived as offering a context where boys can be more open and responsive in class, able to concentrate and participate more, less distracted by girls (Swan 1998), and consequently are better able to achieve.

Other commentators are less sanguine about the benefits for girls and boys of teaching in single-sex contexts. They maintain that single-sex classes reinforce sex-role stereotypes and exacerbate rather than help eradicate sexism, and suggest that some male teachers and some boys welcome single-sex classes because they enjoy the 'boys-own' atmosphere of the classes and the opportunity for male bravado and bonding in such classes (Jackson 1999). Kenway *et al.* (1998) argue convincingly that teachers often normalize and accept sex-based harassment by boys, because – it is maintained – boys are more aggressive, their sexuality is awakening, and boys are slow developers, lacking in maturity and confidence. Equally, some commentators have suggested that schools seem to be unaware of any social, emotional or affective consequences of teaching boys and girls separately in mixed schools (Elwood and Gipps 1999), and others suggest that there are still moral and ethical issues to be resolved if single-sex teaching in mixed schools is to be successful (Parker and Rennie 1997).

Contrasting evidence from English secondary schools

The resurgence of the debate, and the subsequent introduction of single-sex classes in some co-educational schools in England, have occurred despite the lack of any clear agreement about the impact of such classes on boys' and girls' learning. Even where claims are made for its effectiveness, 'researchers question whether these positive effects are attributable to the actual programme or to other factors such as teacher and context specific effects' (Martino and Meyenn 2002: 306). There is a lack of detailed and specific data through time, which restricts informed debate (Elwood and Gipps 1999), and few sustained longitudinal studies with a particular focus on outcomes and on the longer-term effects of such initiatives (Arnot *et al.* 1998).

Work carried out by Sukhnandan *et al.* (2000) and our own in-depth case study (Warrington and Younger 2001; Younger and Warrington 2002) were attempts to evaluate such initiatives. Sukhnandan *et al.* reported that teachers perceived single-sex classes as offering a number of advantages for the teaching of boys: the opportunity to use a variety of teaching strategies which were targeted to boys' needs and interests; a context in which they could challenge boys' stereotypes more effectively; an all-male environment which was more conducive to learning, with fewer distractions and less embarrassment. At the same time, they reported an unease that any adaptations to teaching strategies and curriculum materials 'tended to be in relation to the all-boy classes rather than the all-girl classes' (Sukhnandan *et al.* 2000: 25), with little or no consideration of girls' learning needs.

Our own in-depth study was unusual both because of its longitudinal nature and because it was an intensive study of a school where single-sex teaching had been long standing, since the school's establishment as a co-educational comprehensive in the early 1970s. As such, single-sex teaching was part of the central ethos of the school, across all subjects in Years 7–9, and for core subjects in Years 10–11. We concluded that single-sex teaching was one factor which appeared to contribute to the high achievement levels of *both* girls and boys through time, without apparent accompanying social disadvantages. Both boys and girls construed single-sex classes as safe and secure places for learning, and there was little evidence, from classroom observations or interviews with students, to support the notion of sexist behaviour and of male bonding between boys and male teachers. Girls spoke of a 'hassle-free' environment which was clearly more conducive to learning (Kenway *et al.* 1998; Swan 1998), of being enabled to be themselves, to explore the private and the personal, to develop self-esteem (Smith 1984), within the context of 'normal' heterosexual development (Griffin 1985). It is worth emphasizing that many girls felt *extremely* comfortable within the school environment, and displayed high levels of confidence and maturity (Younger and Warrington 2002). Overall, there were encouraging signs from this in-depth case study to suggest that single-sex teaching, where embedded in the whole school culture, had the potential to contribute both to the raising of academic standards and to the social development of more confident, assured young people, with high levels of self-esteem. In this context, single-sex teaching did not replicate the characteristics identified within a male recuperative discourse, but was more properly related within gender-relational terms, supporting the learning and maturity of both girls and boys, without disadvantage to the other.

Subsequently, we conducted a review of single-sex teaching in 31 comprehensive schools in England (Warrington and Younger 2003). This revealed an ambivalent state of affairs, much more tuned to the male recuperative agenda. It was clear that often schools implemented single-sex classes in an *ad hoc* way, for short time periods, frequently with little preparation and without consideration of the advantages which the distinctiveness of context might bring. Some schools believed it had raised achievement levels, while others did not; some had seen behaviour improve, while in others it had worsened; in some schools, girls were blossoming away from the distractions and the implicit need to help sustain boys' learning; in others, girls and boys resented the single-sex context. In some schools, furthermore, single-sex teaching was abandoned as abruptly as it was introduced, before a sustained time period had elapsed, and without careful evaluation of its benefits or disadvantages. In such contexts, it is not surprising that it was difficult to come to any clear conclusions about the effects on examination and test results, not least because of the diversity of subjects, year groups, sets and length of time the strategy was used.

This review exacerbated our unease about the extent to which single-sex classes might more often contribute to discourses related to male 'disadvantage and repair' than to gender-relational debates. We were disturbed that, in some schools at least, such a strategy focused almost entirely on boys, assumed that girls would learn regardless of context or teacher (Jackson 1999), and sometimes targeted more experienced ('better') teachers to all-boys' classes (Barton 2000; Younger and Warrington 2002). There was emerging evidence, too, of overtly 'boy-orientated' curriculum materials and exemplification through sport which – although developed with enthusiasm and commitment by teachers understandably striving to increase access and interests amongst disengaged boys – assumed that all boys conformed to norms of hegemonic masculinity. Indeed, such an approach often identified some boys as 'surrogate' girls, with the attendant risks of such boys experiencing greater levels of bullying (Askew and Ross 1988; Matthews 1998).

Case study from the Raising Boys' Achievement Project

The Raising Boys' Achievement Project gave us the opportunity to explore these issues in more detail, to try to identify the essence of single-sex teaching in a particularly successful co-educational comprehensive school in southern England, and to attempt to transfer and develop this approach to two schools serving similar socio-economic contexts in Eastern England. Specifically, we were concerned to explore the extent to which *both* boys and girls could benefit from the development of single-sex teaching, and whether such a mode of organization could contribute to the construction of gender-relational approaches to schooling and to students' achievement of academic and social goals.

In the Originator School, single-sex teaching was one of a number of organizational strategies, which aimed to improve the achievement levels of boys and girls within the context of establishing an achievement culture within the school, with high aspirations and expectations of all students. Initially tightly targeted at boys and girls who were perceived as being under-achieving in English at GCSE, single-sex teaching was subsequently expanded to middle ability sets in Mathematics, Science and Modern Languages. Both partner schools had some prior experience of involvement with single-sex teaching in Key Stage 4, but the philosophy underpinning single-sex teaching, and the associated teaching strategies, were less developed than in the Originator School. The rationale underlying the introduction of single-sex teaching also differed: in school B, it focused on improving the achievement of boys in English whereas in school C, the strategy was linked to the perceived under-achievement of girls in Mathematics.

Impact upon achievement

In achievement terms, it is difficult to isolate the impact of single-sex teaching from other variables within any school (Martino and Meyenn 2002), the more so in this triad because single-sex teaching was only one of a whole series of strategies implemented to maximize students' achievements. In the words of one headteacher, 'they all contribute to the whole culture of achievement within the school, of truly believing that it *is* possible'.

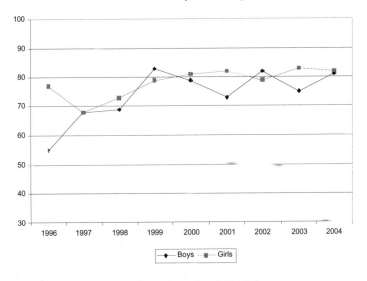

Figure 8.1 Students achieving five(+) A*–C grades, GCSE (%)

In the Originator School, however, single-sex teaching was one of the factors that helped to transform achievement. The scale of this transformation is evident in Figure 8.1, with the performance levels of both girls and boys generally following an upward trajectory, so that by 2004, 82 per cent of girls and 81 per cent of boys had achieved five(+) A*–C grades at GCSE. This is a remarkable transformation, within the context of a stable catchment, an unchanged curriculum and an LEA benchmarking framework which suggested that between 40 per cent and 60 per cent of students should achieve five A*–C grades at GCSE. Furthermore, in particular years, boys had 'out-performed' girls (Figure 8.2).

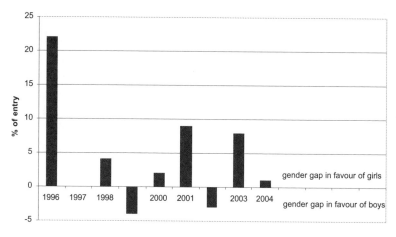

Figure 8.2 Gender gap at GCSE: 1996–2004 Originator School

In more specific terms, both boys and girls in single-sex classes for English in 2001–3 recorded a higher points score in the subject than they obtained overall, although this pattern was not replicated in Maths (Table 8.1); equally, boys' achievements in French were sustained at a level comparable to their performances in other subjects, and did not follow the 'usual' under-performing boys' pattern in modern languages.

Table 8.1: Boys and girls in single-sex classes

	% gaining C(+) in subject	*% gaining 5(+) A*–C grades overall*	*Average points score overall subjects*	*Points score in subject*	*% gaining higher score in subject than their overall average*
Boys in English language	77			5.4	67.7
Boys in English literature	87	81	4.8	5.8	90.3
Girls in English language	80			5.2	63.3
Girls in English literature	97	83	4.8	5.5	80.0
Boys in Maths	59	83	5.0	4.8	27.6
Girls in Maths	48	90	4.8	4.4	22.6
Boys in French	81	88	5.4	5.3	44.0
Girls in French	78	89	4.7	4.7	33.3

Analysis of performance data through time in the partner schools tends to more equivocal conclusions. In both schools, students in single-sex classes for English or Maths were predicted to be on the C/D GCSE borderline, and their interviews with us during their GCSE course suggested they were making uneven and inconsistent progress. Nonetheless, in school B, of the students taught in single-sex classes, all girls passed both English Language and English Literature, compared with 81 per cent of boys for English Language and 56 per cent in English Literature. Equally, when the performance of these boys was analysed, their average points score for English (4.9) was higher than that for other subjects (4.5). In school C, although both boys and girls in single-sex classes performed better in Mathematics than might have been predicted from an analysis of their cognitive ability scores, with typically over 50 per cent of both boys and girls exceeding predictions in any year, this pattern was also apparent from the results of boys and girls, drawn from a similar population in the other half of the year group, and taught in *mixed* classes for mathematics. Definitive claims for the advantages of single-sex teaching on the basis of achievement data are difficult to sustain with any confidence, therefore, although there is clear evidence from the Originator School, and some evidence from one of the Partner schools, of positive impacts.

Learning in single-sex classes: the students' perspective

Previous studies have suggested that students are generally supportive of single-sex teaching, and feel that it has a positive impact on their learning and motivation (Barton 2000; Jackson and Smith 2000; Younger and Warrington 2002). This is particularly so with girls, although boys (initially more ambivalent) generally become more positive once they feel they are achieving at a higher standard. In some contexts, however, studies have shown that boys in particular can feel hostile and resentful of single-sex classes (Kenway *et al.* 1998; Jackson 2002; Warrington and Younger 2003) and feel that the disadvantages outweigh any advantages.

While there was some equivocation and ambivalence in students' responses in this case study, there was more consensus than disagreement across the three schools. Questionnaire returns and interviews suggested that most students agreed that single-sex classes aided their concentration and helped them to feel more confident about their work. They felt they were better behaved in class, and were able to participate more, particularly in terms of being able to ask questions to clarify understanding. Girls and boys felt that the quality of their work was better, and that it was easier to accept praise from teachers. This increased participation by students in lessons and their development of greater levels of confidence confirm observations by Rowe (1998) and by Kenway *et al.* (1998) in their research in Australian schools, by Gillibrand *et al.* (1999) in their study of girls in single-sex Physics classes, and is noted as a significant feature in our own in-depth study of one school (Younger and Warrington 2002).

When asked to identify the two best things about being taught in single-sex classes, girls and boys both stated that it was easier to concentrate because there were fewer distractions from the opposite sex. To girls, these distractions might range from 'the noise generated by immature boys' to the fact that we 'don't have to worry about what we look like if boys are not there'. To boys, it was easier to concentrate when there were no temptations to look at or talk with girls, since in the memorable words of one boy, 'my hormones are not dancing to the beat of the night!' Both girls and boys welcomed the removal of social pressures to perform to an image to sustain femininity or laddishness: 'you don't need to act as though you're really cool, especially when you're not feeling as though you are!' Students felt able to participate more readily, to offer answers and ask questions, to offer opinions because they felt less intimidated:

> You feel braver and less embarrassed in offering answers, because there are no boys to make fun of you when you are wrong

> It gives you a lot more confidence to answer questions in class because there is not so much pressure and embarrassment if you are wrong as there would be with girls about.

Girls and boys wrote of more informal relationships in single-sex classrooms, with teachers tolerating a more relaxed and friendly attitude and being less stressed because there was less off-task behaviour. Girls felt that they learned better because the teachers could *teach* more, with less need to be continually disciplining disruptive boys. Boys felt that they received more teaching and more attention from their teachers because girls were not there to dominate the questioning.

While single-sex classes were seen as having disadvantages, particularly in terms of the possible creation of 'bitchiness and girls' aggressive attitudes to each other when they are taught alone' and because 'in boys' only classes it's sometimes very noisy and a bit too macho, like a pack of wolves searching for a king to rule the pride!', overall there was widespread agreement among both girls and boys that the atmosphere was different and more conducive for learning in single-sex classes. Most of these responses seemed to emphasize the advantages to be gained simply because the class was single-sex. Nonetheless, a significant minority of students did suggest that teachers taught differently when interacting with a single-sex class, and planned a different sequence of activities, taking into account the characteristics of the class:

Teachers are able to adjust their teaching style to suit the sex they are teaching. (girl)

(g)

Half-time in a lesson is a good idea ... the lesson is quicker somehow, you know what you've got to learn, it's all broken down and fast, so a breather halfway through helps you concentrate and keep focused. (boy)

(b)

Boys, in particular, claimed that single-sex classes in English allowed them more freedom to work harder without worrying about stereotypical expectations and their own image, particularly that they were not supposed to enjoy English. They spoke of being able to talk about feelings and express opinions about books and poetry, to target coursework without feeling intimidated by girls, and to study and enjoy the romantic texts:

We don't just do war poems and *Macbeth*, we do Wordsworth too ... it's a challenge, in a way, which Mr J sets us ... to show the girls we're capable of doing it ... but I couldn't talk about these things if there were girls there!

There's more participation in the lesson because he involves all of us, and no one is shy or afraid to express an opinion ... you know other boys won't laugh at you and you don't lose face.

Equally, girls spoke of it being 'far less embarrassing when doing talks if the blokes aren't there to rubbish you', of 'being able to say what you really feel about plays and emotional stuff and things like that' and of there being 'no pressure to be loud and funny in front of the guys!'. Boys, too, acknowledged 'feeling more confident, especially when giving presentations and asking questions', of 'not being nervous and messing up so much when talking about the work' and of being 'not afraid to talk about feelings in poetry and plays'.

Girls' responses were equally positive in the context of Mathematics; they wrote of being 'able to have more confidence in myself, knowing that I can do things and answer questions without boys ridiculing me', of there being 'fewer distractions in the class so the teacher can spend more time teaching' and 'because it separates the badly behaved boys from the well-behaved girls'. In school C, however, boys' reactions to the introduction of single-sex classes in Mathematics were very different to those of the girls, and much more polarized than those of boys in either of the other schools. There was strong antipathy evident in the boys' responses, linked to their apparent belief that they could and would succeed in Mathematics anyway, without any special arrangements:

> We don't need this because we can do it anyway, and in these classes there is too much pressure now to compete against all-girls' groups, and when I want to work, there's too much aggression from my friends.

> This is only to help the girls get a C in Maths, and it's boring without girls in lessons.

Significantly, when asked whether single-sex classes benefited one sex or the other, or both equally, both boys and girls in school C felt that single-sex classes benefited girls more than boys. This mix of emotions – a sense of simmering resentment from some boys, immature hostility from others, arrogance even from others, existed in a context where single-sex classes were originally introduced to support girls', rather than boys' learning.

The perspectives of students in at least two of these schools, and of girls in all three schools, suggest therefore, that single-sex classes can be developed to support the learning of girls as well as boys, rather than discriminating against or undermining girls' achievements. Some questions remain, however. Boys' reactions in both partner schools highlight a common concern about issues of classroom management in single-sex classes. In school C, in particular, boys were explicit about the extent to which all-boys' classes were more challenging for teachers. In some instances, this was because 'there are no girls present, so boys don't worry how they act and behave' or because 'everyone is trying to outshine each other all the time with jokes and distractions'. In this school, boys generally were not attracted to the idea of single-sex teaching because 'when you're with all your mates, then the lesson isn't a lesson at all ... you just talk and mess around ... it gets more rowdy', and 'there are more of us in this group who mess around, so we get into more trouble'. Equally, however, there was a feeling that girls exerted a positive influence in classes, 'you'd miss the girls, because they calm you down, and they help you with the work, too'.

We challenge the notion that girls should be seen as having a supporting and servicing role for boys' learning (Kenway *et al.* 1998; Arnot *et al.* 1999), but macho behaviour can be exacerbated simply through a concentration of numbers, and in some schools, a worsening of boys' behaviour has led to single-sex teaching being abandoned. In such situations, where schools failing to control boys in single-sex classes revert to mixed classes, girls are made to bear the brunt of the failure of the school to develop an effective approach to classroom management and communication. This underlines the inappropriateness of relying on an organizational strategy to address a behavioural problem, without confronting the underlying reasons for that poor behaviour.

What, though, about the position of non-macho boys in this discussion? What about the view that single-sex classes encourage male bonding between male teachers and boys, and reinforce laddishness and hegemonic forms of masculinity (Arnot 1984; Solomon and Harrison 1991; Collins *et al.* 2000; Roulsten and Mills 2000; Martino and Meyenn 2002)? We recognize that this is a difficult issue to explore with boys who feel less identity with other boys. Our interviews with 'non-macho' boys suggest, however, that these boys did not feel exposed in single-sex classes. While, at one level, there *were* hints of more banter and occasional rowdiness in all-boys' lessons, the occasional sexist comment at girls' expense, and discussion about football, such boys told us – without exception – that they felt at ease and comfortable, that they did not experience bullying or aggressive behaviour from other boys, that they were not intimidated by the atmosphere in all-boys' classes:

> My mates and I ... we feel included and at ease, and we all play a part in class.

> The teacher is a man's man, I suppose, he talks about football to some of the boys. I'm not into football, but it's OK ... It's just how it is, because it's only a starter like, for a few minutes ... the atmosphere is so much more relaxed and joyful without girls ... it's great being in the lesson!

It would be nonsense to ignore the reality that homophobia is usually perpetuated by boys against other boys, and that certain boys become more easily targeted and bullied than others (Collins *et al.* 2000; Martino and Meyenn 2001; Martino and Pallotta-Chiarolli 2003). Equally, we recognize the difficulty of probing this issue and getting to the heart of the matter, particularly when we have met individual boys only on a limited number of occasions over a two-year time span. In our ongoing interviews with non-stereotypical boys, however, and in our classroom observations, we encountered no evidence that supported the view that boys-only classes were sites of exclusion and antagonism against such boys. On the contrary, our evidence suggested that such boys felt a greater sense of inclusion and less vulnerability than in some other mixed sex classes.

Teaching in boys-only classes: gender-specific pedagogies?

In earlier studies of single-sex teaching, there is little evidence that teachers explicitly modify their teaching style and strategies to meet any perceived differing needs of boys and girls (Sukhnandan *et al.* 2000; Younger and Warrington 2002). In most schools, there appear to be few pedagogic differences between single-sex and mixed classes. It might be argued that this is a missed opportunity, and that teaching and learning within a single-sex context will only be most effective when they impinge explicitly on teachers' planning, teaching and assessment (Elwood and Gipps 1999; Warrington and Younger 2001).

Within this triad of schools, then, the initial approach was to develop pedagogy for boys-only classes. Clear advice was offered on timing, on pace and variety, on the need for tight parameters but within a context almost of persuasion and identification with the boys, rather than confrontation, on having high expectations. In the words of a female Modern Languages teacher:

> There needs to be a sustained pace, a sense of achievement and plenty of merited praise, tight management techniques which preserve the work ethic and establishes a good listening ethos, an acknowledgement that I won't take nonsense!

A similar approach was evident in English lessons, articulated by the head of department in terms of momentum, short tight activities, and diversity:

> I say to my Year 11 boys : 'We can *still* do one more thing today ... you've got *three* minutes to work this out in pairs, we're going to do five different things in this hour ... aren't you lucky!' They pretend to hate me, but they really like the structure, the security, the expectation, and the praise when they achieve, and they *do* achieve.

Successful teaching and learning in single-sex contexts demanded not only such pedagogic practices in the classroom, however, but these teaching strategies needed to be located within a set of beliefs, attitudes and expectations held by teachers, and be strongly supported by senior managers within each school. Classroom observations tended to confirm that the most successful teachers were those who generated a sense of belief and mutual respect among the students and who offered positive and immediate feedback. Such teachers were prepared to engage with the class, accepting irony and humour and acknowledging where the students were coming from, but establishing a context of clear expectations which were understood by all.

This is delicate because there are dangers that this approach *can* at times disintegrate into a situation where teachers encourage laddishness, where stereotypes *are* reinforced, where female teachers are frivolous with boys. This need not be the case, however, for in other contexts, this approach can establish remarkably successful contexts for learning, regardless of the gender or age of the teacher:

> You need to be able to relate well to challenging boys ... to have high expectations of them, in terms of behaviour, work, their relationship with each other ... to be very, very positive with them, to be upbeat ... I let them know I believe in them ... that I'm committed to them and to their learning ... once I've got that relationship in place, you don't have this roller-coaster of negativity, of disgruntlement.
>
> (female English teacher, school B)

In similar vein, another teacher spoke of the need to establish a formal regime, with very clear and firmly defined classroom parameters, because 'there were some very strong lads in the group, who were quite streetwise and could quite easily have overwhelmed me and group'. But once this had been established,

> then I started to let go, to encourage language conversations, to take more controlled risks ... through tightly focused activities, using humour to challenge and activate them ... with tasks which have a step-by-step progression, which are clear and short term. I find that the whole business of teaching French to boys like this is fascinating ... I love it, I *really* do; I work on making them feel valued.

Faced with assertive behaviour from boys within their classes, the teachers showed they were accessible to the boys, supportive and positively engaged with their learning, encouraging group work and work-related exploratory talk. They used a variety of techniques – occasional humour, an informality of approach, praise and charm – to ensure that learning took place. The essential tone of these classrooms was mutual respect, a shared understanding that learning could at times be sustained within an informal, relaxed context, but equally there was an understanding held by the boys that the teachers were setting the tone and maintaining the ethos of the lessons. Such classes could and were brought sharply to order when it was necessary, by teachers who were aware that it was their responsibility not to cede power or authority to the boys within their classes.

The borderline with an over-aggressive reaction is a narrow one here, of course, just as is the borderline between establishing rapport to support learning and going along with a laddishness that encourages unacceptable stereotypes. But in a succession of lessons in these schools, teachers were creating a collaborative, lively atmosphere for learning, using praise extensively, and offering energetic and directly instructional teaching. Boys who had been disruptive were re-integrated into lessons without further comment, with the acknowledgement that punishment had been issued and taken, and that no 'cult status' or 'sense of difference' would be accorded to the boys by other boys or by the teacher. To the boys, these teachers were outstanding in their ability to create acceptable contexts for their learning:

> Mr J is a bloke who really works for you, remembers what you're going through as boys, who tries to do his best for you, gives you new opportunities, and tries to keep us out of trouble.

> Ms C is a woman who really gets you involved in the text and what you should be learning, who's a nice mix of charm and determination, so you know you can't mess!

With some teachers, too, there was a recognition that students' attention may wander and flag, and that a short natural break in the lesson was useful to aid concentration and consolidate teacher–pupil rapport.

Such teachers were successful in these boys-only classes because they had openly acknowledged the dangers of such a context. There was an acceptance by teachers and boys of the need to accept the individuality of boys, of the dangers of the intimidation of 'non-macho' boys, and a recognition that laddishness in such classes needed to be kept in check rather than encouraged. Teachers gave these boys space to work as individuals, allowed them to express themselves differently, and worked to create a rapport and an ethos which challenged rather than reinforced stereotyping and sexism.

Teaching in girls-only classes: gender-specific pedagogies?

One of the perceived advantages of single-sex classes is the calmer space they provide in which girls can learn without the disruptive influence of boys (Ball and Gewirtz 1997), a space where girls are safer from ridicule, harassment and violence (Kruse 1996) and away from the peacock-like behaviour of some boys (Slater 1996). Nonetheless, such classes can be challenging for teachers, as some girls and their teachers forcefully told us. In the words of one female Science teacher:

> It's high energy teaching when it's all girls together, with different issues to a mixed class ... they can be so bitchy towards each other ... they need calming down at times, getting rid of any arguments they've had, because they don't forget or let go as easily as boys ... one or two girls will usurp the male role, to behave as surrogate boys ... and when you discipline a girl, they retain a grudge for longer than a boy.

Nonetheless, it was true that girls' lessons observed in each school were characterized by a different approach and teaching style, with less explicit challenge to the teacher. Typically, lessons were more self-sustained by the girls themselves, in terms of work effort, motivation, involvement in on-task activities. It was possible for the teacher to adopt a more relaxed style, to be more concerned with individuals and groups, to be less high profile and proactive. Girls offered each other genuine praise and encouragement, supporting each other in learning.

Teachers in each school said that single-sex classes offered clear opportunities and advantages for girls in their learning. In English, for example,

> I've had quite challenging, difficult girls producing extremely high quality work ... work which is coherent, lengthy, well illustrated ... they show they can write in the style of the play, and have really embraced the task and produced outstanding work. It gives them opportunities to gain confidence to ask questions, they get more involved and really talk about the text.

The introduction of single-sex Maths classes in school C had promoted the girls' confidence levels, stimulated dialogue between the girls about Maths, and led to more collaboration in learning. In the words of a female Maths teacher:

> In a girls-only class, there is less intimidation, it's easier to establish a 'can do' culture, you can get real thought, discussion and effort, they're more willing to acknowledge that they don't understand and really pleased when they achieve ... it has allowed their potential to come through.

It is crucial, though, that girls-only classes are constructed as conducive *and* demanding contexts for learning, so that girls are explicitly challenged to achieve more (Sukhnandam *et al.* 2000; Warrington and Younger 2003), otherwise their surface calmness and order can be deceptive, hiding under-achievement and concealing subtly unobtrusive off-task behaviour.

This brings us to the heart of the issue in our discussion of gender-specific pedagogies. The more we have explored this issue of different teaching and learning styles, and the nature of 'boy-friendly' and 'girl-friendly' pedagogies, the more complex the issue has become to us. As will be clear from Chapter 6, we are not convinced that such a sharp and explicit distinction can be made. We have reservations because of our reluctance to generalize about 'boys' and 'girls', and because of our deep unease with the notion that *any* strategy put in place will support the learning of girls *whatever* because they are more acquiescent learners in a school context. Essentially, though, we have reservations because the evidence emerging from this triad and from other case studies within the RBA project suggests that discussion of so-called 'gender-specific' and 'boy-friendly' pedagogies is, in fact, simply discussion about the essence of high quality teaching. We have not seen evidence, despite extensive classroom observations and numerous individual and focus group interviews with boys and girls, that such strategies support the learning of boys more than girls, or are unsuited to girls' learning. As a consequence, we strongly challenge the notion that girls' classes require a less active, less structured, less interactive, less varied pedagogy than boys' classes. In our view, to adopt a more passive, *laissez-faire* pedagogy runs the serious danger of failing to motivate, challenge and engage girls, and to accept lower levels of potential and under-achievement of girls.

Indeed, if single-sex classes are to be perceived within gender-relational contexts, then it is essential that such strategies are put in place for girls-only classes as well as for boys-only classes, to pose appropriate challenges and to combat the danger of making too few demands of girls. Otherwise single-sex classes for girls may unwittingly reinscribe female helplessness, and place more emphasis on 'a nurturing and emotional refuge within which less is expected and from which they are not prepared or required to venture' (Kenway *et al.* 1998: 150).

If single-sex classes, preconditions for implementation?

In some schools there is an ideological opposition to single-sex classes, consistent with the notion that all comprehensive schools must be co-educational in all respects. Our research in these triad schools confirms, however, that

- many boys and girls feel more comfortable in single-sex classes because of the lack of distraction of the other sex;

- many boys and girls feel more able to question, explore issues related to learning, take part in discussion without fear of ridicule or embarrassment;
- many boys and girls feel less pressurized to perform, to 'showboat', once the other gender are not present;
- many boys and girls feel that they produce better quality work.

Equally, it has become clear that single-sex classes are not a universal panacea. Teaching boys and girls in such contexts can be challenging, sometimes demoralizing, and negativity of behaviour can become the norm; in such contexts, the morale of teachers and the learning of pupils can deteriorate rapidly. What, then, are the pre-conditions which must be established and fulfilled if single-sex teaching is to be effective in enabling boys and girls to learn more effectively?

Crucially, there is the need to articulate a coherent and vibrant pedagogy to support such classes. We do not subscribe to the view that there is a boy-specific pedagogy which is different from a girl-friendly pedagogy, but we do acknowledge that single-sex classes, while offering opportunities to generate distinctive classroom contexts in which girls and boys can learn more effectively, can present more pedagogic and management challenges, particularly with some all-boys classes. It is essential to identify appropriate teaching strategies which engage and motivate these students, to ensure that the pedagogy employed makes it worthwhile and valuable for students to turn up for lessons.

Successful implementation of single-sex teaching needs staff to feel involved and supported, to have access to strategies which have proved effective in other contexts, and to have a means whereby they can exchange experiences without feeling threatened or undermined. It is crucial that senior management within the school is actively on board, taking a proactive and high profile role, willing to give clear and unequivocal support. In our experience with the RBA Project, it is not enough for senior managers to adopt a permissive role, facilitating and subsequently monitoring developments. Successful implementation of single-sex teaching needs more active involvement and identification from senior managers, rationalizing the initiative to parents, carers and students, and keeping the issue a high profile one within the school community.

There is a further factor, however, which must be discussed which relates to the wider issue of boys' and girls' achievement at school. In all three schools, the most effective teachers went beyond 'good practice' pedagogic strategies, to establish a sense of togetherness and of common purpose, with informal references – often, but not always, linked to sport, popular culture or to fashion – which helped to sustain the credibility of teacher and to sustain the collaborative sense of working. Humour and informality were used to motivate and engage students in learning, to generate collaboration and a sense of team spirit, and to consolidate a relationship of shared respect and commitment. Yet there was a further aspect of this mutuality of understanding, associated with definition of context. The most effective teaching in single-sex classes took place when common expectations had been clearly established and were accepted by all, when it was understood that learning required high standards of behaviour, work and commitment, and that disruptive behaviour or failure to complete work, especially homework and coursework, would not be tolerated. This mutuality of understanding created a context of high expectation, and particularly a climate in which boys particularly could perform without fear of undermining their own image or losing face with their friends of either sex. The mix of collaboration and engagement with persuasion and requirement enabled them to associate with and publicly acknowledge the aspirations of the school.

Conclusion: cautionary words

Our work on single-sex classes has been a journey of discovery and enlightenment, for us at least! Starting from a sceptical position, sharing the view that comprehensive schools ought by their very title to be inclusive and undifferentiated, we have moved to a position which acknowledges that both girls and boys can gain from single-sex classes. We are clear that such classes on their own are not a panacea for the problems of poor behaviour, disaffection and lack of achievement, but equally we are clear that they *can* provide a positive and successful experience for girls and boys. Central to this, though, is the willingness to sustain, monitor and evaluate single sex as a mode of organization through time, and to develop a classroom pedagogy which is accessible and opens up learning for all students, regardless of gender. While we accept Martino and Meyenn's contention that 'productive pedagogy ... is not so much attributable to the single sex strategy per se, but to the complex dimensions of ... teachers' pedagogical approaches' (2002: 321), we do conclude that single-sex classrooms can offer opportunities to develop a more conducive classroom atmosphere for learning, in which productive pedagogies may be the more better developed. In recognizing this, however, we set our face firmly against a specifically 'boy-friendly' pedagogy, convinced that such an approach has been sustained neither by research nor by classroom experience, and demeans the worth of girls.

As Kruse (1996) points out, 'sex segregated education can be used for emancipation or oppression' and therefore, most importantly, there must also be a willingness, as Kenway *et al.* (1998) and Jackson (2002) argue, to implement gender-reform strategies, to resist strongly any stereotyping of girls and boys in relation to gender, and to challenge any practices and behaviours which reinforce stereotypical gendered roles. Carefully implemented, with the support of teachers at all levels within a school, and within a positive context which has been rationalized clearly through the school community, single-sex classes have the ability to contribute to raising achievement levels in schools, to enhancing the self-esteem and social attributes of girls and boys, to establishing a sociable and enjoyable environment for learning. Carelessly implemented, as an *ad hoc*, almost spontaneous response to issues of male disenchantment and poor achievement, within a recuperative masculinity context, single-sex classes can be a recipe for disaster. At the extreme within such contexts, stereotypes can be exacerbated, gentle boys exposed, and many girls under-valued. Such are the opportunities and the dangers!

9 The Socio-Cultural Key

*A cool person has to have all the right fashion, has to have the
latest clothes, has to, like, set the trend and has to be basically
ahead of everybody else and hang around with other cool people.
Confident.*

(Matt, Year 10)

*It's not good to be a loner; you could become a loser for the
rest of your life. We do fun things, you know with sport, some
productions sometimes, the school's good at encouraging that,
but not with the druggies and people that smoke and stuff ...
at 15, that's so sad!*

(Paul, Year 10)

*Of course you need to be with your mates ... for protection, like
... and when you're interested in summat, and want to work, you
can work together, and tell em to get lost if they start to have a go
at you.*

(Aaron, Year 10)

Our discussion of the factors affecting boys' academic performances at
school (Chapter 2) places considerable emphasis on the impact of laddishness and dominant versions of masculinity, as boys seek to 'learn' masculinity and to become 'real men' within the context of local community norms.
We argue that boys learn to assume roles, to seek acceptable identities
through exploration and negotiation, and to incorporate into their persona
aspects of behaviour, dress, competitiveness and risk-taking that are associated with a laddish culture (Francis 2000a, b; Skelton 2001; Martino and
Pallotta-Chiarolli 2003). Following Jackson (2002), we suggest that implicit
within this culture is the adoption by lads of specific strategies which reduce
the chances of failure and the associated loss of status and esteem within the
group, and the need to assume behaviours and attitudes which avoid the risk
of being labelled as feminine and possibly homosexual.

Versions of masculinity

We acknowledged in Chapter 2 that these notions of masculinity vary in their detail through time and space, and have fluidity and flexibility, so that there is no one version of masculinity. Indeed, different forms of masculinity have been evident in the literature since Willis' (1977) seminal work described the 'lads' and the 'ear'oles'. Similarly, Connell (1989) proposed a threefold typology, of Cool Guys, Swots and Wimps, based on interviews with young working-class men who had recently left school, and Mac an Ghaill (1994) identified different groups of working-class heterosexual males: the Macho Lads, the Academic Achievers and the New Enterprisers, as well as a middle-class group of Real Englishmen, which he encountered in one predominantly working-class school. To Mac an Ghaill, Macho Lads were those who viewed school as a system of hostile authority and meaningless work demands, primarily concerned to 'look after your mates', 'act tough', 'have a laugh', 'look smart' (in a streetwise sense) and 'have a good time' They rejected the official three Rs of reading, writing and arithmetic, and the unofficial three Rs of rules, routines and regulations, and instead got status from the three Fs – fighting, fucking and football. Academic Achievers, described as reminiscent of grammar school scholarship boys, saw academic qualifications as their ticket out of the working classes and envisaged a professional career. To achieve this they adopted a strong work ethic; although positive towards the academic curriculum, they were not entirely pro-school and were critical of some teacher practices. Other teachers and students often positioned Academic Achievers as effeminate and they were ridiculed for their work ethic, hence they did not feel comfortable with middle-class students or some other working-class boys such as the Macho Lads. New Enterprisers formed Mac an Ghaill's third group of boys, who saw and utilized the new vocational routes opening up in school. These students valued rationality, instrumentalism, forward planning and careerism.

It is clear that categories of masculinity differ with social class (Arnot *et al.* 1999) and ethnicity (Sewell 1998) because masculinities are constructed in a given context in relation to general social, cultural and institutional patterns of power (Skelton 2001). The concern of both Connell and Mac an Ghaill with working-class communities is particularly salient, of course, because at least some versions of the 'male under-achievement' debate rest on the (not uncontested) notion that it is among working-class boys (and girls) where the 'under-achievement' is greatest and the issue most polarized. In some parts of England, such communities are those most affected by the collapse of the traditional local manufacturing industry base and deindustrialization in the 1980s and 1990s. These working-class boys can no longer rely on work for their traditional status and power, and see little point in striving for qualifications. To Connell (1989), therefore, 'the authority structure of the school becomes the antagonist against which one's masculinity is cut'. Hence these boys are more likely to reject values that are conducive to academic success such as conformity, work ethic and punctuality, and to devalue academic success, deriving status instead from the admiration of peers when they challenge the school's authority. The historical dimension is important within this context, too; some schools serving working-class catchments have had very frustrating experiences trying to work with and alongside the local community, with working-class people who may feel injured, insulted and disempowered by their own experiences of school (Connell *et al.* 1982), unwilling or unable to enter the school to support their children's own education. Indeed, in some contexts, the hostility of some family members, usually fathers, has encouraged the construction of a confrontational, anti-school laddishness and ladettish-ness among their sons and daughters. As Skelton (2001) points out, it is not that some of these students lack role models and self-esteem, rather that the characteristics of the role models, linked often to power, violence and aggression, are not those which schools are trying to foster. For these boys, their self-esteem is rooted in aspects of behaviour and achievement which might be linked to the informal economy and to aspects of criminality. Thus, it is that societal influences through the labour market, families and peers, as well as the specific institutional practices, all contribute to the con-structions of masculinity within a given school situation.

This view of masculinity (and the same constructions apply to femi-ninity) accepts that there is variety, difference and plurality between and within individuals, and identity is contradictory and fragmentary (Salisbury and Jackson 1996). The sense of identity which boys develop is defined and redefined through discourses and power associated with this process. Institutional practices such as discipline and authority, the pastoral system, the curriculum, teaching styles and school values, school culture and ethos, and competition (Salisbury and Jackson 1996) all contribute to the forms of masculinity that are constructed by boys attending a particular school. Within any discussion of factors which affect dominant forms of masculin-ities and femininities however, emphasis must be placed on the crucial importance of peer group cultures in the process of constructing gender identities in schools as these provide mechanisms through which gender identities are developed and lived out (Skelton 2001). The voices of boys and girls quoted in Chapter 2, from such contrasting settings as inner-city Manchester, commuter belt Southern England and rural East Anglia, confirm this. There are in any school a number of students who exert influ-ence within classrooms in Years 10 and 11 and often impair the learning of others, and who might on occasion be candidates for temporary exclusion. Such students may assume significant roles as key peer leaders within their year group, and be dominant in the school or in the local student commu-nity outside school. In some schools, there is evidence of a growing number of girls within these disengaged sub-groups, but usually they are dominated by boys. While there may be different sub-groups of these students within any school, some with a high profile in sport or in the performing arts, or with a key role in the local youth culture based on one or more of drink, drugs or claimed sexual prowess, these students often share common characteristics. In many contexts, they have a powerful influence which can 'knock on' to other boys and girls, and have a significant impact upon the engagement of others with school. On occasions, they adopt a position on the margins of school life with apparent anti-school traits. Sometimes, too, they acknowledge their own anti-social behaviour in the lower school and their own under-achievement, and claim that they want a 'fresh start'; frequently they are in need of support to accept such a new beginning, however, even when staff feel able to offer such a possibility. Crucially, these students are strongly influential in establishing the peer group norm within a year group, whether it be linked to dress, behaviour, attitude to work and aspirations. How the school responds to them is crucial.

A Socio-cultural case study

In Chapter 5, we defined socio-cultural intervention strategies as those which attempt to change images of laddish masculinity held by the peer group, and the family and community, and to develop an ethos which helps to eradicate the 'it's not cool to learn' attitude among boys. One prime aim of such approaches is to identify key movers within the student body, those who might have a negative influence on peer group attitude, opinion and ethos, and to incorporate these students into the mainstream of the school or to reduce their influence over others by marginalizing their impact. These socio-cultural strategies are not always overt or explicitly articulated, but tend to be implicit and integrated within the whole school culture, to develop an ethos which helps to identify and diminish the importance of anti-work groups; in the words of one headteacher, they are approaches which 'attempt to reframe the students' view of school so that academic success is valued, aspired to and seen to be attainable'.

The schools within the Raising Boys' Achievement Project which focused explicitly on socio-cultural approaches were 11–16 comprehensive schools which served challenging inner-city catchment areas in a metropolitan area in North West England. Their intakes were predominantly white working-class students, though two had a significant proportion of students (up to 25 per cent) from ethnic minority cultures; between 20 per cent and 30 per cent of students in each school were eligible for free school meals. Subsequent expansion of the triad, in a second phase of the Project's work, incorporated three further schools and increased the ethnic and socio-economic diversity of the triad; one phase 2 school, for example, had

44 per cent of its students eligible for free school meals, and another had 35 per cent of its intake with English as an additional language.

The Originator School had been identified during the pilot stage of the RBA project as one of the very few schools nationally where the gender gap had been narrowing significantly through time, and where there was an upward trajectory in the trend of achievement of both girls and boys. The school, therefore, was of particular interest to us, the more so because it served a catchment which had significant aspects of social deprivation within it, and where parental aspirations of education and subsequent employment were limited. The school in its current form dated from 1990 following restructuring within the LEA; at its inception it had a poor reputation and few staff from the previous establishment remained in post. Several long-serving members of staff, including the current head, recalled the early years when the school was not a safe environment; vandalism was rife, the buildings were frequently broken into, fires were not unknown and bullying and fights were commonplace. Incidents in school merely reflected the disaffection and violence in the local community, where levels of unemployment were high following the collapse of the local manufacturing base. Despite great changes in the past ten years within the school community, the locality is still characterized in terms of routine violence and crime, often related to drug dealing, and parental involvement in, and support for, the school are not readily forthcoming. In this context the school aims to create – in the words of its 1997 OFSTED report – a community that is 'non-violent, honest, fair and tolerant'.

The socio-cultural approach implemented in the school has been underpinned by the single-minded determination of the headteacher and her senior management group (SMG) to create an alternative, learning culture for students once they are in school, which contrasts with the norms of the street culture within which many students normally operate. From the outset this acknowledged that education was not valued by the local community because of the perceived long-standing lack of opportunity locally and recognized the extent to which a laddish masculinity and an anti-school ethos had gained ascendancy. There was also a strong belief that tackling the peer group culture was the most significant challenge facing the school if achievement was to be raised. In the words of the headteacher:

> Ten years ago we got 9 per cent A–C and were bottom of the league table. We were publicly vilified. To raise attainment we put lots of things in place like target setting, good teaching and mentoring but most important of all was to try and get into the peer culture.

At one level, the main thrust of these policies has been based on very clearly defined expectations of students and staff, with the head in particular as an indispensable change agent, giving strong leadership and a clear vision. This is articulated through a series of proactive measures related to behaviour, attendance, punctuality, dress and appearance (Figure 9.1) which conveys to all students what it is that is expected of them as students and learners. There is no prevarication, no implicit message, no room for debate; the notion of students as learners is made explicit to all students and to the community. Thus there is a focus on stamping out anti-school behaviour and not allowing students the opportunity to opt out of learning. That this vision to tackle laddish culture has come from Senior Management is important, as Noble and Bradford make clear:

> The acceptance of, or inability to tackle, the anti-swot culture is largely a management responsibility... schools must be, and must portray themselves as, learning organisations. There should be no place for the anti-swot culture, Schools should treat it as they do racism; there should be no tolerance of it. It is an assault upon equal opportunities and results in misery and underachievement.
>
> (2000: 21)

At the same time, there is a recognition that students face barriers to learning and if they are to be successful, as is their entitlement, these barriers need to be removed. Hence there is a complementary emphasis on support and encouragement (Figure 9.1), enabling students to have access to effective and structured teaching within the classroom, offering additional support lessons and resources, enabling students both to settle into the school culture and to contribute to a sense of caring through a 'Guardian Angels' Scheme. This support and encouragement is not always optional, as these comments about extra lessons from a Year 11 boy, who was being specifically targeted due to his anti-school attitude, testify:

B11 You have to [go to them]. You can choose, there's some you can choose to go to but most you have to.

I So it's sort of twist your arm. But that's OK, is it?

B11 Yer, that's fine. As long as I do actually have to get on with it, they don't just want me to come for punishment.

I So how many extra sessions do you end up going to a week on average?

B11 About four.

I That's quite a few then. I mean it's extra hours, isn't it, over what you'd expect to do.

B11 You have to put those extra hours in if you want to get the grades that you want.

Note: I = Interviewer; B11 = Y11 boy.

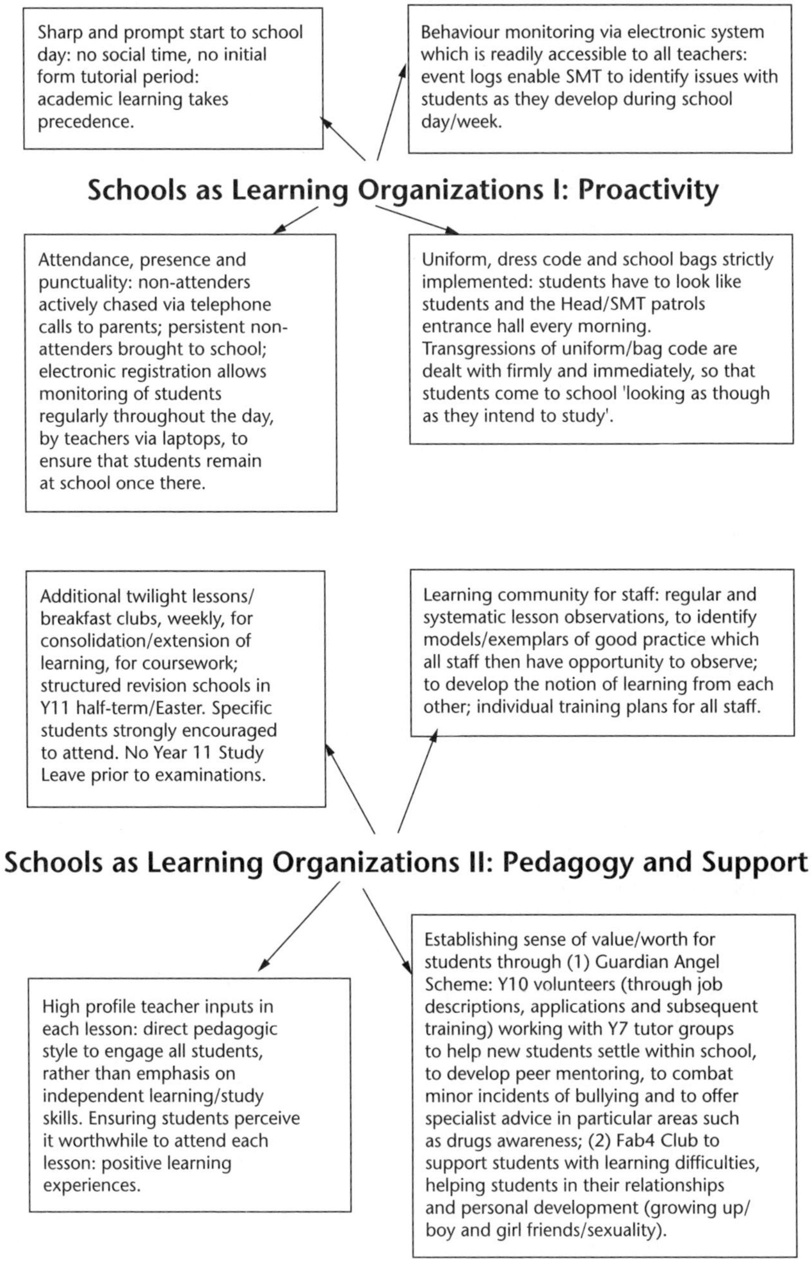

Sharp and prompt start to school day: no social time, no initial form tutorial period: academic learning takes precedence.

Behaviour monitoring via electronic system which is readily accessible to all teachers: event logs enable SMT to identify issues with students as they develop during school day/week.

Schools as Learning Organizations I: Proactivity

Attendance, presence and punctuality: non-attenders actively chased via telephone calls to parents; persistent non-attenders brought to school; electronic registration allows monitoring of students regularly throughout the day, by teachers via laptops, to ensure that students remain at school once there.

Uniform, dress code and school bags strictly implemented: students have to look like students and the Head/SMT patrols entrance hall every morning. Transgressions of uniform/bag code are dealt with firmly and immediately, so that students come to school 'looking as though as they intend to study'.

Additional twilight lessons/ breakfast clubs, weekly, for consolidation/extension of learning, for coursework; structured revision schools in Y11 half-term/Easter. Specific students strongly encouraged to attend. No Year 11 Study Leave prior to examinations.

Learning community for staff: regular and systematic lesson observations, to identify models/exemplars of good practice which all staff then have opportunity to observe; to develop the notion of learning from each other; individual training plans for all staff.

Schools as Learning Organizations II: Pedagogy and Support

High profile teacher inputs in each lesson: direct pedagogic style to engage all students, rather than emphasis on independent learning/study skills. Ensuring students perceive it worthwhile to attend each lesson: positive learning experiences.

Establishing sense of value/worth for students through (1) Guardian Angel Scheme: Y10 volunteers (through job descriptions, applications and subsequent training) working with Y7 tutor groups to help new students settle within school, to develop peer mentoring, to combat minor incidents of bullying and to offer specialist advice in particular areas such as drugs awareness; (2) Fab4 Club to support students with learning difficulties, helping students in their relationships and personal development (growing up/ boy and girl friends/sexuality).

Figure 9.1 Schools as learning organizations

In many respects, it is clear that this holistic approach, attempting to tackle laddishness through a socio-cultural approach, is not unique. It brings together a number of intervention strategies which we have already identified elsewhere in the RBA Project, and which are in place in many schools. What is different here, perhaps, is the sense of cohesion and interdependence between the different strategies, the integration between the different aspects, and the sense of purpose, commitment and direction which is conveyed to students through the vision which the school propagates. Central to this socio-cultural approach is the attempt to transform aspirations and expectations, to generate a sense of what is possible, and to create an achievement culture which offers students an alternative to the culture that often pervades their home lives. Students repeatedly and consistently buy into this vision, as our interviews have shown:

> I I'm getting the impression here, walking around, that there's a big thing with achievement. Is that really high profile in this school?
> $B10_1$ Yer, they have the Achievement Thing most of the time.
> $B10_2$ They don't say you *have* to do well.
> $B10_1$ They give us a choice, but they put it one way. They just try to explain it and make it sound like a good idea.
> $B10_2$ They like to tell us achievement, if we don't have achievement we won't like get a good job or anything.
> $B10_1$ Yer, that's another thing. In assembly they go 'If you don't get your GCSEs you're going to end up at Pandora's Pickles' or something.
> Note: I = Interviewer; $B10_1$ = first Y10 boy; $B10_2$ = second Y10 boy.

In the words of another boy:

> The school does want you to do well. They keep drumming it into your head that if you don't get any GCSEs you're going nowhere so it makes people want to achieve because they want to do summat.

Key leaders and key befrienders

As we have indicated earlier, one of the key challenges facing schools as they attempt to impact upon negative peer group culture relates to their response to specific students who assume significant roles as key peer leaders within their year group, and who are particularly influential in setting images of masculinity and femininity which conflict with the school ethos. It is within this context that the work of this triad has been particularly distinctive and innovative. In essence, the Originator School focused upon attempts to harness the energy of the key image makers in Year 11, to bring these students onside, working with, rather than against, the culture and aspirations which the school was attempting to establish. Two important points must be stressed at the outset about these *key leaders*. These students often had different characteristics and were defined by their resistance to school, their involvement in football or their leadership in social activities, but they were not outright rebels, set on confrontation at every turn. They had the potential to succeed, in the school's eyes, and to become key role models for other students, to lead and influence peer group image and attitude, and to have a significant impact on a group of followers. Second, although the scheme focused initially on boys and notions of laddishness, more recent identification of key leaders included a number of girls, 'ladettes' manifesting the same types of behaviours and attitudes as the laddish boys involved.

The key leader scheme within the Originator School operated at several levels, although the main focus was directed at Year 11, not only because the school felt that students needed most support then, with issues often coming to a crisis point in the autumn term, but also because it was then that the school perceived the students as having the maturity to identify, articulate and negotiate their difficulties. The scheme had several distinct aims and characteristics:

- to help the school develop an ethos of 'it's OK to work';
- to raise key leaders' expectations;
- to get key leaders onside by making them feel special;
- in so doing, to get 'followers' of key leaders onside as they observed the growing work ethic of key leaders;
- to integrate key leaders and their followers into the school ethos, so that there was less likelihood of them opting out.

Key leaders were identified towards the end of Year 10 through staff and departmental meetings, and a relatively small number – usually no more than 20 students – were subsequently confirmed by the Senior Management Group. All members of staff were made aware of the identity of the key leaders, and were asked to be more aware of them around the school, and to acknowledge them positively, to help them feel more integrated within the school. As with Mac an Ghaill's macho men and Connell's cool guys, the characteristics and personalities of these key leaders varied (Figure 9.2), but together they were perceived to exercise a strong impact over others and had the potential to succeed academically.

Each key leader was also allocated a key befriender who made a point of 'looking out' for the student during the school day and in essence acted as an informal mentor. The key befriender was someone with whom the student identified particularly well, and was usually a senior member of staff or a charismatic young teacher able to develop real rapport with the student. Befrienders volunteered because they believed they could work with the student, and often already had a good informal relationship with him or her. Key befrienders were empathetic, identifying with the needs and dispositions of the key leaders, and collaborative in approach. As with the characteristics of most effective mentors (Chapter 7), they had credibility both with the key leaders and with the staff who taught them, and were able to respond immediately to crisis points within the key leaders' experiences, both in and outside school. Equally, though, they were persuasive and with sufficient standing to ensure key leaders' cooperation, in completing coursework, attending extra lessons and working constructively within the school structure. These key befrienders were often the key to the success of the strategy, helping to promote an achievement culture to benefit the students themselves, working to promote and support the students' aspirations while also striving to establish role models which were not physical or stereotypically macho.

The Rebels

The rebels are intelligent students who tend to be on the five A*–C borderline, and who are usually though not exclusively boys. They may tend to bully occasionally and show rebellious behaviour, such as having their hair too short, repeated lateness or no homework. They tend to mock others who work. They are popular, have strong and challenging personalities, and disrupt lessons very easily, but never enough to be excluded. Some staff are intimidated by these characters.

The Clowns

This group of students, usually mostly boys, are immature and silly, and regularly initiate inappropriate behaviour in the classroom. They incite other students, encourage and initiate truancy, and set dares and challenges for other students. They encourage others to follow their lead. Although not necessarily popular, they are powerful and other students want to keep on the right side of them.

The Stars

This final group of students are the positive role models and the stars in school. They are successful and popular, but not thought of as outsiders or swots. The boys among them tend to be good at sport or have good interpersonal skills, and they seek to share their success with others. They are not afraid to help other students with their work.

Figure 9.2 Key leaders in the Originator School

A member of the Senior Management Group, who had acted as a key befriender since the scheme started, suggested that members of staff who were most successful with these types of students were 'those that aren't too concerned with winning every single issue; it is those staff who take the bigger picture of what you want them (the key leaders) to have when they leave school'.

Key befrienders met their key leaders regularly to discuss how things were going and to offer advice and support. Meetings were often contrived to be informal – a chat in the corridor or at the end of a lesson – but could be more or less frequent or more formal depending on need and on the nature of the relationship that developed between the key leader and befriender. There was a dilemma here, however, which needed to be confronted in the first years of the key leader scheme. Initially, students were unaware of their selection as key leaders, and hence often appeared bemused at the amount of attention and support they were receiving, often interpreting it negatively. When the Originator School decided to identify the key leaders explicitly, however, there was a tendency for some of the students concerned to behave arrogantly and to develop an inflated sense of self-importance. In subsequent years, therefore, key leaders were made aware that they were being targeted for support, but they were not explicitly aware of the school's rationale for doing so. The scheme was represented to students, therefore as a form of tightly focused mentoring, and indeed it shared some of the characteristics of quality mentoring defined in Chapter 7; the significant difference, however, was located in the underpinning rationale of the approach, and in the cumulative impact which the school intended the scheme to have on both key individuals and their followers.

Impact of socio-cultural strategies

Longitudinal research in the Originator School over four years suggested that the key leader scheme was very influential in reframing students' experience of school. Not only did attendance rates increase and exclusion rates decrease, but predicted grades increased significantly through the year. The 2003 OFSTED report, for example, identified the low exclusion rate compared to other similar schools and noted the strong effectiveness of exclusion when it *was* used, with very few pupils being excluded more than once.

While interviews through time with key leaders suggested that they did not necessarily enjoy school, they did realize the need for qualifications to 'break out of cycle of poverty in this area' and felt treated in an adult and positive way by the school. Thus, the school was 'alright', and all the key leaders interviewed echoed the view that the school was 'a good school', 'much better than when my mum went here'. Most of them felt that the school wanted them to do well, and that the headteacher was 'a fantastic woman who was right on!!' In the words of one key leader:

> I was a bit shocked when I found out [that the Head was my key befriender] but when I went for my first interview I thought I actually prefer that she is instead of like another teacher because she knows me better and she talks to me and stuff and she helps me along ... It's not like they're doing it to get at me. They're doing it for my benefit so it's OK. If I didn't like enjoy it then – I don't enjoy it because it's school and stuff – but it's like they're doing it, they're trying to help me get my GCSEs that I need so they're doing little things that will help me keep on the straight and narrow ... if you don't do well in school, you're not going to get a decent job and a nice house. You're going to be stuck on the minimum wage and things like that ... they're on my back because they want it to work for me.
>
> (Year 11 key leader 2003/4)

Crucially, there is a sense here that key leaders appreciated that the school was working for them, and there was a feeling of valuing of the school because students knew what they required for their career choice, and saw the school as supporting them to achieve. It was clear to the students involved that the school was committed not to achieving results to raise its own profile, but to help them fulfil their own career ambitions. Interviews with other key leaders also supported the view that the work the school did with them changed their perspective on achievement, and raised their own aspirations:

> School says things like 'come on you can do this'. School says I'm capable of doing it. I don't think that. Well, I am in some things, like, say I was learning a subject in science that I could do, then I'd be able to do it and I'd do it well. But there again now and then we get a thing where I can't do it and then I can't be arsed doing it. That's when I used to get into trouble. I've changed really because last year I would have said, 'No, I'm not doing that' and argue about it. I'd argue back and if I thought I was right, I was right and I wouldn't change my mind ... I've changed this year. I'm trying to do work. I didn't try last year. I've changed because I've realized I've only got a few months left until I leave. I want to do well, get good grades, for what I want to do anyway. I want to do graphic design at college and I need a C in everything.
>
> (Year 11 key leader 2002/3)

Comments such as these suggested that in most cases key leaders did feel valued and supported. Expectations had been raised, and the students wanted to achieve and had clear goals in mind. The key leaders felt supported by the well-developed careers programme in the school, and gained a sense of motivation and impetus as they realized that their career goals *were* attainable and not unrealistic. Furthermore, it could be argued that the scheme provided a programme of emotional literacy, as integral to the approach as the development of self-discipline; the boys were learning how to negotiate with dignity, how to deal with put-downs, how to develop assertiveness skills and how to manage anger. Working with the boys in this way allowed them to re-construct their identity as learners and indeed as boys, so that they identified with, rather than resisted, the culture and aspirations that the school was trying to establish.

Likewise, most members of staff interviewed during the project identified the scheme as a key factor in raising achievement in the school. There was an underpinning belief that the scheme was immensely successful in ensuring that key leaders and many of their followers left school with good qualifications which both reflected their potential and enabled them to meet their career aspirations through both further and higher education. In the words of one experienced key befriender:

> Over the years there has been a considerable success rate. A kid from three years ago was here being interviewed for the lab tech job the other day. Another one from the same year, I had to go to his house on the day of his science exam to try and get him into school, well, he came in for the others and now he's at Salford University. They know that if they leave school with nothing, then when they emerge from the bad times they have nothing. By working with them, they don't leave here with nothing. Even moderate cases at other establishments would possibly be written off and truant because of the situations they're in. At this school there are outlets and it can be managed.

We must remind ourselves at this stage, however, of the underpinning rationale of the key leaders scheme, and of the idea that if the key leaders of any year group can be persuaded to accept the achievement ethos of the school, then their followers will be more likely to see achievement as acceptable, and there will in turn be a cumulative effect upon the whole year group. Any evaluation of the key leaders scheme, therefore, must be framed not only within the context of the impact upon the key leaders themselves, but on the impact of the strategy upon their followers and indeed upon all the students in the year. At the same time, it is clear that the key leaders scheme will only be effective when it is located within the broader socio-cultural context of the whole school; it cannot be transposed into contexts where certain pre-conditions are not already in place (Figure 9.1). This increases the complexity of evaluating the specifics of the key leader scheme itself, however, since invariably it is difficult to disentangle the impact of the key leader scheme from the wider socio-cultural context in which it operates.

These reservations notwithstanding, it is clear from achievement data over the last decade that, despite the challenging socio-economic characteristics of the catchment area, the school has been able to transform the achievement levels of its students (Figure 9.3), and to dramatically change its reputation.

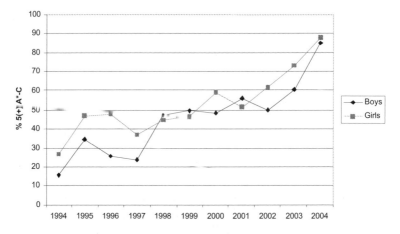

Figure 9.3 GCSE results by gender at Originator School

Of particular interest is the pattern of achievement since 1997, when socio-cultural initiatives were refined and the key leaders strategy developed more explicitly, within a whole school socio-cultural context. Since then, the achievement trajectory for both boys and girls has been sharply upward; in 1997 only 23.8 per cent of boys and 36.9 per cent of girls achieved at the benchmark grade level at GCSE. In the period 1998–2001, boys' achievements improved at a faster rate than that of girls, so that by 2001 56 per cent of boys and 51 per cent of girls achieved five or more A*–C grades, and boys outperformed girls in three of those four years. Although the period 2002–4 saw a reversal to the typical national pattern, with the gender gap within the school favouring girls, the overall transformation in achievement continued, so that in 2004 88 per cent of girls and 85 per cent of boys achieved at the benchmark grade level.

The achievement profile of successive cohorts of boys and girls within this school, against the background of a stable catchment area and a curriculum structure which has remained largely unchanged over this time period, shows a remarkable transformation. The gender gap has indeed reverted to type, but this must be seen alongside the dramatic acceleration in the rate of girls' achievements in recent years, and the fact that the highest ever proportion of boys achieved the higher level GCSE grades in 2004. Given the catchment area of the school, it is remarkable that in successive cohorts, more boys and girls within the school have achieved five or more higher level passes than within the country generally, and that achievement levels have risen so markedly to the 2004 peak. As we emphasized in Chapter 3, this is a more meaningful measure of a successful school, working on gender equity issues within an inclusive context.

Diffusion to the wider triad

Initial discussions with both the Originator School and partner schools within this triad suggested that the impact of the key leader strategy upon achievement and motivation within the Originator School was such as to justify attempts to translate it into the partner schools. Not only did the strategy appear innovative and different, but it appeared to be easily transferable, in its essence, to other schools in similarly challenging inner-city contexts. With hindsight, however, these assumptions were shown to be both naïve and simplistic, as the process of innovation transfer revealed.

Although the partner schools appeared to be similar to the Originator School both in terms of their inner city catchments and in their characteristics as learning organizations, it soon became clear that there were significant differences of approach and ethos. In both schools, the introduction of the key leader strategy, as a new initiative, rested heavily upon one key player (in both cases a deputy head) within the senior management team, and support from the rest of the SMG – and crucially from the headteacher – seemed permissive rather than proactive. As a consequence, the strategy was not promoted as vigorously as it had been in the Originator School, and in each school only a limited number of key befrienders volunteered to participate. Significantly, too, there was some staff resistance to the strategy, particularly in one partner school where the idea that those boys who were problematic in terms of their behaviour and performance should receive special support was anathema to the prevalent staff culture. Indeed, some influential members of staff, 'key leaders' within the staff as it subsequently emerged, appeared to find it difficult to accept that the school should implement a strategy which required them actively to seek out and praise individual students for good behaviour and meritworthy achievement, to 'catch them doing good rather than catching them doing bad!', in the words of the school coordinator of the project. As a consequence of this staff reluctance, members of the SMG and Learning Mentors assumed the key befrienders role. This in itself proved to have significant consequences in the partner school contexts, since members of the SMG were perceived by the student key leaders as having primarily a managerial and disciplinary function, while the Learning Mentors who were assigned roles as key befrienders were not seen, by either the students themselves or many members of staff, to have sufficient status or to offer appropriate role models for the student key leaders.

In retrospect, there were also issues with the identification of the key leaders themselves, mainly because early discussions between the Project team and the triad schools did not place enough emphasis on defining the essential characteristics of key leaders. Initial selection of key leaders within the partner schools, therefore, tended to focus upon students who had a significant impact and influence on others, but who were also confrontational in many aspects of their behaviour, or perceived as 'lost causes' in terms of attitudes, aspirations and conflict, rather than stressing their potential to be positive influences on other students. This intensified the difficulty of getting the strategy accepted in the partner schools, since in the words of the school coordinator in one of the partner schools: 'It's an uphill task persuading staff to be pleasant and accessible to kids who give you a lot of grief the whole time; it simply doesn't make sense to them!'

Despite the unremitting efforts of the school coordinators in both partner schools, therefore, the key leader strategy was only established after some considerable delay, and against a somewhat unpromising background. Indeed, staff resistance and hostility, together with competing priorities and staff retention issues generally in one partner school, were such that that school was forced to withdraw at the end of the first year of the project.

In the other partner school, the strategy slowly began to take root and to become more accepted, and in the second year of the project it become evident that the key leader strategy was having some impact, albeit more directly on the identified students themselves and on their immediate associates, rather than on the whole of year group. Interviews with these individuals suggested that they recognized they could do better and needed help to achieve this and that they were beginning to reflect more thoughtfully upon their attitudes to school and their subsequent aspirations. Significantly, some key leaders spoke of trying to control their own behaviour and of the help which the school had given to support them in this, and of trying to avoid conflict and confrontation by mixing with a wider and more diffuse group of people. From the perspective of the school coordinator, the scheme was beginning to be embedded within the whole school, and had been effective in improving the attendance rates of key students; disciplinary referrals for key leaders had decreased, and predicted grades were beginning to increase, although from a low base. In this context, the most significant impact upon achievement was in the higher percentages of girls and boys achieving one A*–G grade at GCSE (Figure 9.4).

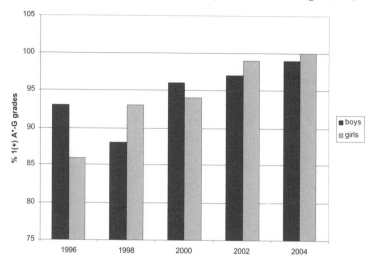

Figure 9.4 Partner school: % girls and boys achieving 1(+) A*–G grades, 1996–2004

   The potential of the key leaders strategy, as evidenced in the Originator School, and the cautious signs of transformation in the continuing partner school, suggested to us that there was scope to prolong the life of the triad into a third year of research and intervention, and to extend the number of schools involved. Thus, three schools in similar socio-economic contexts in the same metropolitan area joined with the Originator and the remaining partner school, to trial the socio-cultural initiatives in general and the key leader strategy in particular. It might be argued, with some justification, that a one-year period is inadequate for the trialling of such a complex set of strategies. Ideally, of course, we would agree, and the extension was certainly of insufficient scope to allow us to evaluate the impact of the strategy upon performance data. We were, however, able to analyse the impact of the strategies upon students' attitudes, through an attitudinal survey which was administered to students in all the schools at the beginning and end of their year 11 schooling (Table 9.1).

   Three significant aspects of students' attitudes (their engagement with school, their sense of self as student and their academic self-concept) were identified and assessed through factor analysis. In each case, there is a statistically significant upward trend in the scores recorded by the key leaders and by their followers, greater than that recorded in the year group as a whole. We must be somewhat cautious in interpreting these data, because of the small sample size of key leaders and their followers, and because of inter-school variations, but nonetheless, there are some interesting outcomes:

- In terms of students' engagement and the support they perceived they received from teachers, the analysis suggests that the key leaders and their followers did not disengage during Year 11, as their prior behaviour suggested they might, and that both groups became *more* engaged with their schooling during the year. It is interesting to note, too, that the perceived level of engagement and support of these two groups of students increased at a greater rate during the year than that perceived by other male students in the year, so that the marked perceptual differences noted at the beginning of the year had become minimal by the end of Year 11.
- Students' sense of self/students' academic self-concept: both key leaders and their followers saw themselves more as students and developed more confidence as learners during the course of the year. Although the end-of-year attitudinal scores of the key leaders and their followers remain lower than the rest of the boys within the year group, there have apparently been significant positive changes in attitudes of these targeted students during the year, greater than evidenced in the rest of the year group.

Taken together, this analysis does indicate, however tentatively, that the schools were becoming more successful in beginning to transform students' culture and generating more appropriate attitudes and behaviours in their Year 11 students.

Table 9.1 Engagement of male key leaders and their followers

	Students' engagement/ perceived support from teachers		Students' sense of self: behaving appropriately as a student		Students' academic self-concept	
	Mean scores at start of Year 11	*Mean scores at end of Year 11*	*Mean scores at start of Year 11*	*Mean scores at end of Year 11*	*Mean scores at start of Year 11*	*Mean scores at end of Year 11*
Key leaders	34.2	39.3	16.7	18.5	13.9	15.5
Followers	32.8	38.3	17.0	19.0	14.0	15.3
Other male students	38.5	38.7	20.7	20.7	15.7	15.9
	Possible range of scores 15–60		*Possible range of scores 7–28*		*Possible range of scores 6–24*	

Pre-conditions for successful implementation of socio-cultural strategies

Discussions of many of the strategies which have been developed and refined during the course of the RBA Project have stressed the need for the careful identification and implementation of a set of pre-conditions, which are essential if the various strategies are to have maximum effectiveness in raising achievement levels of boys and girls. Nowhere is this more evident than in the implementation of complex socio-cultural strategies which attempt to address issues of laddishness and anti-school cultures, particularly when, as our experiences working with this triad of schools have constantly reiterated, the schools are facing values within the community and the home which are sometimes directly oppositional to those which the schools are striving to promote.

Crucial within these pre-conditions is the establishment of an achievement culture within the school, a culture which embraces all students. In two of the six schools within the extended triad, the relative lack of success of the key leader strategy appeared to stem, at least in part, from the lack of such a culture. Among a minority of staff who were significantly influential upon staffroom opinion, there appeared to be low expectations of students, and a focus on behaviour management rather than the promotion of learning. Staff appeared willing to support those students who were motivated and engaged in learning, but did not see it as their responsibility to offer positive opportunities to those that were anti-learning. Students not identifying with the aims and aspirations of the school tended to be written off, and there was little inclination to offer fresh starts, through the key leader strategy, to students who were constantly challenging teachers' roles, denying the opportunity to teach and other students the opportunity to learn. Not surprisingly, then, the scheme had almost no impact in terms of changing the attitudes or improving the achievement of the students involved. Students had internalized their own lack of value, did not see the key leader strategy as changing that value in any significant way, and continued to work against rather than with the school. Low staff expectations reinforced this lack of achievement and lack of self-value among the students. In one school, for example, staff seemed unable to recognize the validity of prior attainment data which suggested that 45 per cent of the cohort had the potential to achieve five A*–C GCSE grades and to work with students towards this target, predicting instead that only 33 per cent of the year group would achieve it. Boys inevitably dominated the list of those students thought to be incapable of meeting the target grades, but across both boys and girls, previous attainment data seemed to suggest that under-achievement was an endemic issue in these schools.

Schools in more deprived socio-economic environments also battle against a long-standing lack of educational aspirations within the communities they serve. Some schools – and their teachers – are seen as unworldly, not connected with the real world which their students experience, out-of-touch with the informal grey economy in which some of their parents operate. 'The boys need to want to achieve more', one headteacher told us; 'attendance is an issue through Year 11 and we cannot keep them', admitted another, 'because the boys work illegally in family businesses or with a friend of a friend!'. Equally, though, to some parents and their sons and daughters, education is not valued because it fails to offer real, viable opportunities to which they can relate, and increasingly it is perceived to bring – through fees and loans – real financial cost. The curriculum is seen to fail, still, to address the needs of these students, with a classroom pedagogy that is dull, boring and oppressive.

As is clear from Figure 9.1, where the key leaders scheme is most successful it is located within a series of proactive whole school approaches, which emphasize the school as a place of learning, and which – crucially – take time to develop and embed. These approaches place emphasis on raising aspirations and offering encouragement and support, on the one hand, and on a more prescriptive, demanding approach on the other. Students are offered entitlement and the possibility of achievement, which can be transformative and liberating for them; at the same time, high expectations and tough demands are made of them. Thus, it is essential that students see the school as a place where they come to work, where the focus first and foremost is on learning, where they expect to achieve and have confidence in the staff to help them reach their aspirations. Schools need to be places where – in the words of one headteacher – 'you know that you can work and not be name-called for it, a place where it can be cool to be clever'. Certainly our work with this triad shows that where these preconditions do not exist, the key leaders scheme is unlikely to achieve its potential. If many students within the school hold values contradictory to achievement, and if a significant minority of the staff do not identify with the sense of what is possible, then much work must be done first in managing behaviour and getting the focus on learning. Thus, at an earlier stage, the Originator School had explicitly to address issues of uniform policy and dress code, to clarify its expectations about students' attendance, punctuality and behaviour, to widen the support offered to students in terms of out-of-hours clubs for homework, coursework and revision, and to reassess classroom pedagogy so that lessons were structured, accessible and worthwhile for all, in order to establish and sustain a culture of achievement and expectation within the community.

As we have emphasized, though, there are also critical aspects of the key leader scheme itself which impact strongly upon its effectiveness. There needs to be a clear understanding of the criteria for the selection of the students themselves, an explicit recognition that key leaders, although they may offer challenge in terms of behaviour, attitude and motivation, must have the potential to accept the support offered by the scheme and to work eventually with the aims and aspirations of the school, rather than perpetually defying and confronting. It is important, too, that the aims of the key leader scheme are carefully articulated, that staff understand that it is not simply an enhanced form of mentoring, but a strategy which offers wider support and encouragement, trying to generate a 'feel-good' factor, which encourages the wider participation of key leaders in whole school activities and peer group leadership.

Self-evidently, too, the key leaders need to have the capacity to lead others, to influence and be accepted by the peer group. This requires heads of year and form tutors to have a real knowledge of the students within their year group, and of the strengths of social interactions within groups, rather than a superficial knowledge based on staffroom talk and behavioural records. Otherwise, inappropriate key leaders might be identified, as in one school where, though interviews with the key leaders suggested that the strategy had impacted considerably on their attitudes, aspirations and on their approach to their school, peer pressure was too great for them to be able to acknowledge this in public, and thus they had tended to revert to type in terms of classroom behaviour and demeanour around the school. This is a dilemma in itself, in that while it is understandable that constructions of masculinity and laddishness affect these students' presentations of their own images and attitudes, it is crucial – if the key leader strategy is to become really effective – that these boys acknowledge changes in their own behaviour and aspirations, and are prepared and confident enough to have these changes recognized by others. If this confidence does not exist, then their very identification as key leaders might be questionable. Here, though, is the nub of the issue, for it is increasingly recognized that laddish and macho behaviour is often a defence mechanism against feelings of inadequacy and defencelessness, an act of bravado and defiance, rather than one which is rooted in self-assurance and confidence; such behaviour does not always reconcile with peer leadership and constrictive role modelling.

Equally, the identification of key befrienders is of fundamental importance. They need to know the students informally as well as formally, to have the credibility to encourage, to raise issues and to be listened to by the key leaders, to be able to 'read' their students so that early and fitting interventions can be appropriately timed, so that student anger and disaffection, if it arises, can be well managed. Our work with these triads suggests that this role, if it is to be effective, is time-consuming and demanding: key befrienders need to be in regular contact with their students, to be accessible, to establish rapport and respect. We have encountered individual learning mentors who have carried through the role with sensitivity and imagination, but more often it is senior members of staff whose experience, confidence and status within the school community enable them to fulfil this difficult role with distinction and effectiveness. Certainly, where the scheme has been less effective, it has been in contexts where staffing issues have restricted the selection of experienced staff as befrienders, and where they have not been easily and consistently accessible to their key leaders.

10 Gender and Achievement in Special Schools
Ruth Kershner

The Raising Boys' Achievement Project's work in special schools allowed us to consider the connections between concerns about the comparability of boys' and girls' achievement in mainstream schools, concerns about low attainment in general, and the identification of pupils with special educational needs (SEN). It has long been acknowledged that more boys than girls are identified as having SEN. DfES statistics show that over 106,000 boys in primary and secondary schools had a statement of SEN (around 28 in every 1,000 boys) compared with 41,000 girls (around 11 in 1,000 girls) (DfES 2004f). However additional evidence points to boys with statements beyond Key Stage 1 achieving better results than girls with statements, except in English at Key Stage 3 (DfES 2004g: 62) – raising questions about how the factor of gender actually operates in mainstream procedures for assessment and additional support.

The 'gender factor' has applied notably in the identification of pupils with certain types of SEN, such as emotional and behavioural difficulties (Evans *et al.* 2004). This is often explained in terms of boys' classroom behaviour being more socially disruptive than girls', leading to earlier referral to support services and SEN assessment procedures. Past evidence has suggested similar effects for ethnicity and social class in the area of learning difficulties, pointing to systematic bias in schools and society (Tomlinson 1982). Yet these trends do not entirely explain why an individual pupil may be identified as having special educational needs and perhaps being transferred to a special school. Pupils with apparently similar learning needs can be found in very different mainstream and special school settings.

The assessment of pupils' special educational needs is localized, involving a multi-professional, individualized process of decision-making, taking parental and pupil wishes into account (DfES 2001b), and the point at which special educational provision is made and the nature of this provision differs spatially. Local education authorities even vary in their basic conceptualizations and terminology, such as their definitions of 'moderate learning difficulties' (Norwich and Kelly 2005). The result is a complex, differentiated system of special classes, units, schools and support services in each local area in which gender balances in number and achievement change to some extent from year to year partly in response to changing local circumstances and procedures.

The outcomes of this identification and placement process can have significant consequences for the pupils involved. Norwich and Kelly (2005) found in their survey of pupils' perspectives on special provision that there were differences in the ways in which secondary pupils identified as having learning difficulties in mainstream and special schools perceived their education. Secondary boys in special schools were least satisfied with their school placement, while mainstream boys felt more positive about their school placement even though they felt that they were receiving less help in class. More special school boys preferred to be in the mainstream than special school girls. So the type of school placement matters particularly to many boys, perhaps explained partly by boys' greater likelihood of exclusion from mainstream schools as well as differences in their social networks outside school.

One of the main issues here is that many pupils who transfer in Year 7 from primary school to special school could equally remain in mainstream secondary education in a different location. This applies particularly to pupils placed in broad categories such as 'moderate learning difficulties' (MLD). With regard to teaching and learning for pupils identified as having SEN, it is not at all clear what, if anything, is 'special' for any individuals or groups of pupils. While certain claims are made for areas such as sensory impairment, autistic spectrum disorders and specific or profound and multiple learning difficulties, in the main there is little evidence of a need for distinctive curriculum design and pedagogies for separate categories or areas of SEN (Davis and Florian 2004; Lewis and Norwich 2005). The pedagogic principles for all pupils are largely the same, although the details of practice may differ lesson by lesson in different settings. One of the reasons for this is the acknowledged overlap of difficulties for most individual pupils identified as having SEN, making a simple categorization and labelling process impossible. In this context, gender is just one among many other interacting factors to consider for pupils in special schools.

Gender, achievement and special education

There is an identifiable but not extensive field of research connecting gender with disability, learning difficulty and special education. Some work draws explicitly on socio-cultural understandings of gender. McDonagh (2000) demonstrates how historical studies of literary representations of men and women with learning disabilities have indicated contrasting emphases on either diminished male incapability or disruptive female sexuality. Benjamin examines the connections between social constructions of masculinity and femininity and constructions of special educational needs, asserting that 'SEN is a gendered phenomenon' (2003: 247) which must be understood as such in developing inclusion.

Biological accounts of boys' developmental difficulties are also found in the literature. Skårbrevik (2002), writing in the Norwegian context, suggests the need to take into account the phase of education in examining gender differences and SEN, proposing that genetic or biological differences come to the fore in the pre-school years while later identifications depend more on social factors and pedagogical mismatches. There is a widespread view that boys are generally more vulnerable to adverse biological experiences from infancy (Freides 2001), and many more boys than girls fall into categories or syndromes associated with SEN such as autistic spectrum disorders. Herbert's (2005) comprehensive review of developmental problems in childhood and adolescence refers to gender in discussing a wide range of areas, from attention deficit/hyperactivity disorder, specific reading difficulties and Duchenne muscular dystrophy to anorexia and suicide risk (although it should be noted that girls are sometimes more at risk than boys). Gender has been put forward as a key factor in children's resilience over time, although evidence now suggests the existence of gender differences in responses to childhood adversity rather than, as previously thought, a protective or compensatory effect of being female rather than male (Fergusson and Horwood 2003).

One of the main problems in reviewing research evidence in this field is the difficulty in gathering reliable and valid evidence of overall gender differences in attainment, inclusion and special provision. Any use of quantitative data in this field raises significant technical issues about categorization, measurement, completeness and accuracy (Florian et al. 2004). However, research has suggested that gender variations do exist between schools in the ways that special educational needs budgets are allocated and in the implementation of SEN procedures and support (Hill 1994; Daniels et al. 2000; Vardill and Calvert 2000). Croll and Moses (2000) note that the overall gender ratio (more boys than girls) for pupils in Key Stage 2 (7–11 years old) identified with SEN did not change substantially between 1981 and 1998 in spite of growing concerns about 'male under-achievement' in the 1990s. They did, however, find an increasing proportion of boys regarded as having emotional and behavioural difficulties in that time.

The tendency of teachers to regard more boys as having SEN does not seem to be a simple matter of gender stereotyping and categorization. There are strong, complex connections between pupils' classroom behaviour, learning and achievement, and Cline and Ertubey (1997) found that giving teachers more contextual information helps to reduce the impact of gender on teachers' judgements about individual children. The interactions between different areas of SEN are evident. For example, different rates of SEN referral for learning difficulties can arise via observed differences in classroom behaviour which are exacerbated by peer pressure, cultural clashes and psychological processes of motivation and 'self-worth protection' (Jackson 2002). A consequence of the acknowledged difficulties with 'boys' behaviour' in schools can be that while girls may be numerically under-represented in special schools, those that are identified as having learning or behaviour difficulties are likely to have more severe problems than the boys in the same setting. They may even have their special needs as young women ignored altogether (Malcolm and Haddock 1992). From the boys' point of view, the problem can be one of undue assumptions about learning difficulties on the basis of difficult classroom behaviour. Daniels *et al.* (2000) found that boys are given proportionally more and higher status SEN support in mainstream settings, but they may not receive support clearly matched to their needs (e.g. being given additional reading instruction as a response to inappropriate behaviour). This points towards a need for further research with a gender perspective on teaching and learning processes for pupils receiving special support, an area not well covered in the literature.

In addition to the conceptual difficulties of carrying out research in the area of gender and special educational needs, there are some significant methodological and ethical issues to be taken into account. These relate, for example, to the small numbers, the problems in communicating with pupils with certain types of SEN, and the difficulties which can arise in gaining informed consent in the special school context. There are also questions about the role of research in responding to hidden agendas and wish fulfilment for pupils, parents and teachers who face considerable daily challenges in teaching and learning. With regard to this last point, it is important to emphasize that the relatively hidden issues of gender in the field of special education can be of central personal and lifelong importance for the pupils involved. In special schools there can be significant problems for male and female pupils in developing gender identity, experiencing relationships and benefiting from sex education – particularly for pupils with the most severe learning, physical and emotional difficulties. There can also be long-term implications for men and women with learning difficulties in their post-school experiences, relationships, learning and employment (Riddell *et al.* 2001).

The focus of inquiry for the special schools

At the outset of the RBA Project, it was not clear whether a 'gender gap' existed in special schools, or what its nature might be, and one of the first research tasks was to formulate appropriate research questions for the special school context. This need to identify questions about boys' achievement quickly led to the realization that a key factor lies in the data that are used to measure the progress of pupils with special educational needs. The most recent approaches for this type of measurement have involved the development of the P Scales for identifying attainments below Level 1 in the National Curriculum (DfEE 2001). However, one of the main features of the special school research proved to be a widening understanding of 'progress' from a narrowly curriculum focused quantitative definition towards a broader qualitative assessment of achievement in academic, social and personal terms.

The research with pupils at secondary level involved three special schools for pupils with moderate learning difficulties (all of which included a wide mix of pupils with learning, behavioural, sensory and physical difficulties). From the special school perspective, involvement in the research required a willingness to ask whether enough of the right sort of work was being done to raise boys' (and girls') achievement in a setting where it could be argued that the whole focus is on supporting pupils whose achievement is low compared to their peers. Asking about boys' achievement could therefore be seen as a rather radical question about gender bias in special schools, which are commonly perceived as environments where boys and girls are somewhat detached and protected from the ordinary social pressures.

Case studies of school-based inquiries

The three schools focused on different aspects of boys' writing, self-esteem, expectations and engagement in learning in Years 9–11. The pupils involved in these projects included some who had transferred from mainstream schools into Year 7 and some concurrently involved in inclusion programmes with neighbouring secondary schools. The schools were also concerned in different ways with staff and whole school development, closely connected with the research process.

Case study 1: Focusing on teaching and learning English in Years 10 and 11, in the wider context of whole school development

Initial discussions with staff at this school, which served an extensive rural area in East Anglia, helped to identify an area of interest in pupils' writing, particularly in their understanding of writing and what they perceived as 'good writing'. Interviews with pupils in Years 5, 8 and 10 suggested that many pupils focused on the technical aspects of writing, commonly emphasizing neatness rather than content. However, the interviews also showed that pupils recognized that they were involved in writing across the curriculum and outside school, which was promising for developing their motivation and learning in all aspects of writing in the future. Subsequent research was centred on exploring the range of teaching approaches which might support improvements in boys' writing.

The first year of the project involved working with Year 10 pupils, none of whom were achieving higher than Level 2 to 3 in English. Most of the pupils took a cautious approach to writing, unadventurous with vocabulary or spelling in case they made mistakes. The class teacher involved took an integrated approach to teaching English, including careful scaffolding of tasks over a period of several weeks leading to a specific genre outcome. She catered for diversity in the pupils' learning preferences by using visual and aural approaches, making learning objectives explicit and aiming to help pupils develop self-evaluation strategies.

The research focused on close monitoring of the pupils' responses to teaching, particularly their increasing capacity to write confidently, to talk about their writing and to understand that writing is meant to reflect their own thoughts, ideas and feelings. At three points in the year samples of writing were analysed, and the pupils were interviewed about their attitudes to writing and the processes of their learning. In the first year it was found that all of the pupils had made significant moves in their approach to writing, their attainment levels, their independence, pride and assurance as writers and their abilities to talk about their knowledge of the writing process. Assessments at the end of Year 10 showed that four of the six boys involved had moved at least two NC sub-levels during the year and one pupil had moved a whole writing level (in contrast to the expected timescale of two years for this rate of progress). Analysis of the writing showed developments in overall fluency and assurance, the technicalities of spelling and punctuation, and the range of different types of text tackled. The teaching strategy had also helped the pupils to work collaboratively. This progress continued as the pupils went into Year 11. Periodic reviews indicated that all the pupils continued to comment on the content and meaning of their writing, and they talked about the importance of planning, taking notes and reading through their work carefully. Teacher assessment at the end of the year showed that two of the boys had maintained the gains made during the previous year and that four of them had made a third or two-thirds of a level more progress.

In the second year, however, the new Year 10 group did not replicate the previous year's experience of greater control over writing or their progress in developing a metalanguage to talk about writing. The pupils remained preoccupied with the surface features of handwriting and spelling, and the discernible progress was only in terms of handwriting and control of sentences and paragraphs. The particular special needs of these pupils and the relationships within the group seemed to hinder the boys' progress, raising a question about whether young writers need to have a sense of personal control to underpin their control of writing. Despite the teacher's efforts, the boys in the second cohort did not move very far towards greater independence as learners or writers, although importantly, the girls made very significant gains both in assurance and independence and in writing levels – pointing towards the need to look for distinctive features in this second group of boys.

Case study 2: Focusing on boys' self-esteem and engagement in learning

This West Midlands school was involved in the project under the guidance of the headteacher. The starting point was his observation that in the last few years the school had received a large influx into Year 7 of pupils (mainly boys) who might be described as 'not typically MLD' (moderate learning difficulties), but who were streetwise, disaffected and somewhat resentful of their special school placement when their primary friends had gone to local secondary schools. The focus of research was on the progress of a small group of boys in Year 9, all of whom showed notably good sporting prowess, but whose academic attainment levels were not significantly different from other pupils in this school where approximately 20 per cent achieve levels 3–4 in English and 4–5 in Maths and Science at Key Stage 3. In Year 11, boys' attainment is at least equal to girls' and higher in some subjects. The focus group's attainment levels ranged between 2–4 in English, and between 3–4 in Maths and Science, having risen from 1–2 in English and 2–3 in Maths and Science in Year 7. Observations of the pupils' general behaviour and attitude to school, together with the assessment of the educational psychologist, supported the headteacher's view that low self-esteem and disaffection were significant factors for these pupils. The broad research question asked whether the current ethos of the school and the learning/teaching environment offered enough to effect a change in these pupils' attitudes and self-esteem so as to significantly change their academic and social achievement.

The research involved the headteacher in identifying current strategies, continuing support and evaluating progress, rather than introducing a specific intervention for the identified group of boys. Support strategies were identified at different levels:

- some directly with individual pupils (e.g. counselling);
- some embedded in the school practice (e.g. Good Work assemblies);
- some at the wider family and social context (e.g. parent liaison; appointment of School Welfare Officer).

The aims were variously directed at:

- behaviour management (e.g. rewards for appropriate behaviour);
- social relationships and role modelling (e.g. working with head-teacher; buddy system);
- metacognitive understanding of learning aims and expectations (e.g. target setting and visible evidence of progress; clear expression of expectations to pupils);
- emotional support (e.g. counselling; calm, positive discussion of feelings);
- self-concept and motivation (e.g. sports activities).

Although the pupils' experiences of inclusion in local secondary schools for certain examination courses demonstrated both social and academic progress over time, there was continuing evidence of behavioural and attitudinal difficulties within the research group. In the headteacher's view this was partly exacerbated by the difficulties of transfer from Year 9 to Year 10 (in terms of curriculum, class size and teaching style). For example, for five boys the total recorded behaviour incidents in Year 9 was 22, while in the first term of year 10 the total was already 19. Attendance of four of the pupils had dropped by about 10 per cent compared to Year 9. From previous experience with that age-group the headteacher expected the pupils' confidence, behaviour and attitudes to improve as they saw evidence of their examination achievement in Year 11 – a key goal for pupils and teachers in Key Stage 4 in this school setting.

Case study 3: Focusing on expectations and inclusion

This school, located in a large expansion town in East England, focused on a group of pupils who were perceived to be under-achieving. The deputy headteacher found in a whole-school review of core subject attainment using P Scale data, that certain boys in the Year 9/10 emerged with a distinctive (comparatively high) profile. His hypothesis was that some pupils in school come to expect too little of themselves in academic terms in a context where they are necessarily provided with the emotional and social support required to avoid exclusion. At the time a small number of individual pupils were successfully joining the local secondary school for specific subjects (such as art) in an informally developed inclusion programme. The identification of this group of Year 9/10 pupils raised the possibility of developing a more active inclusion programme for a larger number of pupils. The key goal was to evaluate the effects of inclusion on raising pupils' expectations and achievement.

It was clear from the start that there would be a number of implications and requirements for developing the inclusion programme. These were seen to include not only the financial implications of implementing a more formal and extensive connection with local secondary schools, but also the motivation and justification for doing so. Inclusion might be justified on several grounds, but there would also be sticking points – including parents' views and preferences. It was seen as vital here to understand the pupils' own perceptions and opinions as well as those of other people. To this end, the Key Stage 4 coordinator took responsibility for introducing a more systematic discussion with pupils at regular interviews, using an 'attitude to school' questionnaire format. Some questions proved to be particularly revealing as when a question about being encouraged at home to do well helped three pupils to begin to talk about their difficulties in this respect.

The development of the inclusion programme was tackled at different levels, including work with pupils, parents, local school contacts, resources and practical issues, and funding. Through time, improvements were seen in attainment (for example, four boys taking GCSE courses), pupils' self-esteem, staff–pupil relationships, home–school relationships, attitudes of other pupils, and raised staff expectations. Several of the pupils commented:

When I walk in [to the secondary school] I feel a little bit nervous but I have the confidence as well to do it on my own.

The maths is all right. It makes made me feel good to be chosen.

I like harder work because it is a challenge.

Teachers are encouraging me more now.

There was growth in the local inclusion network of mainstream and special schools, and increased LEA funding. The school became interested exploring further the two-way process of reintegrating pupils where appropriate and offering support to mainstream pupils who were at risk of becoming non-attenders. However, there were also costs to weigh up in considering the ongoing time investment, financial difficulties and practical demands of managing inclusion, with one of the main issues for future consideration being adequate staffing levels for teachers and learning support assistants to facilitate what is seen to be a good way forward in school.

Some issues from the case studies

One of the dilemmas in special school provision is to do with the *balance of support and expectation* for pupils who are likely to have experienced failure in the mainstream system. This issue was at the heart of the inclusion programme in case study 3, and in case study 2 the perceived danger had been that pupils' experiences of failure in Year 6 and transfer to special school, compounded by difficulties in home life and early developmental experience, would produce low self-esteem and subsequent disaffection from school. The headteacher believed that in these circumstances a pupil would not perceive themselves as a 'whole, rounded person who had achieved to the best of their abilities'.

In the end, the question points to how we understand 'achievement' for pupils in special schools, and how that relates to the balance of support and expectation. This becomes crucial for pupils in Key Stage 4, looking towards life after school. The issue of measuring attainment in special schools loomed large in our minds from the start of the project. It became clear that managing quantitative performance data could present many problems in the special school setting. For example, in the school featured in case study 1, the deputy headteacher identified nine different uses of the P Scales, ranging from feedback to teachers, target-setting and parental reports to school improvement planning and accountability. One of the main problems for her rested in deciding how to organize the data to allow these various outputs while also incorporating the qualitative understanding that allows proper understanding of what it means for pupils, teachers, parents and other agencies. The headteacher in case study 2 was similarly employed in developing a wide view of 'achievement' beyond the systematic gathering of detailed attainment data. In talking about his pupils' progress, he made a point of noting their involvement in football training, in organizing tournaments in five-a-side football and pool, and in unprompted 'acts of kindness', such as showing empathy to and comforting a bereaved pupil.

The implication of these broad definitions of achievement is that social, emotional and academic development are closely connected – an argument strongly supported in current psychological thinking. In gaining this wide picture of pupils' progress in school, many different techniques were used to collect evidence. These included attitudinal questionnaires, analysis of pupils' writing, classroom observation and video recordings, attendance monitoring, meeting notes, behaviour incident records, collection and analysis of P Scale data and individual and group interviews. The range of data gathering approaches gives an indication that to look at 'achievement' is to look carefully at several different perspectives of the pupil in several different contexts. This supports the view that achievement and progress are the results of collaboration between pupils, teachers and other people in contact, not just reflections of pupils' personal effort and ability. Indeed, the headteacher in case study 2 reflected at the end of the study that the research reinforced his beliefs about the importance of establishing a relationship with children in order to affect anything in their lives and learning – suggesting that efforts to raise achievement centrally involve this relationship and not just the pupil's own efforts and capabilities.

This multi-level perspective and broad view of 'achievement' is clearly important in balancing social, emotional and academic support and expectation. However, establishing the security and achievement of pupils must be weighed up against their day-to-day experiences of scrutiny and surveillance in the special school setting. Special schools are often small-scale enterprises compared to other schools, with many staff around all the time. The close monitoring that helps many pupils to learn in mainstream schools is likely to be experienced differently by pupils for whom close monitoring in a previous school experience resulted in detailed SEN assessment and ultimately special school placement. The perceived value of monitoring achievement needs to be examined in the light of pupils' actual experiences and their views of what it means for them.

It is also important to sustain initiatives over time, and to manage the subtle challenges in teaching, learning, curriculum development and professional development which are involved. For example, in the writing project in case study 1, the two year groups differed not only in levels of achievement but also in their capacity to use a metalanguage to talk about the content and intentions of their writing. Where the boys in the first group noticeably grew in confidence and a sense of self-efficacy, most of the boys in the second group failed to thrive in these respects. The girls' improvements, however, indicate that it is likely that there were no great differences in the teaching approaches used, but that the nature of the learners and their needs is a key factor in success. This is a strong indicator of the 'specialness' of special education. While some of the successful approaches used in mainstream education can be equally effective in both types of school, the special nature of the learners themselves means that initiatives to improve boys' writing need to take account of individual learning needs. One conclusion could be that the familiar mainstream strategy of focusing on the meaning of writing as the motivation for teaching and learning may have to be put aside where pupils' technical difficulties are overwhelming and 'success' has to be evaluated individually.

Factors such as staffing and curriculum balance are crucial longer-term issues for consideration. A key point here, though, is that the focus is on particular pupils in a specific school context, not general policies for pupils with SEN in general. The school is an important variable in decision-making, mediating between the individual aspects of pupils' special educational needs and the wider social, political and economic influences on educational practice. The evaluation of 'what works' and what changes are required has to be contextualized in the realities of school life – acknowledging what is done well in that context and what to do next.

Final thoughts

The case studies confirmed that special school teachers attend closely to pupils as individuals, drawing on detailed knowledge of each pupil's pattern of difficulties in learning and behaviour often linked to a combination of sensory, physical, medical and social factors. This individualized approach makes it difficult to analyse broad gender trends and patterns of attainment in special schools, and it takes a constructive, reflective and effortful approach to isolate gender as an area of research interest. However, it should be no surprise to discover some relevant 'gender factors'. Special schools are not divorced from mainstream education and the wider world. Socio-cultural beliefs and pedagogic practices inevitably filter between special and mainstream schools. Parents, teachers and other school staff have perspectives and expectations that cross the boundaries. Pupils may be on inclusion programmes with local mainstream schools and they may have friends, club activities and jobs in the local area.

The findings from the special school projects suggest that a gender impact on the achievement profile in special schools is almost inevitable given the social and biological factors involved, but it is complex, interactive and not easily discernible. It changes from year to year and it occurs for a number of different reasons. However, a simple 'gender' distinction fails to tell the whole story, especially when combined with the slippery definitions of special educational needs and a concern for social justice. As Daniels *et al.* (2000: 64) remark:

> categories are analytical tools with which we understand the social processes we seek to monitor and ultimately change ... We know that boys and girls are not treated in the same way. We do not know whether this is fair. It may well be that we should seek to establish new forms of difference rather than impose sameness.

The question of sameness and difference is central to the discussion of special school practices. Without attempting to generalize too widely, it seems clear from our case examples in Key Stages 3 and 4 that while boys with learning and behavioural difficulties in special schools are in some danger of losing confidence and momentum in their learning, there are useful steps that can be taken over a period of time. Approaches to teaching can match those found to be helpful in mainstream schools, but the variability of pupils' individual needs and the intrinsic nature of certain areas or types of SEN add significant layers to the special school teachers' knowledge and decision-making. There may also be certain contextual factors relating specifically to special schools. New curriculum developments set challenges as well as opportunities (e.g. 14–19 changes and alternative curriculum initiatives). The current inclusion strategy calls on special school staff to make links beyond the school while also contributing to their own school as a learning organization (DfES 2004b). The special school teachers in the project also had specific concerns about the content of initial teacher training and new teachers' skills with pupils with special educational needs.

It is not clear, however, that there exists an entirely separate set of 'special school' issues or practices. This conclusion matches other research findings which provide little evidence for a separate special education pedagogy and suggests that the priority is to use special education knowledge to develop inclusive pedagogy in the current policy context (Davis and Florian 2004). The research presented here suggests that understanding gender factors in combination with special educational needs applies to pupils in any educational setting, and deciding to examine these in particular school contexts can have unexpected, challenging and rewarding results for all involved.

A number of key conclusions can be drawn, then, from the RBA project's work within special school contexts:

- Being willing to ask challenging questions in school: 'Special educational needs' are complex and multifaceted in nature, varying also as a function of gender, ethnicity, cultural practices, social class and the specific school contexts of teaching and learning. It can seem difficult or apparently irrelevant for special school teachers to focus directly on gender when the pupil population in most special schools is so diverse, but a willingness to do so can produce valuable insights when close links are established with teachers' professional concerns, aims and practice. This is the value of 'driving from the bottom'.
- Using a broad concept of 'achievement' with equally broad approaches to gathering data: it is essential to work with a broad, interactive and contextualized understanding of 'achievement' and use an equally broad range of qualitative and quantitative approaches to investigation and measurement – weighing specific performance data against the broadening achievement of individuals. This close attention to pupils' individual achievements and differences also helps to provide a better understanding of the complex processes operating for all pupils in school.
- Using combined, multilevel strategies for intervention: interventions are likely to involve combinations of identifiable strategies, with implications at different levels of the school system and beyond. Strategies directed at transfer between different subjects and contexts may be of particular relevance for pupils in special schools.

- Planning for maintenance while acknowledging the likelihood of uneven progress: the maintenance of most new initiatives requires an investment of time and energy with planning and support in staffing, whole-school development and relationships with pupils and parents. There are likely to be phases of development, often starting with very small steps of progress. It is necessary to integrate new strategies with current interests, policies and priorities, acknowledging the likely impact of pupil cohort changes from year to year.
- Making explicit connections between mainstream and special school practices and procedures: gender may help to explain in general terms why some pupils enter special schools. However, gender in itself does not explain why individual pupils enter special education. Some of the boys who achieve less well in mainstream schools will enter special education, but not all of them. This points to the need for further research on the SEN decision-making processes with explicit reference to the effectiveness of strategies used for raising boys' achievement in mainstream schools.
- Extending collaboration and shared professional development between special and mainstream school colleagues: boys are also boys in special schools, often with full social lives outside school hours. Certain 'mainstream' social and educational influences and practices apply to them, and certain special school teaching strategies seem to match and perhaps extend the approaches for raising achievement being developed in mainstream schools. This is a case for extending the special–mainstream collaboration and shared professional development already in place in many LEAs.

We acknowledge in Chapter 5 that our fourfold classification of intervention strategies (pedagogic, individual, organizational and socio-cultural) is to some degree an artificial construct, and that the strategies are not mutually exclusive; there will be inevitable overlap between the categories in different contexts. This is nowhere better illustrated than in the special schools, where individual and organizational considerations underpin all initiatives, and where it is frequently impossible to separate pedagogic considerations from individual ones, or socio-cultural issues from organizational initiatives; the need for integration of approach is paramount.

11 Policy Directions within an Inclusive Context

In developing policy and advocating intervention strategies which might address the apparent under-achievement of students in secondary schools, we need to be cautious, and alert to the danger of making bold and simplistic assertions. It is important, therefore, to restate a number of perspectives which have become of central importance to us as we have worked on the Raising Boys' Achievement Project:

- *Diversity*: at a simplistic level, the 'boys' under-achievement' debate ignores the diversity of gender constructions which exist within schools and societies, and within which boys and girls operate. Discussions which explore the 'reasons for under-achievement' (Chapter 2) must acknowledge that while many boys negotiate a position with respect to the locally dominant masculinity, which preserves their image and status, some boys *also* devise coping strategies which enable them to achieve; girls do likewise within popular versions of femininity. While these coping strategies are often implicit, they are recognized and articulated by girls and boys, as part of the legitimized local culture, and adopted by some students as part of the strategies which enable them also to achieve and to further their own aspirations. There is a danger, then, in the academic discourse about 'boys' under-achievement', of assuming uncritically that many students identify publicly with an agenda of disengagement. Our work suggests that in some schools this is not the case, with many boys and girls accepting the ethos and aspirations of the school.
- *Multiplicity*: equally, we recognize that in some secondary schools, a gender regime has been established, by staff and students, which values a multiplicity of gender constructions (Chapter 5). This is not blind to the rejection and exclusion which some gay boys and girls experience, but it is clear that in some contexts, gay boys (more so, perhaps, than gay girls) have been recognized *and* accepted as different, seen to have strengths and perspectives to

offer, and incorporated within the 'gender multiculturalism' (Lingard and Douglas 1999) which the school has developed.

- *Under-achievement*: the current emphasis on performance and measures of value-added has raised expectations in some schools and challenged deep-rooted assumptions, held by some teachers, parents and students, about what can be achieved and what is possible, but equally, we must not allow target-setting, from an ever early age, to lull us into the presupposition that current patterns of achievement reflect stable differences in young people's potential which are pre-determined. As we point out in Chapter 3, such a view of ability can lead to students receiving low levels of challenge and intellectual stimulation, and cumulative under-achievement might be the outcome. We emphasize, too, the inappropriateness of framing this discussion within the context of 'under-achievement', when achievement levels in schools – when measured against public examination results – are continually rising.

- Inclusivity: assessment data *do* suggest that more boys than girls currently 'under-achieve' in secondary school, but such 'under-achievement' occurs at all ability levels, and impacts upon girls as well as boys. Girls remain marginalized and invisible in some co-educational schools, and demeaning assumptions are often made about their compliance and their potential. There remains, as we point out in Chapter 4, a powerful and disturbing mismatch between the levels of educational achievement of girls at school and university, and the experiences of many women in our wider society. In our view, therefore, the debate about the gender gap and the 'under-achievement' of boys needs reconceptualizing in terms of promoting achievement for all students. Where this has been the motive force, the gender gap of itself may well not close in the short or medium terms, since 'under-achieving' girls may benefit as much from strategic developments as 'under-achieving' boys.

It is self-evident, then, that this issue of 'under-achievement' is complex and multi-layered. This complexity is exacerbated where schools have a particularly diffuse student intake, in terms of social class, disability, ethnicity and learning needs, as our work with schools in different socio-cultural and socio-economic contexts has revealed only too starkly. Identities of masculinity are then inter-twined with a wide range of ethnic, racial and national identities (Archer and Yamashita 2003; Archer, L. 2004), become tangled with social class variables and with localized images, aspirations and role models (Nayak 2001; Skelton 2001), and can be overlain by self-perceptions. The intersection, in specific localities, of factors of social class, ethnicity and gender (Gillborn and Mirza 2000) adds further dimensions to the intensity of the issue, and exacerbates the sense of challenge which schools face as they try to work with the communities to energize and release potential.

Revisiting the interventions

This acknowledgement that the debate is sophisticated and intricate alerts us against accepting apparent solutions which are short-term and narrowly focused. Indeed, our discussions of the various intervention strategies which we have helped develop, monitor and refine during the span of this project (Chapters 6–10) reveal how all of the strategies are inevitably interwoven and inter-connected. Although we have developed the four-fold typology (pedagogic, organizational, individual and socio-cultural) to emphasize the distinctiveness of different approaches, it has never been our argument that these are free-standing or independent of each other. Indeed, there are frequently pre-conditions for the successful implementation of one strategy which are derived from another. Pedagogic interventions, for example, are unlikely to be effective if certain organizational pre-conditions have not already been established (Chapter 6). Equally, socio-cultural interventions need schools to be proactive as learning organizations and to offer specific pedagogic styles and learning support (Chapter 9) if their transformative potential is to be maximized. Indeed, as made clear in Chapter 5, the inter-linkages between the intervention strategies were one of the challenges we faced in the project, since while some of the approaches in Originator Schools were explicit, other aspects were much more implicit and had become imbued within the culture of the school (Younger *et al.* 2002).

Our work with secondary schools during the course of this project suggests that this analysis through time, with different cohorts of students and in different school localities, is crucial if real and enduring change is to be effected. This is not to say that, in certain circumstances, short-term changes cannot be put into place, but we argue that such changes will have only a limited lasting effect on achievement. The *Breakthrough Project* (DfES/NPDT 2003), for example, worked with the National Primary Care Development model devised from experiences in health care and General Practice in England, to raise boys' achievements through a programme of work which was designed to help teachers make 'rapid, systematic and sustainable improvements' (2003: 16). Giving 124 exemplars of change ideas linked to aspects such as leadership and environment, teaching and learning methods, mentoring and targeted interventions, the Breakthrough project required participating schools to monitor and report attainment, motivation and attendance measures on a monthly basis to track improvements. Currently, the outcomes of such an ambitious project are unclear, but we have reservations, partly because there is little clear evidence to support the project's claim that the changes advocated 'have been tried, tested and implemented *effectively in many successful secondary schools'* (DfES/NPDT 2003: 5: our italics), and partly because we doubt whether the short-term strategy developed within the health care context can be transferred effectively to this complex issue of boys' apparent under-achievement. Indeed, the notion that the intervention strategies addressing such a complex issue can be monitored for effectiveness each month, and subsequent changes then put in place, reinforces our view that this is an oversimplistic approach. Such a view is reinforced by an analysis of much of the exemplification offered to schools, which is centrally located in the recuperative masculinity field and is very boy-focused.

We argue, therefore, that intervention strategies will be most effective when they are developed not within a recuperative masculinity context, but rather address the issue of apparent under-achievement through sustained work with schools, which is developed in the longer term, which takes careful account of different contexts and localities, and which addresses the needs and interests of boys and girls in gender-relational frameworks. Such a view is founded on our experiences of working with schools which are successfully addressing this issue through following an approach which is integrative and holistic, developing strategies within a well-articulated and coherent whole school ethos. At the same time, there is in these schools an identification of the essence of specific intervention strategies, so that analysis can be focused on the specifics of each intervention strategy in turn, and important pre-conditions for transfer and implementation established. It is to a summary of each of these intervention strategies which we will now turn.

Pedagogic approaches

The essence of successful pedagogic approaches, in the eyes of many of the boys and girls we interviewed, is linked to the environment for learning which teachers and students develop together, the rapport they establish with each other, the extent to which 'respectful pedagogies' (Martino and Pallotta-Chiarolli 2003: 209) are established in classrooms. This mutuality of interest places responsibility upon both teachers *and* students:

> If schools are to improve student motivation for learning and reduce behaviour problems and exclusions, there needs to be an effective *dialogue* between staff and students about how to achieve a culture of mutual respect, not just one which adheres to rules of conduct.
>
> (Riley and Docking 2004: 179)

At one level, this acknowledges the attractiveness of short, structured, varied activities in lessons, where there is a degree of support and appropriate challenge to interest and motivate. Equally there is a recognition that students need opportunities, over and again, to talk to each other and to discuss their learning, that sometimes they do not learn because they have not understood *rather* than they have not listened to teachers' instructions, that students and teachers need opportunity to 'talk themselves into understanding' (the Bullock Report, 1975). This cross-references to teaching strategies advocated by the pro-feminist *'Boys Talk'* (MASA 1996), such as role play, hot seating, value and opinion walk continuums, graffiti sheets and journal writing. Thus students speak of the appeal of lessons where: 'You can loosen up a bit more ... some teachers don't like a silent room, and they encourage talk, and that helps learning' (Year 11 boy, West Midlands school).

Respectful pedagogies acknowledge, too, that students do have different profiles in their modes of learning and understanding, which may vary according to time, place and teacher, and that frequently the preferred modes of successful learners do not coincide with preferred modes of learning of disengaged students. As we make clear in Chapter 6, however, we have reservations with an uncritical adoption of work on preferred learning styles. We remain unconvinced of the strength of the evidence to support some of the claims made; we feel there is insufficient acknowledgement of the difficulties involved in defining the learning styles which are accessed by different types of pedagogic activities; we suggest there are dangers implicit in a simplistic interpretation of accelerated learning and multiple intelligences which reduces a complex and multi-faceted issue to a series of concerns related to defining and indulging students' *particular* preferred learning styles.

Equally, however, we do recognize the potential of such an approach to pedagogy when it is properly focused, and when it is located within a framework which emphasizes the processes of learning *and* teaching, and the multiplicity of learning styles involved. This reiterates the mutuality theme associated with 'respectful pedagogies', particularly the need for a variety of activity, with teachers at times planning to access different learners through differentiated activities, and students recognizing and accepting that at times they need to work in learning styles which they might favour less readily, to develop this aspect of their learning profile. In such a context, there is more emphasis on facilitating and enabling learning than on indulging supposedly preferred learning styles.

In terms of actual pedagogy, there is little that is startling or innovative which emerges from students' accounts of quality teaching. Rather, their expectations relate to teachers' ability to establish connections with them, to create a context for learning which is both informal and accessible, to make learning fun: 'he understands where we come from and what we're talking about ... he has "light" rules ... we do the work because he's a good teacher who treats us properly!' (Year 11 girl, Hampshire school). Mutual respect and reciprocity are at the heart of the matter. Students value most highly teachers who show confidence in them and are committed to their learning, who generate self-belief in the students they teach, and convey a sense of enthusiasm and involvement in the work planned for them. In such situations, students recognize the dedication which the teacher is showing to their learning, and acknowledge their dependence:

> It's obvious she does actually care about us as people ... she's interested in us and talks to us properly ... she doesn't put a downer on us ... we feel we *have* to do well, to work for her, to live up to her expectations ... we don't want to let her down because she doesn't let us down.
>
> (Year 11 boy, Sandwell school)

Crucially, these boys and girls – in their identification of successful contexts for learning and teaching – recognize boundaries and indeed value them. In the memorable words of a Year 10 Asian boy in Wolverhampton: 'You wouldn't even think about "pratting around" in Ms P's classes ... but she only has a *real* go at us when we need it! She's safe.'

It is vital to many students that teachers can establish and maintain an ordered classroom for learning, where expectations are well defined and consistently and justly applied, and where teachers are seen to be fair and reasonable. Boundaries also have to be respected by teachers, however; while informality is welcomed, the 'trendy', 'cool' teacher can become despised if they are ineffective in other ways: 'Some teachers try to get close to us, they use "trendy" language which isn't cool any more, they don't keep discipline, they're sad! It's cringing and very embarrassing, just like when your dad thinks he'll talk to your friends!' (Year 11 boy, Norfolk school). Such is the challenge which emerges from these students' views of high quality teaching and teachers. In the view of these students, teachers need to be accessible and informal within clearly defined parameters, to avoid overstepping the line of familiarity, to offer encouragement and support without making the praise too obvious, to raise expectations and aspirations and to create a sense of self-belief in students without 'putting too much pressure on'. This is both demanding and encouraging; it is based on the reality of students' perspectives, on their construction of what *is* possible from their own experiences of teachers and as learners. While the motivation of some teachers is questioned: 'why some teachers want to teach defeats me ... they seem so bored, so we're bored!' (Year 11 girl, North-West England school), there is equally a sense of wonder at the dedication, energy, generosity and enthusiasm shown by so many teachers:

Mr X is a brilliant teacher. He makes the subject fun. He shares all his time and energy between the whole group, not just the boys, nor just the girls. He doesn't flirt at all. He's just a really good teacher, humorous as well.

(Year 11 boy, Cambridgeshire school)

In the words of Rudduck and Flutter, then, 'the qualities that matter to pupils tend to be as much related to how they are treated as how they are taught' (2004: 78).

Whole school organizational issues

Our work on the RBA project has confirmed that single-sex teaching has the potential to motivate and impact positively on the academic achievements of boys and girls. Many boys and girls have valued the experience, and felt more able to question, receive praise and take part in learning activities without fear of ridicule or embarrassment. Equally, though, as we explore in Chapter 8, context is vital, in avoiding stereotypes and the creation of antagonisms against 'different' boys and girls, in maintaining a curriculum which is inclusive for both boys and girls, in developing an effective teaching pedagogy which is not gender-biased, and in creating a sense of rapport, mutual support and collaborative working within single-sex classrooms. It is crucial, too, that single-sex teaching is situated within the ethos of the whole school, with positive and proactive support from senior managers, if it is to be most effective.

Equally, organizational strategies must establish a whole school environment which expects, acknowledges and applauds achievements. In some schools, for example, a leadership (or prefects') system in Year 11 is a key element in affecting both the motivation and self-esteem of students, and subsequent achievement levels (Younger *et al.* 2002). Giving responsibility is regarded as an essential tool in countering any culture of under-achievement, and the leadership system has become a very strong aspect of the ethos of these schools, accessible to all students and based upon high standards of behaviour, work and homework, appearance, and duties carried out conscientiously. Although a prefect system is sometimes seen as elitist, based upon student popularity or passivity (Martino and Pallotta-Chiarolli 2003), the open access to the position in these schools, based upon clearly defined and publicly accepted criteria, meant that the role was prized by virtually all students. In one school, for example, some boys spoke of the feeling of being valued highly within the school, of being *enabled* to show care and concern for others, and of coming to recognize that it was acceptable and legitimate to care and to achieve. Students appreciated being given responsibility, and felt that the school was acknowledging a coming of age, and offering independence and trust. In return, the students offered commitment and involvement, and felt more ready to identify with the aspirations of the school.

A further characteristic of organizational strategies is the emphasis on a high quality of aesthetics around the school environment, with high priority placed on the appearance of the school, particularly on the visual in terms of wall displays of students' work (both in classrooms and in public areas around the school):

> This school is better than my old school, it's more human. It's interested in us and our achievements, it's for us. The way the teachers teach us means we enjoy school. Our work is valued and the walls everywhere are covered with our work, from all of us, even the head's office, there's no space left.
>
> (Year 10 boy, Peterborough school)

Public recognition of success was also high, through Achievement Boards which carried photographs and pen portraits of boys and girls who had achieved success not only in the academic, but also in the sporting, drama, musical and community contexts. Numerous public displays celebrated the achievements of previous cohorts, including photographs of elated students receiving their results and statements made by them about their futures, indicating how the school had helped them to achieve their goals. The aim was to make lads and ladettes proud to be publicly acclaimed and recognized for their achievements, and to establish acceptable and non-stereotypical role models for other students.

A central and recurring theme in our consideration of whole school issues has been, not surprisingly, the role of school leaders and senior staff in establishing an achievement ethos. In some contexts, staff and students have described the forceful impact of a new headteacher, challenging and transforming the aspirations held by many students and their parents and by some staff (Chapter 7), and creating pedagogic scenarios where worthwhile learning activities take place in classrooms (Chapters 8 and 9). Students are *very* clear about the qualities needed in effective headteachers:

> He's always about, always interested, he seems to know us really well; his door is nearly always open at lunchtime, and we can go in and talk to him; if he's not there, there's a sheet showing what he's doing that day, you know, visiting another school perhaps ... and a sheet when we can book to see him the next day. *And* he really seems to love learning!
>
> (Year 11 girl, Norfolk school)

She's really cares and gives her time; she's always in the revision clubs like. We're on really good terms with her because she knows us, she's concerned about us, you know like as people ... she's a good source of advice too, about all sorts of things.

(Year 11 boy, North West England school)

Once again, there is identification here with students which gives them a sense of value and worth, a high level of visibility, an encouraging presence at break-times and lunch-times, with words of support and engagement in informal exchanges with students. In these schools, headteachers have set the tone, offered a rapport to students which contributes to achievement, offered a sense of vision to staff and shown the determination and persistence to see the vision to fruition. There is also a sense of independence in these schools, a confidence to define the local agenda within their own terms and to redefine national priorities so that they can be aligned with the philosophy and ethos of the school. In each of these schools, students are prioritized as people; in different contexts, there are nuanced differences of approach, but the underlying theme, a sense of mutual valuing to foster and support achievement, is common, and there is consistency and uniformity of outcome.

The impact of these organizational strategies reinforces our belief that 'under-achieving' boys and girls are not likely to respond if schools simply concentrate on adopting narrowly focused and quick-fix solutions in isolation from the ethos of the whole school. Students need to feel that the school's ethos is enabling for them, and constructed with their real interests and aspirations in mind, rather than disempowering them or being imposed upon them. Such an ethos has to be consistently enacted through most staff – teachers, administrative and learning support staff – inside and outside the classrooms, if it is to impact positively on students. Thus, students show more willingness to acknowledge the validity of the school's vision and to collaborate with teachers when a rapprochement has been reached with them, when they are able to rationalize and internalize the regime and policies of the school, when rules are seen to have a purpose and logic. Equally, students' resistance, and subsequent lack of engagement in learning, are more likely when rules and regulations are seen to be petty and purposeless, with the emphasis on authority and control for the sake of it rather than in a common agreed purpose.

Thus, issues such as school uniform, hair length, punctuality, consistency of policy towards behaviour, can become flashpoints and foci of conflict, and take on real meaning for students. While most students we interviewed accepted the legitimacy of a reasonable dress code, and acknowledged that the wearing of uniform did help to construct their identity as learners: 'Yeah, uniform does kind of help you remember you're at school ... you're not worrying about fashion, having to buy all the right clothes ... it's not a big stress each day like oh no, what have I got to wear?' (Year 10 boy, East Midlands school), there was a strong resistance in those schools where the detail of the dress code became, in the students' views, obsessional:

> It's too strict, you know ... ties in a certain way, top buttons done up, shirts tucked in, no highlights ... and the punishments for breaking it are too severe ... it's taken to such an extreme, and it doesn't matter, does it, as long as we look smart?
>
> (Year 11 girl, Wolverhampton school)

Hair style, length and colouring, were a particular *bête noire* of students in some schools:

> Now they've done the hair thing for boys as well ... not too long or too short. So it's not just clothes. The clothes you can change when you go home and get into some of your own stuff, but you can't grow or shrink hair whenever you want.
>
> (Year 11 boy, Hampshire school)

Martino and Chiarolli-Pallotta (2003), in documenting similar concerns of boys in the Australian context, note that where schools insisted on a rigid uniform, it became a visual marker of resistance to school authority for many boys, and generated shifting students' strategies of resistance which meant that rules had constantly to be rewritten or redefined. We encountered similar reactions from students in some schools, as summarized by Josh: 'There are stupid rules to rebel against ... it gives you comradeship against the teachers' (Year 10, Yorkshire school).

We are not arguing here that these issues are insignificant in contributing to the school culture and ethos. Indeed, in Chapter 8, we acknowledge that intervention strategies which are based around a particular mode of organization such as single-sex teaching will only be effective when certain school structures and conventions are in place which sustain the school primarily as a place of learning and work. What is noticeable, however, is that these issues can readily become focused sites for conflict in some schools, and direct student and teacher energy away from learning and teaching, and by generating resistance from some students, detract from attempts to construct a caring, achievement-oriented ethos.

Individualized approaches

In Chapter 3, we argued that there are very real dangers, in the current educational climate, of focusing resources on a narrow cohort of students, whose achievements impact significantly on schools' attainment profiles, on their improvement indices and subsequently on their league table positions. In so doing, we have accepted Gillborn and Youdell's (2000) warnings about a new-IQism, and recognized that such an approach, by focusing on 'benchmark borderline' students, frequently devotes more time and support to boys than to girls. At the same time, however, we suggested in Chapter 7 that it *is* possible to develop an approach to target-setting and mentoring which is accessible to students regardless of ability, gender and potential achievement, and which can support students' sense of membership of school and develop their own sense of agency, so that they develop increasing responsibility for their own learning.

The development of such an approach is not without its difficulties: it needs to be structured around detailed and reliable data, which reflect in part historic trends within the school. At the same time, there has to be a recognition that historic trends might embody expectations that are universally too safe and too low, and may incorporate systematic and wide-ranging under-achievement of many students. To be transformative of achievement, therefore, there needs to be an honest and rigorous re-appraisal of expectations, which might mean challenging both the legitimacy of value-added data *and* entrenched staff expectations of the real capabilities of students in particular schools.

Equally, given our discussion in Chapter 2 on contributory factors to under-achievement, and our emphasis on the importance of image and attitude in establishing acceptable models of masculinity and femininity, it is very clear to us that effective mentoring needs to be both collaborative and assertive. The most successful mentoring which we have observed offers a mix of styles from mentors, offering support and guidance, on the one hand, but challenging and demanding, on the other. In such situations, mentors establish and sustain rapport with students, offering general encouragement and support, outlining specific strategies for work and revision, negotiating issues as a third party with subject teachers, and gaining credibility and respect from students. At the same time, such mentoring must be framed within a context which allows those disengaged students to protect their own images and their own construction of masculinity and femininity, to give those students a way of engaging with targets which they frequently acknowledge they need, and indeed, want to meet. They need to be enabled to further their own aspirations, without endangering their own social standing in the peer group. In the words of one head-teacher:

> The best mentors are those who give students a sense of protection, a reason for working; they can blame someone else for having to behave and work, they can rationalise to their mates that they have no choice other than to work because the mentor is monitoring their own progress closely ... they can preserve their self-image in this way.

Many discussions with school colleagues during the Raising Boys' Achievement Project have made us aware that this direct, almost confrontational, aspect to mentoring, does not rest easily with the ethos of some schools. As shown in Chapter 7, however, it *has* been effective in other schools in helping to engage and motivate the disengaged students. In such contexts, it has enabled students to achieve without loss of status and self-esteem, and in so doing, it has helped to transform long-standing patterns of achievement within the school. It has changed perceptions about what *is* possible for boys and girls who might have low prior attainment and of whom staff might historically have low expectations. But, in our experiences, this assertive aspect of mentoring will not be effective if it is isolated from collaborative aspects of mentoring. If students do not believe that mentors are exercising a genuine care and concern for their welfare and achievements, and are not offering them real and effective strategies for learning which will support their own aspirations and ambitions, then mentoring will be seen as counter-productive and condescending. Mentoring must not only be rooted in a concern for students, as individuals, rather than focused upon a concern with raising achievement levels within the school 'for the school's own sake'; it must also be seen by students as having this as its central purpose.

Socio-cultural approaches

It seems to us that a fundamental starting-point, if we are to meet this challenge of raising boys' achievement within a gender equity framework, is the need to understand clearly the motives and behaviours of those students (girls as well as boys) who establish acceptable peer group norms, in terms of image, outlook, aspiration and mindset. It is clear that these students establish standards of behaviour, dress, attitude and opinion which have to be met, sustained and publicly avowed by those boys and girls wishing to gain membership of the group. As discussed in Chapter 2, notions of laddishness and conforming to the demands and expectations of hegemonic masculinity contribute powerfully to such group rules, and frequently override the ambitions and genuine feelings of individual boys; there is emerging evidence, too, that issues of ladettishness are impacting upon an increasing number of girls. These pressures are so powerful, we suggest, that they represent the central challenge which schools must overcome if they are to address 'under-achievement' issues. This is a vital concern, too, because our extensive interviews with individual students suggested that they frequently *did* want to achieve, and wanted the school to help them to take a position and assume an image which would help them to achieve. There is a dilemma here, then, for individual students, as they try to chart an accepted role for themselves, and to negotiate a way through a series of contradictions. Frosh *et al.* identify similar issues: 'Most boys were struggling to negotiate the canonical narrative which opposes popular/hegemonic masculinity and being seen to work hard' (2002: 223). Hence our emphasis, in the title of Chapter 9, on the socio-cultural *key*. Whatever the potential of pedagogic, individual and organizational approaches, this potential will only be maximized in school contexts which have addressed socio-cultural issues, and provided frameworks within which students feel secure to work without losing self-esteem as a member of the group.

As also indicated in Chapter 9, however, these dilemmas and contradictions can be worked out if the school provides structures and frameworks which enable key boys and girls to work and achieve without loss of self-esteem and status within the peer group. This aspect of self-esteem is crucial, since it is not that these students lack self-esteem, but that their self-esteem is constructed through behaviours, achievements and conventions which are often oppositional to those of the school (Skelton 2001). Their badges of masculinity and femininity embody difference and challenge, and are threatening to some teachers who neither understand nor tolerate them (Majors 2001). Their disengagement leads to the lack of any achievement which the school values, and thus while their social esteem might be rising, their self-esteem as learners drops.

Hence the significance of the key leaders/key befrienders scheme, which is predicated on the conviction that these key leaders can be integrated within the school ethos and persuaded that academic achievements are attainable and liberating. At the same time, there is the belief that these key leaders can be harnessed to become a powerful force for positive change within the whole school. Our research suggests that it is vital that senior staff in schools, particularly those in key pastoral roles, know their year groups well enough to be able to identify, shrewdly and perceptively, those students who really *are* the key leaders in any year. This is no easy task, since this group of students may exhibit different characteristics from school to school, and while it is unlikely to be conformist, it need not necessarily be identified in terms of outright challenge and an anti-work culture. In one school, for example, the key leaders, mostly male, were characterized by arrogance and a strong charismatic presence which drew in significant numbers of high achieving girls. In another, the dominant group were described as 'bright sporty white working-class boys *and* girls who have been persuaded to see achievement as cool'. In a third school, the key players were seen as 'certainly not high flyers ... a dozen boys and girls in all, who were attention-seeking and easily abusive when not handled well, more likely to be confrontational but not *that* problematic in terms of getting them on board'. In each case, alert and accurate identification of those individuals and small groups of students in leadership roles within the peer group had enabled each school to respond to these students, to identify staff who were best positioned to work with them and for them, and to provide credible leadership for these students within the school.

This discussion relates back to the starting-point of this chapter, and our caution against regarding the different strategies within our four-fold typology as independent of each other. The socio-cultural context is a highly complex one, and so many aspects of the school's life contribute to it. The school's approach to target-setting and mentoring can enable key students to identify with *or* to reject the support which the school is offering; the teaching styles of all the staff who teach these students can increase their involvement in learning *or* alienate them further; single-sex teaching can open up new contexts for learning *or* it can degenerate and restrict learning; any student leadership system can increase a sense of valuing, foster self-esteem and integrate these students *or* it can add to disenchantment and disengagement where it is not accessible to these students. All of these aspects contribute directly to creating a community where achievement, in all its forms, is viewed as a legitimate goal, and where boys and girls develop more confidence and self-esteem as learners.

Conclusion

> We shall not cease from exploration
> And the end of all our exploring
> Will be to arrive where we started
> And know the place for the first time.
>
> (T.S. Eliot, Little Gidding)

We have attempted, through this focus on secondary schools in different parts of England, to explore the distinctiveness of practice-oriented work in schools which appears to have been successful in raising the achievements of students, both boys and girls, and to identify pre-conditions which appear necessary if that practice is to be successfully transferred into other schools. At the same time, we have tried to frame this exploration within a context which is informed by theoretical-oriented research both on masculinities and laddishness, and by reference to the needs and legitimate interests of girls. Working together with school colleagues, we have analysed, refined and subsequently developed these intervention strategies within gender inclusive and gender-relational contexts. Throughout, we have tried to develop approaches to raising achievement which are seen to be relevant and realistic within daily school practice, but which are consistent with the insights and understandings provided by the theoretical base, to allow each to inform the other in meaningful ways.

We are convinced, however, that – in some senses at least – we have arrived back where we started, in that the more we have explored this issue of raising (boys') achievement, the more complex and multi-faceted it has become. If we place more emphasis on issues of ethnicity, social class and disability, then the issue becomes even more complex, and we are very aware that we have had insufficient scope or resource to place enough emphasis on these important aspects. *'Do we know the place better?'* is, of course, the crucial question. We hope that readers will feel that we do and that *they* do, that we have opened up the theoretical base in an accessible and meaningful way, and that readers can identify with the complexity of the issues we outline in our first four chapters. We have tried to identify a coherent philosophical approach to the issue, which is articulated and consistently developed in the practice-based Chapters (6–10). Our intention has been to develop an approach which challenges some current notions of under-achievement, and which is true to the concepts of diversity, multiplicity, and inclusivity which we summarize at the start of this chapter.

Certainly, we feel *we know the place better* because we are clear in our own minds, on the basis of an analysis of practice and outcomes through time, that this issue of raising (boys') achievements is a much more challenging issue than is assumed by many of those who offer solutions within the recuperative masculinity field. Such an approach is attractive, as Lingard and Douglas point out in their incisive critique of the approach, because it offers 'simple and seemingly commonsense answers to complex issues' (1999: 153), but with them, we question whether mechanistic and narrowly-defined approaches have real impact on longer-term learning, attitudes and engagement. On the contrary, our experiences within the Raising Boys' Achievement Project lead us to assert that changes which are to have real and long-term impact, on practice within schools and on individuals as learners through their life cycle, take time to become embedded if they are to be sustained and work effectively. We question, too, whether short-term approaches within the recuperative masculinity context enable boys to address and change issues of behaviour, relationships and aspirations, which girls tell us they would particularly welcome. There is a danger in all these approaches of exacerbating what Kenway *et al.* (1998) call the 'hope and happening gap'!

We know the place better, too, we suggest, because in advocating and helping to develop approaches which are more gender-inclusive and which promote gender equity, we have arrived at a number of intervention strategies which are informed by a number of common principles. In these approaches, there is a fundamental recognition that if disengaged and perhaps under-achieving boys and girls are to be more fully engaged with schooling and with learning, they need both to feel secure and valued within the school context, and to be enabled, through persuasion, support and direction, to develop a sense of esteem and self-worth as learners and as people. Crucially, the school has to open up aspirations and raise expectations, to show that achievement can lead to new opportunities which might not be part of the community or peer group tradition of expectation.

Such an approach can help students to develop a sense of agency which offers choice and confers responsibility, to identify with the school's aims and aspirations for them as students, and thus to develop a sense of belonging and membership of school. But this sense of agency and belonging will not be generated in the short term; again, in our experience, it evolves in those schools where there is a clear sense of vision and determined leadership, and a commitment to persist and sustain initiatives through time, where successful practice can be informed by – and subsequently informs – the theoretical base.

Finally, we think *we know the place better* because we have a better idea of the nature of the challenges which schools need to face if they are to raise the achievement of more disengaged students within a gender inclusivity context:

1   to value the individual, genuinely and in practice, without stereotyping, gender-blindness or pre-suppositions about attitude, behaviour or potential for achievement;
2   to develop a holistic approach which integrates pedagogic, individual, organizational and socio-cultural interventions and with which most staff, whatever their role in the school, can identify;
3   to balance persuasion and collaboration, on the one hand, with assertiveness and direction, on the other, so that students feel that the school places value and worth on them for themselves, while at the same time it does not expose them through a loss of self-esteem and self-image;
4   to address issues of laddish and ladettish behaviour, so that boys and girls are allowed and enabled, even, to construct defence mechanisms to protect their own sense of self-worth, in ways which are recognized and acknowledged implicitly as such by the school rather than openly challenged;
5   to avoid developing approaches to raising boys' achievement which problematize boys and label all boys as 'a problem', thereby perpetuating a myth, establishing a vicious cycle of downward expectations within boys and some teachers themselves, and adding to the feelings of resentment and exclusion which some boys carry.

References

Anon (1998) Grim reading for males, *The Guardian*, editorial, 6 January.

Apple, M. (2001) *Educating the 'Right' Way: Markets, Standards, God and Inequality*. London and New York: RoutledgeFalmer.

Archer, J. (2004) The trouble with 'doing boy', *The Psychologist*, 17: 132–6.

Archer, J. and Lloyd, B.B. (2002) *Sex and Gender*. Cambridge: Cambridge University Press.

Archer, L. (2004) *Race, Masculinity and Schooling*. Buckingham: Open University Press.

Archer, L. and Yamashita, H. (2003) Theorising inner-city masculinities: 'race', class, gender and education, *Gender and Education*, 15: 115–32.

Arnot, M. (1984) How shall we educate our sons? in R. Deem (ed.) *Co-education Reconsidered*. Milton Keynes: Open University Press.

Arnot, M. (2002) *Reproducing Gender? Essays on Educational Theory and Feminist Politics*. London: RoutledgeFalmer.

Arnot, M., David, M. and Weiner, G. (1996) *Educational Reforms and Gender Equality in Schools*. Manchester: Equal Opportunities Commission.

Arnot, M., David, M. and Weiner, G (1999) *Closing the Gender Gap: Postwar Education and Social Change*. Cambridge: Polity Press.

Arnot, M., Gray, J., James, M. and Rudduck, J. (1998) *Recent Research on Gender and Educational Performance*. London: Office for Standards in Education.

Arnot, M. and Weiner, G. (eds) (1987) *Gender and the Politics of Schooling*. London: Hutchinson.

Askew, S. and Ross, C. (1988) *Boys Don't Cry: Boys and Sexism in Education*. Milton Keynes: Open University Press.

Aveling, N. (2002) 'Having it all' and the discourse of equal opportunity: reflections on choices and changing perceptions, *Gender and Education*, 14: 265–80.

Ball, S. and Gewirtz, S. (1997) Girls in the education market: choice, competition and complexity, *Gender and Education*, 9: 207–22.

Barker, B. (1997) Girls' world or anxious times: what's really happening at school in the gender war? *Educational Review*, 49: 221–8.

Baron-Cohen, S. (2003) *Men, Women and the Extreme Male Brain.* London: Penguin.

Barton, A. (2000) Raising boys' achievement in modern foreign languages through single-sex grouping, paper presented at the British Educational Research Association Annual Conference, University of Cardiff, September.

Bell, D. (2004) The achievement of girls, speech to the Fawcett Society, 8 March.

Benjamin, S. (2003) Gender, 'special educational needs' and inclusion, in M. Nind, K. Sheehy and K. Simmons (eds) *Inclusive Education: Learners and Learning Contexts.* London: Fulton.

Benioff, S. (1997) *A Second Chance: Developing Mentoring and Education Projects for Young People.* London: Commission for Racial Equality/Crime Concern.

Biddulph, S. (1998) *Raising Boys: Why Boys are Different – and How to Help Them Become Happy and Well-Balanced Men.* Sydney: Finch.

Black, P. and Wiliam, D. (1998) *Inside the Black Box: Raising Standards through Classroom Assessment.* London: King's College School of Education.

Blankenhorn, D. (1996) *Fatherless America: Confronting Our Most Urgent Social Problem.* New York: HarperCollins.

Bleach, K. (1998) *Raising Boys' Achievement in Schools.* Stoke-on-Trent: Trentham Books.

Blunkett, D. (2000) quoted in 'Single sex classes to help failing boys', *The Observer*, 20 August.

Boaler, J. (1997) Reclaiming school mathematics: the girls fight back, *Gender and Education*, 9: 285–305.

Bohan, J. (1997) Regarding gender: essentialism, constructionism and feminist psychology, in M. Gergen and S. Davis (eds) *Towards a New Psychology of Gender.* London: Routledge.

Bornbolt, L., Goodnow, J. and Cooney, G. (1994) Influence of gender stereotypes on adolescents' perceptions of their own achievement, *American Educational Research Journal*, 31: 675–92.

Bradford, W. (1996) *Raising Boys' Achievements.* Kirklees: Kirklees Education Advisory Service.

Bright, M. (1998) 'Girls really are better than boys – official', The *Observer*, 4 January.

Browne, R. and Fletcher, R. (eds) (1995) *Boys in Schools: Addressing the Real Issues – Behaviour, Values and Relationships.* Sydney: Finch.

Bullock Report (1975) *Language for Life.* London: DES.

Burgess, A. (1990) Co-education: the disadvantage for girls, *Gender and Education*, 2: 91–5.

Butler, J. (1990) *Gender Trouble: Feminism and the Subversion of Identity.* London: Routledge.

Byrne, E. (1999) *Social Exclusion.* Buckingham: Open University Press.

Cameron, D. (1998/99) Could do better, *Trouble and Strife*, Winter 1998/99: 46–53.

Carrington, B. and Skelton, C. (2003) Re-thinking 'role models': equal opportunities in teacher recruitment in England and Wales, *Journal of Education Policy*, 18: 253–65.

Clark, A. and Trafford, J. (1995) Boys and modern languages: an investigation of the discrepancy in attitudes and performance between boys and girls in modern languages, *Gender and Education*, 7: 315–25.

Cline, T. and Ertubey, C. (1997) The impact of gender on primary teachers' evaluations of children's difficulties in school, *British Journal of Educational Psychology*, 67: 447–56.

Coffield, F., Moseley, D., Hall, E. and Ecclestone, K. (2004) *Should We Be Using Learning Styles? What Research Has to Say to Practice*. London: Learning and Skills Research Centre.

Cohen, M. (1996) Is there space for the achieving girl? in P. Murphy and C. Gipps (eds) *Equity in the Classroom: Towards Effective Pedagogy for Girls and Boys*. London: Falmer Press.

Cohen, M. (1998) 'A habit of healthy idleness': boys' underachievement in historical perspective, in D. Epstein, J. Elwood, V. Hey and J. Maw (eds) *Failing Boys? Issues in Gender and Achievement*. Buckingham: Open University Press.

Colley, H. (2003a) Engagement mentoring for 'disaffected' youth: a new model of mentoring for social inclusion, *British Educational Research Journal*, 29: 521–42.

Colley, H. (2003b) *Mentoring for Social Inclusion: A Critical Approach to Nurturing Mentor Relationships*. London: RoutledgeFalmer.

Collins, C., Kenway, J. and McLeod, J. (2000) *Factors Influencing the Educational Performance of Males and Females in School and their Initial Destinations after School*. Adelaide: Deakin University.

Connell, R. (1989) Cool guys, swots and wimps: the interplay of masculinity and education, *Oxford Review of Education*, 15: 291–303.

Connell, R. (1995) *Masculinities*. Cambridge: Polity Press.

Connell, R. (2000) *The Men and the Boys*. Cambridge: Polity Press.

Connell, R., Ashenden, D.J., Kessler, S. and Dowsett, G.W. (1982) *Making the Difference: School, Families and Social Divisions*. London: George Allen and Unwin.

Connellan, J., Baron-Cohen, S., Wheelwright, S., Batki, A. and Ahluwalia, J. (2000) Sex differences in human neonatal social perception, *Infant Behaviour and Development*, 23: 113–18.

Covington, M.V. (1998) *The Will to Learn: A Guide for Motivating Young People*. Cambridge: Cambridge University Press.

Croll, P. and Moses, D. (2000) *Special Needs in the Primary School: One in Five?* London: Cassell.

Daniels, H., Hey, V., Leonard, D. and Smith, M. (2000) Issues of equity in special needs education as seen from the perspective of gender, in H. Daniels (ed.) *Special Education Re-formed: Beyond Rhetoric?* London: Falmer Press.

Davis, P. and Florian, L. (2004) *Teaching Strategies and Approaches for Pupils with Special Educational Needs: A Scoping Study.* London: DfES.

Davies, L. (1984) *Pupil Power.* Lewes: Falmer Press.

Davison, K.G. (2000) Boys' bodies in school: physical education, *The Journal of Men's Studies,* 8: 255–66.

Deem, R. (1980) *Schooling for Women's Work.* London: Routledge and Kegan Paul.

Deem, R. (1984) *Co-education Reconsidered.* Milton Keynes: Open University Press.

Delamont, S. (1999) Gender and the discourse for derision, *Research Papers in Education,* 14: 3–21.

Delamont, S. (2000) Review essay: three inequalities in search of a solution? *British Educational Research Journal,* 26: 423–4.

DfEE (2000) *The Connexions Strategy Document.* Nottingham: DfEE.

DfEE (2001a) *Supporting the Target Setting Process.* London. DfEE.

DfES (2001b) *Key Stage 3: The National Strategy.* London: DfES.

DfES (2001c) *Special Educational Needs Code of Practice.* London: DfES.

DfES (2002) *The Autumn Package, 2002: Pupil Performance Information.* London: DfES.

DfES/NPDT (2003) *National Education Breakthrough Programme for Raising Boys' Achievement in Secondary Schools.* London/Manchester: DfES Innovation Unit/National Primary Care Development Team.

DfES (2004a) *Key Stage 2 to GCSE/GNVQ: The Value Added Pilot.* London: DfES.

DfES/The London Challenge (2004b) *Key Stage 3 National Strategy: Ensuring the Attainment of Black Caribbean Boys.* London: DfES.

DfES (2004c) *Participation Rates in Higher Education for the Academic Years 1999/00–2002/03,* SFR07/2004.

DfES (2004d) www.standards.dfes.gov.uk/thinkingskills/resources. Accessed 9 August, 2004.

DfES (2004e) *The Autumn Package, 2004: Pupil Performance Information.* London: DfES.

DfES (2004f) *Statistical First Release (SFR 44/2004).* London: DfES.

DfES (2004g) *Removing Barriers to Achievement: The Government's Strategy for SEN.* London: DfES.

DfES (2005) *National Curriculum Assessment and GCSE/GNVQ Attainment by Pupil Characteristics in England, 2004.* London: DfES. 29005: www.dfes.gov.uk/rsgateway/DB/SFR/s000564. Accessed 25 February.

Dunn, R. (2003) Epilogue: so what? in R. Dunn and S. Griggs (eds) *Synthesis of the Dunn and Dunn Learning Styles Model Research: Who, What, When,*

Where and So What – the Dunn and Dunn Learning Styles Model and its Theoretical Cornerstone. New York: St John's University.

Dweck, C.S. (1986) Motivational processes affecting learning, *American Psychologist*, 41: 1040–8.

Dweck, C.S. (1999) *Self-Theories: Their Role in Motivation, Personality and Development*. Hove: Taylor and Francis.

Eliot, T.S. (1944) *Four Quartets*. London: Faber and Faber.

Elwood, J. and Gipps, C. (1999) *Review of Recent Research on the Achievement of Girls in Single-sex Schools*. London: Institute of Education.

Epstein, D., Elwood. J., Hey, V. and Maw, J. (1998) *Failing Boys? Issues in Gender and Achievement*. Buckingham: Open University Press.

Epstein, D. and Johnson, R. (1998) *Schooling Sexualities*. Buckingham: Open University Press.

Evans, J., Harden, A. and Thomas, J. (2004) What are effective strategies to support pupils with emotional and behavioural difficulties (EBD) in mainstream primary schools? Findings from a systematic review of research, *Journal of Research in Special Educational Needs*, 4: 2–16.

Faulkner, J. (1991) Mixed-sex schooling and equal opportunities for girls: a contradiction in terms?, *Research Papers in Education*, 6: 197–223.

Fennema, E. (1996) Scholarship, gender and mathematics, in P.F. Murphy and C.V. Gipps (eds) *Equity in the Classroom: Towards Effective Pedagogy for Girls and Boys*. London: Falmer Press.

Fergusson, D.L. and Horwood, L.J. (2003) Resilience to childhood adversity: results of a 21-year study, in S.S. Luthar (ed.) *Resilience and Vulnerability: Adaptation in the Context of Childhood Adversities*. Cambridge: Cambridge University Press.

Finney, J. (2003) From resentment to enchantment: what a class of thirteen year olds and their music teacher tell us about a musical education, *International Journal of Education and the Arts*, 4: 1–23.

Fisher, J. (1994) The case for girls-only schools, *Education Review*, 8: 49–50.

Fitz-Gibbon, C.T. (1996) *Monitoring Educational Indicators Quality and Effectiveness*. London: Cassell.

Florian, L., Rouse, M., Black-Hawkins, K. and Jull, S. (2004) What can national data sets tell us about inclusion and pupil achievement? *British Journal of Special Education*, 31: 115–21.

Foster, V. (1992) Different but equal? Dilemmas in the reform of girls' education, *Australian Journal of Educaton*, 36: 53–67.

Foster, V., Kimmel, M. and Skelton, C. (2001) 'What about the boys?' An overview of the debates, in W. Martino and B. Meyenn (eds) *What about the Boys? Issues of Masculinity in Schools*. Buckingham: Open University Press.

Francis, B. (2000a) *Boys, Girls and Achievement: Addressing the Classroom Issues*. London: Routledge Falmer.

Francis, B. (2000b) The gendered subject: students' subject preferences and discussions of gender and subject ability, *Oxford Review of Education*, 26: 35–48.

Francis, B. and Skelton, C. (2001) *Investigating Gender: Contemporary Perspectives in Education*. Buckingham: Open University Press.

Frank, B., Kehler, M., Lovell, T. and Davison, K. (2003) A tangle of trouble: boys, masculinity and schooling – future directions, *Educational Review*, 55: 119–33.

Freides, D. (2001) *Developmental Disorders: A Neuropsychological Approach*. Oxford: Blackwell.

Frosh, S., Phoenix, A. and Pattman, R. (2002) *Young Masculinities*. Basingstoke: Palgrave.

Gallagher, A.M. (1997) *Educational Achievement and Gender: A Review of Research Evidence on the Apparent Under-achievement of Boys*. Department of Education, Northern Ireland: Research Report No. 6.

Gardner, C., Grove, J. and Sharp, D. (1999) *Solihull Boys Achievement Project*. Solihull: Solihull Metropolitan Borough Council.

Gardner, H. (1983) *Frames of Mind*. New York: Basic Books.

Gardner, H. (1999) *Intelligence Reframed: Multiple Intelligences for the 21st Century*. New York: Basic Books.

Gilbert, P. and Gilbert, R. (1998) *Masculinity Goes to School*. London: Routledge.

Gilbert, P. and Gilbert, R. (2001) Masculinity, inequality and post-school opportunities: disrupting oppositional politics about boys' education, *International Journal of Inclusive Education*, 5: 1–13.

Gillborn, D. and Mirza, H.S. (2000) *Educational Inequality: Mapping Class, Race and Gender, a Synthesis of Research Evidence*. London: Office for Standards in Education.

Gillborn, D. and Youdell, D. (2000) *Rationing Education: policy, practice, reform and equity*. Buckingham: Open University Press.

Gillibrand, E., Robinson, P. and Brawn, R. (1999) Girls' participation in physics in single-sex classes in mixed schools in relation to confidence and achievement, *International Journal of Science Education*, 21: 349–62.

Gipps, C. (1996) Review and conclusions: a pedagogy or a range of pedagogic strategies? in P. Murphy and C. Gipps (eds) *Equity in the Classroom: Towards Effective Pedagogy for Girls and Boys*. London: Falmer Press.

Gipps, C. and Murphy, P. (1994) *A Fair Test? Assessment, Achievement and Equity*. Buckingham: Open University Press.

Gold, K. (1995) Hard times for Britain's lost boys, *New Scientist*, 4 February.

Golden, S. (2000) *The Impact and Outcomes of Mentoring*. Slough: NFER.

Golden, S. and Sims, D. (1999) *Evaluation of the National Mentoring Network Bursary Programme 1998/99*. Slough: NFER.

Goldstein, H. (2001) Using pupil performance data for judging schools and teachers: scope and limitations, *British Educational Research Journal*, 27: 433–42.

Gorard, S. (2000) *Education and Social Justice*. Cardiff: University of Wales Press.

Gorard, S., Rees, G. and Salisbury, J. (1999) Reappraising the apparent underachievement of boys at school, *Gender and Education*, 11: 441–54.

Gorard, S., Rees, G. and Salisbury, J. (2001) Investigating the pattern of differential achievement of boys and girls at school, *British Educational Research Journal*, 27: 125–39.

Gordon, T. (1996) Citizenship, difference and marginality in schools: spatial and embodied aspects of gender construction, in P. Murphy and C. Gipps (eds) *Equity in the Classroom: Towards Effective Pedagogy for Girls and Boys*. London: Falmer Press.

Goss, P. (2003) The gender mix among staff in schools for pupils with severe and profound and multiple learning difficulties and its impact, *British Journal of Special Education*, 30: 87–92.

Gray, J., Goldstein, H. and Jesson, D. (1996) Changes and improvements in schools' effectiveness: trends over five years, *Research Papers in Education*, 11: 35–51.

Gray, J., Goldstein, H. and Thomas, S. (2003) Of trends and trajectories: searching for patterns in school improvement, *British Educational Research Journal*, 29: 83–8.

Gray, J., Hopkins, D., Reynolds, D., Wilcox, B., Farrell, S. and Jesson, D. (1999) *Improving Schools: Performance and Potential*. Buckingham: Open University Press.

Gray, J. and Wilcox, B. (1995) *Good School, Bad School: Evaluating Performance and Encouraging Improvement*. Buckingham: Open University Press.

Gregorc, A.F. (1985) *Style Delineator: A Self-Assessment Instrument for Adults*. Columbia: Gregorc Associates Inc.

Griffin, C. (1985) *Typical Girls? Young Women from School to the Job Market*. London: Routledge and Kegan Paul.

Griffiths, M. (1998) Social justice in school, *British Educational Research Journal*, 24: 301–16.

Guardian, The (1998) Grim reading for males, *The Guardian*, Editorial, 6 January.

Gurian, M. (1998) *A Fine Young Man: What Parents, Mentors and Educators Can Do to Shape Adolescent Boys into Exceptional Men*. New York: Jeremy P Tarcher/Putnam.

Gurian, M. (2001) *Boys and Girls Learn Differently!* San Francisco: Jossey-Bass.

Hall, E. (2004) Researching learning styles, *Teaching Thinking*, Spring: 28–35.

Halstead, M. (1991) Radical feminism, Islam and the single-sex school debate, *Gender and Education*, 3: 263–78.

Hammersley, M. (2001) Obvious, all too obvious? Methodological issues in using sex/gender as a variable in educational research, in B. Francis and C. Skelton (eds) *Investigating Gender: Contemporary Perspectives in Education*. Buckingham: Open University Press.

Hannan, G. (1997) *The Gender Game and How to Win It*. London: G. Hannan.

Hannan, G. (1999) *Improving Boys' Performance*. London: Folens.

Harker, R. (2000) Achievement, gender and the single sex/coed debate, *British Journal of Sociology of Education*, 21:203–18.

Harris, S., Wallace, G. and Rudduck, J. (1995) 'It's not just that I haven't learnt much. It's just that I don't understand what I'm doing': metacognition and secondary school students, *Research Papers in Education: Policy and Practice*, 10: 254–71.

Hart, S., Dixon, A., Drummond, M.J. and McIntyre, D. (2004) *Learning without Limits*. Maidenhead: Open University Press.

Hawkes, T. (2001) *Boy Oh Boy: How to Raise and Educate Boys*. Sydney: Pearson Education.

Hay McBer (2000) *Research into Teacher Effectiveness*. London: DfEE.

Hayes, D. (2002) Wanted – more male primary teachers, *Times Educational Supplement*, 22 April.

Haywood, C. and Mac an Ghaill, M. (2003) *Men and Masculinities*. Buckingham: Open University Press.

Head, J. (1996) Gender identity and cognitive style, in P.F. Murphy and C.V. Gipps (eds), *Equity in the Classroom: Towards Effective Pedagogy for Girls and Boys*. London: Falmer Press.

Henry, J. (2002) Anxiety as able girls are demoted, *Times Education Supplement*, 18 January.

Henry, J. (2003) 'Ladette' culture blamed for rise in young girls being locked up, *Daily Telegraph*, 7 September.

Herbert, M. (2005) *Developmental Problems of Childhood and Adolescence: Prevention, Treatment and Training*. Oxford: BPS Blackwell.

HESA (Higher Education Statistics Agency) (2004) *Qualifications Obtained By and Examination Results of Higher Education Students at Higher Education Institutions in the UK for the Academic Years 2002/3*. London: HESA.

Hey, V., Creese, A., Daniels, H., Fielding, S. and Leonard, D. (2000) Questions of collaboration and competition in English primary schools: pedagogic sites for constructing learning, masculinities and femininities, paper presented to British Association Educational Research Conference, Cardiff, September.

Hill, J. (1994) The paradox of gender: sex stereotyping within statementing procedure, *British Educational Research Journal*, 20: 345–55.

Hillman, J. and Pearce, N. (1998) *Wasted Youth*. London: IPPR.

Hirom, K. and Mitchell, G. (1999) The effect of mentoring on the academic achievement of boys, paper presented to BERA Annual Conference, Sussex, September.

House of Representatives Standing Committee on Education and Training (2002) *Boys: Getting It Right: Report on the Inquiry into the Education of Boys*. Canberra: Parliament of the Commonwealth of Australia.

Jackson, C. (1999) Underachieving boys? Some points for consideration, *Curriculum*, 20: 80–5.

Jackson, C. (2002) 'Laddishness' as a self-worth protection strategy, *Gender and Education*, 14: 37–51.

Jackson, C. (2003) Motives for 'laddishness' at school: fear of failure and fear of the 'feminine', *British Educational Research Journal*, 29: 583–98.

Jackson, C. (2004) 'Wild' girls? An exploration of 'ladette' cultures in secondary schools, paper presented at British Educational Research Association Conference. Manchester, September.

Jackson, C. and Smith, I. (2000) Poles apart? An exploration of single-sex and mixed-sex educational environments in Australia and England, *Educational Studies*, 26: 409–21.

Jackson, D. and Salisbury, J. (1996) Why should secondary schools take working with boys seriously?, *Gender and Education*, 8: 103–15.

James, M. (1998) *Using Assessment for School Improvement*. London: Heinemann.

Johannesson, I.A. (2004) To teach boys and girls: a pro-feminist perspective on the boys' debate in Iceland, *Educational Review*, 56: 33–42.

Jones, B. and Jones, G. (2001) *Boys' Performance in Modern Foreign Languages*. London: CILT.

Kehily, M.J. (2001) Issues of gender and sexuality in schools, in B. Francis and C. Skelton (eds) *Investigating Gender: Contemporary Perspectives in Education*. Buckingham: Open University Press.

Kehily, M.J. and Nayak, A. (1997) Lads and laughter: humour and the production of heterosexual hierarchies, *Gender and Education*, 9: 69–87.

Kenway, J. (1995) Masculinities in schools: under siege, on the defensive and under reconstruction? *Discourse: Studies in the Cultural Politics of Education*, 16: 59–79.

Kenway, J. (1997) Taking stock of gender reform policies for Australian schools: past, present and future, *British Educational Research Journal*, 23: 329–44.

Kenway, J. and Fitzclarence, L. (1997) Masculinity, violence and schooling: challenging 'poisonous pedagogies', *Gender and Education*, 9: 117–33.

Kenway, J. and Willis, S. with Blackmore, J. and Rennie, L. (1998) *Answering Back: Girls, Boys and Feminism in School*. London: Routledge.

Kershner, R. (2003) Intelligence, in J. Beck and M. Earl (eds) *Key Issues in Secondary Education*. London: Continuum.

Klein, P. (2003) Rethinking the multiplicity of cognitive resources and curricular representations: alternatives to 'learning styles' and 'multiple intelligences', *Journal of Curriculum Studies*, 35: 45–81.

Kolb, D.A. (1999) *The Kolb Learning Style Inventory*, version 3. Boston: Hay Group.

Kruse, A-M. (1996) Single-sex settings; pedagogies for girls and boys in Danish schools, in P. Murphy and C. Gipps (eds) *Equity in the Classroom: Towards Effective Pedagogy for Girls and Boys*. London: Falmer Press.

Lafrance, M. (1991) School for scandal: different educational experiences for females and males, *Gender and Education*, 3: 3–13.

Lamb, C. (1996) Gender differences in Mathematics participation in Australian schools: some relationships with social class and school policy, *British Educational Research Journal*, 22: 223–40.

Lebor, O. (2003) Boys' 'under-achievement' in Malaysian schools and universities, personal correspondence, March 2003.

Lee, A. (1996) *Gender, Literacy, Curriculum: Rewriting School Geography*. London: Taylor and Francis.

Lee, V. and Marks, H. (1992) Who goes where? Choice of single-sex and coeducational independent secondary schools, *Sociology of Education*, 65: 226–35.

Lee-Potter, E. (2003) Rescue plan for the weaker sex, *Secondary Education*, 3 April.

Lees, S. (1993) *Sugar and Spice: Sexuality and Adolescent Girls*. London: Hutchinson.

Leonard, D. (1996) The debate around co-education, in S. Kemal, D. Leonard, M. Pringle and S. Sadeque (eds) *Targeting Underachievement: Boys or Girls*. London: Institute of Education, CREG.

Lewis, A. and Norwich, B. (eds) (2005) *Special Teaching for Special Children? Pedagogies for Inclusion*. Maidenhead: Open University Press.

Lingard, R. and Douglas, P. (1999) *Men Engaging Feminisms: Pro-Feminism, Backlashes and Schooling*. Buckingham: Open University Press.

Lucey, H. (2000) Social class, gender and schooling, in B. Francis and C. Skelton (eds) *Investigating Gender: Contemporary Perspectives in Education*. Buckingham: Open University Press.

Mac an Ghaill, M. (1994) *The Making of Men: Masculinities, Sexualities and Schooling*. Buckingham: Open University Press.

MacBeath, J., Demetriou, H., Rudduck, J. and Myers, K. (2003) *Consulting Pupils: A Toolkit for Teachers*. Cambridge: Pearson Publishing.

Macrae, S. and Maguire, M. (2000) All change, no change: gendered regimes in the post-sixteen setting, in J. Salisbury and S. Riddell (eds) *Gender, Policy and Educational Change*. London: Routledge.

Mahony, P. (1985) *Schools for the Boys? Co-education Reassessed*. London: Hutchinson.

Majors, R. (2001) *Educating Our Black Children*. London: RoutledgeFalmer.

Malcolm, L. and Haddock, L. (1992) "Make trouble: get results": provision for girls in support services, *Educational Psychology in Practice*, 8: 97–100.

Martino, W. (1995) Boys and literacy: exploring the construction of hegemonic masculinities and the formation of literate capacities for boys in the English classroom, *English in Australia*, 112: 11–24.

Martino, W. (1999) 'Cool boys', 'party animals', 'squids' and 'poofters': interrogating the dynamics and politics of adolescent masculinities in school, *British Journal of Sociology of Education*, 20: 239–63.

Martino, W. (2001) 'Powerful people aren't usually real kind, friendly, open people!' Boys interrogating masculinities at school, in W. Martino and B. Meyenn (eds) *What about the boys? Issues of masculinity and schooling*. Buckingham: Open University Press.

Martino, W. and Berrill, D. (2003) Boys, schooling and masculinities: interrogating the 'right' ways to educate boys, *Educational Review*, 55: 99–117.

Martino, W. and Meyenn, B. (2001) *What about the boys? Issues of masculinity and schooling*. Buckingham: Open University Press.

Martino, W. and Meyenn, B. (2002) 'War, guns and cool, tough things': interrogating single-sex classes as a strategy for engaging boys in English, *Cambridge Journal of Education*, 32: 302–24.

Martino, W. and Pallotta-Chiarolli, M. (2003) *So What's a Boy? Addressing Issues of Masculinity and Schooling*. Buckingham: Open University Press.

MASA (Men Against Sexual Assault) (1996) *Boys-Talk: A Program for Young Men about Masculinity, Non-Violence and Relationships*. Adelaide: Kookaburra Press.

Matthews, B. (1998) Co-education, boys, girls and achievement, in K. Bleach (ed.) *Raising Boys' Achievement in Schools*. Stoke-on-Trent: Trentham Books.

McDonagh, P. (2000) Diminished men and dangerous women: representations of gender and learning disability in early- and mid-nineteenth-century Britain, *British Journal of Learning Disabilities*, 28: 49–53.

McDowell, L. (1997) *Capital Culture: Gender at Work in the City*. Oxford: Blackwell.

McDowell, L. (2003) *Redundant Masculinities?* Oxford: Blackwell.

Mills, M. (2001) *Challenging Violence in Schools: An Issue of Masculinities*. Buckingham: Open University Press.

Morrison, I., Everton, T. and Rudduck, J. (2000) Pupils helping other pupils with their learning: cross-age tutoring in a primary and secondary school, *Mentoring and Tutoring*, 8: 187–200.

Murphy, P. (1996) Defining pedagogy, in P. Murphy and C. Gipps (eds) *Equity in the Classroom: Towards Effective Pedagogy for Girls and Boys*. London: Falmer Press.

Murphy, P. (1998) Boys are not the only ones which lose out, *Guardian Education*, 13 January.

Myers, K. (2000) *Whatever Happened to Equal Opportunities in Schools? Gender Equality Initiatives in Education.* Buckingham: Open University Press.

Nayak, A. (2001) 'Ice white and ordinary': new perspectives on ethnicity, gender and youth cultural identities, in B. Francis and C. Skelton (eds) *Investigating Gender: Contemporary Perspectives in Education.* Buckingham: Open University Press.

Nayak, A. (2003) 'Boyz to men': masculinities, schooling and labour transitions in de-industrial times, *Educational Review*, 55: 147–59.

Nayak, A. and Kehily, M.J. (1996) Playing it straight: masculinities, homophobias and schooling, *Journal of Gender Studies*, 5: 211–30.

Nieto, S. (1994) Lessons from students: creating a chance to dream, *Harvard Educational Review*, 64: 392–426.

Noble, C. and Bradford, W. (2000) *Getting it Right for Boys ... and Girls.* London: Routledge.

Noble, C., Brown, J. and Murphy, J. (2001) *How to Raise Boys' Achievement.* London: David Fulton.

Norwich, B. and Kelly, N. (2005) *Moderate Learning Difficulties and the Future of Inclusion.* Abingdon: RoutledgeFalmer.

O'Brien, L. (1991) *SOS: Strengthening of Skills.* Rockville, MD.: Diagnostic Studies Inc.

OFSTED (2003) *Boys' Achievement in Secondary Schools.* London: OFSTED/HMSO.

Ohrn, E. (2001) Marginalization of democratic values: a gendered practice of schooling? *International Journal of Inclusive Education*, 5: 319–28.

Osler, A. and Hill, J. (1999) Exclusion from school and racial equality: an examination of government proposals in the light of recent research evidence, *Cambridge Journal of Education*, 29: 33–62.

Osler, A., Street, C., Lall, M. and Vincent, K. (2002) *Not a Problem? Girls and School Exclusion.* London: National Children's Bureau/Joseph Rowntree Foundation.

Osler, A. and Vincent, K. (2003) *Girls and Exclusion: Rethinking the Agenda.* London: RoutledgeFalmer.

Parker, L. and Rennie, L. (1997) Teachers' perceptions of the implementation of single-sex classes in co-educational schools, *Australian Journal of Education*, 41: 119–33.

Phillips, A. (1998) Close schools for girls, *The Guardian*, 6 January.

Phoenix, A. (2001) Racialisation and gendering in the (re)production of educational inequalities, in B. Francis and C. Skelton (eds) *Investigating Gender.* Buckingham: Open University Press.

Pickering, J. (1997) *Raising Boys' Achievement.* Stafford: Network Educational.

Plummer, G. (2000) *Failing Working-Class Girls.* Stoke-on-Trent: Trentham Books.

Pollard, A., Triggs, P., Broadfoot, P., McNess, E. and Osborn, M. (2000) *What Pupils Say: Changing Policy and Practice in Primary Education.* London: Continuum.

Pyatt, G. (2002) Cross-school mentoring: training and implementing a peer mentoring strategy, *Mentoring and Tutoring,* 10: 171–7.

Quirke, J. and Winter, C. (1995) 'Best friends': a case study of girls' reactions to an intervention designed to foster collaborative group work', *Gender and Education,* 7: 259–81.

Reay, D. (2001) 'Spice girls', 'nice girls', 'girlies' and tomboys: gender discourses, girls' cultures and femininities in the primary classroom, *Gender and Education,* 13: 153–66.

Redman, P. and Mac an Ghaill, M. (1996) Schooling sexualities: heterosexual masculinities, schooling and the unconscious, *Discourse,* 17: 243–56.

Reid, K. (2002) Mentoring with disaffected pupils, *Mentoring and Tutoring,* 10: 153–70.

Riddell, S. (1998) Boys and under-achievement: the Scottish dimension, *International Journal of Inclusive Education: Special Issue on Boys' 'Under-Achievement',* 2: 169–86.

Riddell, S., Baron, S. and Wilson, A. (2001) Gender and the post-school experiences of women and men with learning difficulties, in B. Francis and C. Skelton (eds) *Investigating Gender: Contemporary Perspectives in Education.* Buckingham: Open University Press

Riding, R. (2002) *School Learning and Cognitive Style.* London: David Fulton.

Riley, K. and Docking, J. (2004) Voices of disaffected pupils: implications for policy and practice, *British Journal of Educational Studies,* 52: 166–79.

Robinson, P. and Smithers, A. (1999) Should the sexes be separated for secondary education – comparisons of single-sex and co-educational schools? *Research Papers in Education,* 14: 23–49.

Roulsten, K. and Mills, M. (2000) Male teachers in feminised teaching areas: marching to the men's movement drums, *Oxford Review of Education,* 26: 221–37.

Rowan, L., Knobel, M., Bigum, C. and Lankshear, C. (2002) *Boys, Literacies and Schooling: The Dangerous Territories of Gender-Based Literacy Reform.* Buckingham: Open University Press.

Rowe, K. (1998) Single-sex and mixed-sex classes: the effects of class type on student achievements, confidence and participation in mathematics, *Australian Journal of Education,* 32: 180–202.

Rudduck, J. (1994) *Developing a Gender Policy in Secondary Schools.* Buckingham: Open University Press.

Rudduck, J., Chaplain, R. and Wallace, G. (1996) *School Improvement: What Can Students Tell Us?* London: David Fulton.

Rudduck, J. and Flutter, J. (2000) Pupil participation and pupil perspective: carving a new order of experience, *Cambridge Journal of Education*, 30: 75–89.

Rudduck, J. and Flutter, J. (2004) *How to Improve your School*. London: Continuum.

Salisbury, J. and Jackson, D. (1996) *Changing Macho Values: Practical Ways of Working with Adolescent Boys*. London: Falmer Press.

Salisbury, J. and Riddell, S. (2000) *Gender, Policy and Educational Change*. London: Routledge.

Sewell, T. (1998) *Black Masculinities and Schooling: How Black Boys Survive Modern Schooling*. Stoke-on-Trent: Trentham Books.

Sharma, S. and Meigham, R. (1980) Schooling and sex roles: the case of GCE O level maths, *British Journal of Sociology of Education*, 1: 193–216.

Sharpe, S. (1976) *Just Like a Girl: How Girls Learn to Be Women*. London: Penguin.

Shaw, J. (1984) The politics of single-sex schools, in R. Deem (ed.), *Co-education Reconsidered*. Milton Keynes: Open University Press.

Sims, D. (2002) Mentoring young people: benefits and considerations, *Topic*, 27: 1–5.

Sims, D., Jamison, J., Golden, S. and Lines, A. (2000) *Running a Mentoring Programme: Key Considerations*. Slough: NFER.

Skårbrevik, K.J. (2002) Gender differences among students found eligible for special education, *European Journal of Special Needs Education*, 17: 97–107.

Skelton, C. (2001) *Schooling the Boys: Masculinities and Primary Education*. Buckingham: Open University Press.

Skelton, C. (2003) Typical boys? Theorising masculinity in educational settings, in B. Francis and C. Skelton (eds) *Investigating Gender: Contemporary Perspectives in Education*. Buckingham: Open University Press.

Skelton, C. and Francis, B. (2003) *Boys and Girls in the Primary Classroom*. Buckingham: Open University Press.

Slater, A. (1996) The lost boys, *Managing Schools Today*, January: 24–6.

Smith, A. (1997) *Accelerated Learning in the Classroom*. Stafford: Network Educational Press.

Smith, A. (1998) *Accelerated Learning in Practice: Brain-based Methods for Accelerating Motivation and Achievement*. Stafford: Network Educational Press.

Smith, A. (2001a) What the most recent brain research tells us about learning, in F. Banks and A. Shelton Mayes (eds) *Early Professional Development for Teachers*. London: David Fulton.

Smith, A. (2001b) The strategies to accelerate learning in the classroom, in F. Banks and A. Shelton Mayes (eds) *Early Professional Development for Teachers*. London: David Fulton.

Smith, E. (2002) Failing boys and moral panics: perspectives on the under-achievement debate, *British Journal of Educational Studies*, 51: 282–95.

Smith, E. (2003) Understanding underachievement: an investigation into the differential attainment of secondary school pupils, *British Journal of Sociology of Education*, 24: 575–86.

Smith, S. (1984) Single-sex setting, in R. Deem (ed.) *Co-education Reconsidered*. Milton Keynes: Open University Press.

Solomon, J. and Harrison, K. (1991) Talking about science based issues: do boys and girls differ?, *British Educational Research Journal*, 17: 283–94.

Sommers, C.H. (2000) *The War Against Boys: How Misguided Feminism Is Harming Our Young Men*. New York: Simon and Schuster.

Stanworth, M. (1981) *Gender and Schooling*. London: Century Hutchinson.

Stanworth, M. (1987) Girls on the margins: a study of gender divisions in the classroom, in G. Weiner and M. Arnot (eds) *Gender under Scrutiny*. London: Hutchinson.

Stables, A. (1990) Differences between pupils from mixed and single-sex schools in their enjoyment of school subjects and in their attitudes to science and to school, *Educational Review*, 42: 221–30.

Sukhnandan, L., Lee, B. and Kelleher, S. (2000) *An Investigation into Gender Differences and Achievement: Phase 2: School and Classroom Strategies*. Slough: NFER.

Sutherland, M. (1999) Gender equity in success at school, *International Review of Education*, 45: 431–43.

Swan, B. (1998) Teaching boys and girls in separate classes at Shenfield High School, Brentwood, in K. Bleach (ed.) *Raising Boys' Achievement in Schools*. Stoke-on-Trent: Trentham Books.

Taber, K. (1992) Girls' interactions with teachers in mixed physics classes: results of classroom observation, *International Journal of Science Education*, 14: 163–80.

Teese, R., Davies, M., Charlton, M. and Polesel, J. (1995) *Who Wins at School? Boys and Girls in Australian Secondary Education*. Melbourne: University of Melbourne.

Thomas, S. and Mortimore, P. (1996) Comparison of value-added models for secondary school effectiveness, *Research Papers in Education*, 11: 5–33.

Thorndike, R.L., Hagen, E. and France, N. (1986) *Cognitive Abilities Test: Administrative Manual*. Windsor: NFER-Nelson.

Thornton, M. and Bricheno, P. (2002) Staff gender balance in primary schools, paper presented to BERA Annual Conference, Exeter, 12–14 September.

Tinklin, T. (2003) Gender differences and high attainment, *British Educational Research Journal*, 29: 307–25.

Tinklin, T., Croxford, L., Ducklin, A. and Frame, B. (2001) *Gender and Pupils' Performance in Scotland's Schools*. Edinburgh: University of Edinburgh Press.

Tomlinson, S. (1982) *A Sociology of Special Education*. London: Routledge and Kegan Paul.

Treneman, A. (1998) Will the boys who can't read still end up as the men on top? *Independent*, 5 January.

University of Durham Curriculum, Evaluation and Management Centre (2003) *YELLIS: Year 11 Information System*. Durham: University of Durham.

Van Houtte, M. (2004) Why boys achieve less at school than girls: the difference between boys' and girls' academic culture, *Educational Studies*, 30: 159–73.

Vardill, R. and Calvert, S. (2000) Gender imbalance in referrals to an educational psychology service, *Educational Psychology in Practice*, 16: 213–23.

Volman, M., Van Eck, E. and Ten Dam, G. (1995) Girls in science and technology: the development of a discourse, *Gender and Education* 7: 283–91.

Walby, S. (1997) *Gender Transformations*. London: Routledge.

Walden, J. (1991) Gender issues in classroom organisation and management, in C. McLaughlin, C. Lodge and C. Watkins (eds) *Gender and Pastoral Care*. Oxford: Blackwell.

Walkerdine, V. (1989) *Counting Girls Out*. London: Virago.

Warrington, M. and Younger, M. (1999) Perspectives on the gender gap in English secondary schools, *Research Papers in Education*, 14: 51–77.

Warrington, M. and Younger, M. (2000) The other side of the gender gap, *Gender and Education*, 12: 493–508.

Warrington, M. and Younger, M. (2001) Single-sex classes and equal opportunities for girls and boys: perspectives through time from a mixed comprehensive school in England, *Oxford Review of Education*, 27: 339–56.

Warrington, M. and Younger, M. (2003) 'We decided to give it a twirl': single-sex teaching in English comprehensive schools, *Gender and Education*, 15: 339–50.

Warrington, M., Younger, M. and McLellan, R. (2003) Under-achieving boys in English primary schools?, *Curriculum Journal*, 14: 184–206.

Warrington, M., Younger, M. and Williams, J. (2000) Student attitudes, image and the gender gap, *British Educational Research Journal*, 26: 393–407.

Watson, S. (1997) Single-sex education for girls: heterosexuality, gendered subjectivity and school choice, *British Journal of Sociology of Education*, 18: 371–83.

Weaver-Hightower, M. (2003a) The 'boy-turn' in research on gender and education, *Review of Educational Research*, 73: 471–98.

Weaver-Hightower, M. (2003b) Crossing the divide: bridging the disjunctures between theoretically oriented and practice-oriented literature about masculinity and boys at school, *Gender and Education*, 15: 407–21.

Weiner, G. (1994) *Feminisms in Education*. Buckingham: Open University Press.

Weiner, G., Arnot, M. and David, M. (1997) Is the future female? Female success, male disadvantage, and changing gender patterns in education, in A. Halsey, H. Lauder, P. Brown and A. Wells (eds) *Education: Culture, Economy and Society*. Oxford: Oxford University Press.

West, A. and Pennell, H. (2003) *Underachievement in Schools*. London: RoutledgeFalmer.

West, P. (1996) Boys, sport and schooling: an Australian perspective, paper presented at University of Cambridge Faculty of Education, 7 November.

White, J. (1998) *Do Howard Gardner's Multiple Intelligences Add Up?* London: Institute of Education: Perspectives on Education Policy.

Whitty, G. (2001) Education, social class and social exclusion, *Journal of Education Policy* 16: 287–95.

Whitty, G., Power, S. and Halpin, D. (1998) *Devolution and Choice in Education*. Buckingham: Open University Press.

Whyte, J. (1985a) *Girl Friendly Schooling*. London: Methuen.

Whyte, J. (1985b) *Girls into Science and Technology*. London: Routledge.

Wilkinson, H. (1994) *No Turning Back: Generations and the Gender Quake*. London: Demos.

Willis, P. (1977) *Learning to Labour: How Working Class Kids Get Working Class Jobs*. Aldershot: Saxon House.

Wirth, J. and Klieme, E. (2003) Computer-based assessment of problemsolving competences, *Assessment in Education: Principles, Policy and Practice*, 10: 329–45.

Wise, D. and Lovatt, M. (2001) *Creating an Accelerated Learning School*. Stafford: Network Educational Press.

Woods, P. (1990) *The Happiest Days? How Pupils Cope with School*. Basingstoke: Falmer Press.

Woodward, W. (2000) Single-sex lessons plan to counter laddish culture, *The Guardian*, 21 August.

Yates, L. (1997) Gender equity and the boys debate: what sort of challenge is it?, *British Journal of Sociology of Education*, 18: 337–47.

Younger, M. and Warrington, M. (1996) Differential achievement of girls and boys at GCSE: some observations from the perspective of one school, *British Journal of Sociology of Education*, 17: 299–313.

Younger, M. and Warrington, M. (1999) 'He's such a nice man, but he's so boring, you really have to make a conscious effort to learn': the views of Gemma, Daniel and their contemporaries on teacher quality and effectiveness, *Educational Review*, 51: 231–41.

Younger, M. and Warrington, M. (2002) Single-sex teaching in a co-educational comprehensive school in England: an evaluation based upon students' performance and classroom interactions, *British Educational Research Journal*, 28: 353–74.

Younger, M., Warrington, M. and McLellan, R. (2002) The 'problem' of 'under-achieving boys': some responses from English secondary schools, *School Leadership and Management*, 22: 389–405.

Younger, M., Warrington, M. and Williams, J. (1999) The gender gap and classroom interactions: reality and rhetoric? *British Journal of Sociology of Education*, 20: 327–43.

Index

ability
  notions of 41–3
accelerated learning 73
  ALPS 73–4,
achievement boards 178
achievement for all 61, 100,
  165–6, 169, 186
achievement levels
  at key stage 4, 19
  differences by ethnicity 36
  improvement trajectory 65
  in special schools 161, 166–7
  social class differences in 36
Aveling, N. 50
Archer, J. 20
Arnot, M. 21, 33

backlash against feminist
  successes at school 18
benchmark grades at GCSE 35,
  38–9, 181
Blunkett, D., 25
boys
  as risk-takers 135
  attitudes 6–7, 10–12, 21–4
  authenticity of voices 2, 9–14
  behaviour in special schools
  160
  'boy-friendly' teaching
  strategies 55, 73, 119, 127–9,
  133
Boys-Talk Program 69, 175,

coping strategies 171
dilemma to girls 3
discourse on 18–19
disregard for authority 20
engagement with school
151–2
feminisation of 17
narrowness of interests 22
'other' boys in single-sex classes
126
out-of-school 3
perspectives on single-sex
classes 122–6
pseudo-confidence 6
rites of passage, 17
role models,29, 56
role-players 5
seating arrangements 55–6
sense of helplessness 8–9
subject choice 28
under-achievement 2, 13–14,
16–18, 37–8, 99, 172, 185
Breakthrough Programme for Boys
55, 173
Bright, M. 16
Bullock Report 175

Coffield, F. 75, 92
cognitive ability tests 41
Cohen, M. 30
Colley, H. 96
competition 67

Connell, R. 22, 136
Connexions, 94

Daniels, H. 168
DfES
  Autumn Package 39, 42
  performance tables 39
  system of vocational
    qualifications 39
  website on learning styles 75
deindustrialisation 47, 136
differential rates of improvement
  63
dilemmas in working on boys'
  achievement 60–1
discourse of derision 61

educational triage 38
emotional literacy 147
equal opportunities 18, 47–9, 116,
  185
ethnicity, 62

femininities 29
feminist/feminism 18, 46, 47, 48,
  60, 68, 71, 175
Francis, B. 4, 19, 22
Frank, B. 28
Frosh, S. 27, 183

gender equity debate 17, 185
gender:
  diversity of constructions 171
  gender relational approaches
    69–71, 118, 134, 174, 184, 185,
    gender specific pedagogy 72–3,
    92–3, 127–131
  homogeneity 62
multiculturalism 172
  multiplicity of gender
    constructions 171
  'the other' 21, 177
gender gap 16, 30–3, 6,
  by subject 33–4

contextualisation 36
  interpretation 37
  politician's error 35
  other side of 50–4
Gilbert, P. 23
Gillborn, D. and Youdell, D. 39, 43
girls
  achievement levels 46–7
  breadth of interests 22
  career patterns 48, 49, 52
  confidence in single–sex classes
    118
  in labour market 49
  in special schools 160
  in trouble 57
  Into Science and Technology
    Project 48
  invisibility 57–8
  marginalised in classrooms 48,
    52
  out-performing boys 33–4
  perspectives on single-sex
    classes 122–6
  self-exclusion 58
  subject choice, 29 51–2
  under-achieving 62, 172, 185
  views of boys 4–6
Gorard, S. 35
Gray, J. 16, 41,
Guardian Angels Scheme 140–1

Hall, E. 74
Hart, S. 43
heterosexuality 27
homophobia 126
hyper-heterosexual identify 27

inclusivity 60
individual strategies 69–70,
  94–113, 170, 180–2
intervention strategies 67–70
  embedded 174, 185, 186
  interlinkage of 173
  revisited 173–84

Jackson, C. 25, 26, 28, 133, 135, 160
Jackson D.,19

Kehily, M. 27
Kenway, J. 131, 133
Kershner, R. 42
kinaesthetic
  learning 76–82
  outcomes 89–92
  teaching styles 78–82
Kruse, A-M 133

labour markets 20
laddishness 135, 186
  as a defence strategy 25–6
  as avoidance of the feminine 26–8
  behaviour 24, 52–3
  culture 139–40
  image 29, 114, 182,
learning styles 76–8, 82–4, 175–6,
Lee-Potter E16
Lingard B, 50
London Challenge 76

Mac an Ghaill, M. 6, 136, 143
MacBeath, J. 3
macho behaviour 125
Majors, R. 23
male repair agenda 67–8
Martino, W. 27, 28, 117, 133, 174
masculinity
  as a performance 23
  badges of 23
  hegemonic 21, 68, 119, 135, 182,
  multiple masculinities 29, 136–138
  recuperative 67–8, 70–1, 118, 134, 174, 185
mentoring
  assertive 105–8, 181
  collaborative 103–5, 181

criteria for successful 94–5, 181,
impact on achievement 97–9
Learning Mentors 96, 150
link with data 103
National Mentoring Network 94
negotiated with teachers 102
pre-conditions for successful 108–13, 181
role of senior staff in 111–2
strengths of 107–8
  structure of 101–3
  students' perspectives 6, 100–1, 112, 181
  within RBA Project 96–7
Mills, M. 23
multiple intelligences 73–4, 82–8, 89–92
Myers, K. 18

new IQ-ism 43, 181
new knowledge economy 47
Noble, C. 140

organisational strategies 69–70, 116–134, 170, 177–80
Originator Schools 46, 66–8, 76–7, 82–4, 99, 119–20, 139, 143, 173
  outcomes of strategies 80–2, 84–8

partner schools 66–8, 82–4, 130, 149
pedagogic strategies 69–70, 72–93, 170, 174–7
  approaches 72–93, 141
  outcomes: cautionary words 88–9
  enabling factors 89–92
  gender-specific 72–3, 92–3, 127–131, 132, 133
  respectful 174–5
potential data 114
prefect system 177

pro-feminist approaches 68–9,
70–1, 175

Raising Boys' Achievement Project
15, 46, 60–5, 76, 95, 119, 131,
138, 150, 157, 160–1, 182, 186
research design 65–6, 160–1, 184
Riley, K. 174,
Rudduck, J. 2, 14, 61, 64, 177,

school
aesthetics 178
culture and ethos 108–13,
119–26, 140–2, 180, 183
leadership 111–2, 132, 153–6,
186
schools as learning organisations
proactivity 141–2
pedagogy and support 141
self-esteem and self-worth 114,
136–7, 160, 183, 185
sense of agency 14, 185–6
sex-based harassment by boys 52
Skelton, C. 19, 68
single-sex classes 54, 116, 177
advantages 131–2
affective issues 117
boys'-only atmosphere 117
classroom management in 125,
128–9
effect on classroom
environment 118
evaluation of 117–9
impact on achievement 119–22
preconditions for
implementation 131–3
proactive role of senior staff
132
reinforcing sex-role stereotypes
117, 128
successful teaching in 127–31,
132
students' perspectives 122–6

Smith, A. 75
Smith, E. 42
social class 62, 136–7
socio-cultural strategies 69–70,
135–156, 170, 182–4,
case study 138–142
effect on achievement 148–9,
151, 153
evaluation in partner schools
149–152
holistic approach 142, 186
impact of 145–49
impact on students' attitudes
151–2
intervention strategies 138
key befrienders 142, 144, 146,
155, 183
key leaders 142–44, 154–5, 183
preconditions for successful
153—6
proactive measures 140–2
rationale 147
students' perspectives on 145–7
special schools 157–8
boys' behaviour in 160
boys' self-esteem and
engagement in learning 163–4
boys' writing in 161–3
case studies in 161–5
different types of learning
difficulty 158
dilemmas in provision 165–6
ethical issues 160
expectations 164
gender factor in 157, 159
identification and placement
process 158
inclusion 64–5, 169
links with mainstream schools
164–5, 170
more boys in 159
multilevel strategies 169
P scales 161, 166

previous research 158–60
understanding of achievement
in 166–7, 169
strategies for boys 53, 133
dangers of 64
quick-fix 179
student leadership systems 177
Sukhnandam,L. 95

target-setting 94, 109–10, 111,
181
targets and expectations 108
teaching
qualities of outstanding 175–6,
178–9
textbooks
sexist language in 48
Treneman, A. 46

under-achievement 77, 99, 172,
174, 179, 182
biological explanations of 20–1
debate 136

difficulties of definition 41–2
intersection of ethnicity, social
class and gender 172, 184
moral panic about 46
revisited 40–3, 44

value-added measures 16, 40–1,
44, 172, 181
limitations of 41, 181
VAK (visual, auditory,
kinaesthetic) strategies 74–5,
77, 80

Warrington, M. 26, 28, 35, 42
Weaver-Hightower, M. 17
Weiner, G. 18, 64
Willis, P. 136
Younger, M. 26, 35, 42

LEARNING WITHOUT LIMITS

Susan Hart, Annabelle Dixon, Mary Jane Drummond and Donald McIntyre

- Why do some teachers insist on teaching without recourse to judgements about ability?
- What are the key principles on which they draw as they organize and provide for learning?
- What is the significance of their alternative approach for classrooms in the 21st century?

This book explores ways of teaching that are free from determinist beliefs about ability. In a detailed critique of the practices of ability labelling and ability focused teaching, *Learning without Limits* examines the damage these practices can do to young people, teachers and the curriculum.

Drawing on a research project at the University of Cambridge, the book features nine vivid case studies (from Year 1 to Year 11) that describe how teachers have developed alternative practices despite considerable pressure on them and on their schools and classrooms. The authors analyze these case studies and identify the key concept of transformability as a distinguishing feature of these teachers' approach. They construct a model of pedagogy based on transformability: the mind-set that children's futures as learners are not pre-determined, and that teachers can help to strengthen and ultimately transform young people's capacity to learn through the choices they make. The book shows how transformability-based teaching can play a central role in constructing an alternative improvement agenda.

This book will inspire teachers, student teachers, lecturers and policy makers, as well as everyone who has a stake in how contemporary education and practice affect children's future lives and life chances.

Contents
Part one: The problem in context - Why learning without limits? - What's wrong with ability labelling? - Researching teachers' thinking and practices - Part two: The case studies - nine teachers in action - Part three: Towards an alternative model - The principle of transformability - From principle to practice - The contexts of teaching for learning without limits - Pupils' perspectives on learning without limits - An alternative improvement agenda - Conclusion - Index.

192pp   033521259X (Paperback)   0335212603 (Hardback)

TEACHERS, PARENTS AND CLASSROOM BEHAVIOUR
A Psychosocial Approach

Andy Miller

'Andy Miller's Teachers, Parents and Classroom Behaviour is the most useful, insightful and coherent account of understanding and managing behaviour in schools that I have read. It is also superbly written, making it a pleasure to read... if you buy only one book this year, then it should be this one.' *Educational Psychology in Practice*

'This elegantly crafted book contains thought-provoking implications for all branches of applied psychology, as well as educationists and policy makers ... With an increasing focus in education on evidence-based practice, this book will be a valuable resource for practicing and trainee teachers and educational psychologists ... [It] offers an extremely timely contribution to current developments in education.' *The Psychologist*

'I found the book fascinating and it has led me to think differently in a variety of situations ... It has also impacted my views on the school ethos and teacher relationships. I will be recommending this book to members of the senior management team and staff who work with pupils with behavioural problems.' *Young Minds Magazine 68/2004*

The behaviour of students in schools is a matter of great concern. Legislation, media coverage and 'test cases' are flooding into the public consciousness at an increasing pace. The relative responsibility of teachers and parents is a particularly prominent and contentious issue.

This book examines the reasons why strong statements of mutual recrimination and blame often occur in this area, before looking at policies and practices which are co-operative, preventive and proactive in nature.

But this is not solely another book of tips and techniques. In addition to describing strategies with a proven evidence base, it also demonstrates, within a coherent framework, how and why these approaches achieve their aims.

This book provides an in-depth understanding of key psychological factors for those in schools struggling in this vexed and pressing area and for that widening group of professionals charged with working in partnership to bring about demonstrable change.

Contents

Introduction- Part one: The Context of Difficult Behaviour in Classrooms – Emerging perspectives on behaviour in classrooms – Difficult behaviour in classrooms: the psychosocial perspective – Part Two: Working with individual students, teachers and parents – The evidence base – Strategies with individual students: the evidence base and major challenge – Strategies with teachers and parents: an evidence base and a major challenge – Consulting with teachers-and parents – Part three: Teacher and Pupil Cultures- Teacher culture and difficult behaviour in classrooms – Pupil culture and difficult behaviour in classrooms – Teacher, student and parent perspectives on behaviour: clash and concordance – Part four: Grasping the nettle: Coherent psychosocial interventions – Intervening within staff cultures – Across the great divide – Intervening with teachers and parents – Conclusion – References – Index.

2003   216pp   0335211569 (Paperback)   0335211577 (Hardback)

FAILING BOYS?
Issues in Gender and Achievement

Debbie Epstein, Jannette Elwood, Valerie Hey and Janet Maw (eds)

'... a breath of fresh air in a climate of sweaty panic over the 'underachievement' of boys.' – Education Review

Failing Boys? Issues in Gender and Achievement challenges the widespread perception that all boys are underachieving at school. It raises the more important and critical questions of which boys? At what stage of education? And according to what criteria?

The issues surrounding boys' 'underachievement' have been at the centre of public debate about education and the raising of standards in recent years. Media and political responses to the 'problem of boys' have tended to be simplistic, partial, and owe more to 'quick fixes' than investigation and research. Failing Boys? provides a detailed and nuanced 'case study' of the issues in the UK, which will be of international relevance as the moral panic is a globalised one, taking place in diverse countries. The contributors to this book take seriously the issues of boys' 'underachievement' inside and outside school from a critical perspective which draws on the insights of previous feminist studies of education to illuminate the problems associated with the education of boys.

This will be a key text for educators, policy makers, students and teachers of education, sociology, gender studies and cultural studies and others interested in gender and achievement.

Contents

Part one: Boys' underachievement in context- Schoolboy frictions – Feminism and failing boys – 'A habit of healthy idleness' – Boys' underachievement in historical perspective – Part two: Different constructions of the debate and its under-currents – Girls will be girls and boys will be first – 'Zero tolerance', gender performance and school failure – Breaking out of the binary trap – Boys' underachievement, schooling and gender relations – Real boys don't work – Masculinities, 'underachievement' and the harassment of sissies – Part three: Boys, which boys? – Loose canons – Exploding the myth of the 'black macho' lad – Boys underachievement, special needs practices and equity – Part four: Curriculum, assessment and the debate – Language and gender, who, if anyone, is disadvantaged by what? – Gendered learning outside and inside school influences on achievement – Index.

1998 208pp 0335202381 (Paperback)

SO WHAT'S A BOY?
Addressing Issues of Masculinity and Schooling

Wayne Martino and Maria Pallotta-Chiarolli

This book focuses on the impact and effects of masculinities on the lives of boys at school. Through interviews with boys from diverse backgrounds, the authors explore the various ways in which boys define and negotiate their masculinities at school. The following questions and issues are addressed:

- What does it mean to be a 'normal' boy and who decides this?
- How do issues of masculinity impact on boys from culturally diverse backgrounds, indigenous boys, those with disabilities and boys of diverse sexualities?
- What issues of power impact on these boys' lives and relationships at school?
- What effects do these issues have on boys' learning at school?

Through problematizing and interrogating the question of what makes a boy a boy, this fascinating title offers recommendations and indicates future directions for working with boys in school.

Contents
Preface – Part one: Normalization and schooling – 'So what's a boy?': normalizing practices and borderland existences – 'You have to be strong, big and muscular': boys, bodies and masculinities – 'That's what normal boys do': bullying and harassment in the lives of boys at school – 'Getting into the cool group is like passing an exam': boys talk about friendships at school – Part two: Diverse masculinities – 'It was never openly talked about': the experiences of sexually diverse students at school – 'If you're a wog you're cool, but if you're Asian you get picked on': multiple masculinities and cultural diversity – 'One of the main problems at school would be racism': indigenous boys, masculinities and schooling – 'You're not a real boy if you're disabled': boys negotiating physical disability and masculinity in schools – Part three: Sites of intervention – 'There's no opportunity for guys to get down and think about what they're doing and why they are doing it': boys interrogating 'masculinity' in schools – 'It's the politics of my school that upsets me': the rhetoric and realities of school policies, structures and pedagogies – 'It's not the way guys think': interrogating masculinities in English and physical education – 'So what's a healthy boy?': health education as a site of risk, conformity and resistance – Conclusion – References – Index.

2003 256pp 0335203817 (Paperback)